To my dearest Josh —

Very best wishes for your continued health, happiness and spiritual growth.

In affection,

Ramon Grosfoguel

The Spirit of Mishnaic Law
Tractate Berachot

Volume 1
Chapters One through Four
Pages 1-256

Reuven Grodner

Copyright © Gefen Publishing House
Jerusalem 1989/5750

All rights reserved. No part of this publication may be translated, reproduced, stored in a retrieval system or transmitted, in any form or by any means, electronic, mechanical, photocopying, recording or otherwise, without expressed written permission from the publishers.

Photo Typeset by Gefen Ltd.

Volume I

ISBN 965-229-045-9

First Edition 1989

Gefen Publishing House Ltd.
P.O.B. 6056, 91060 Jerusalem

Gefen Books
3 Station Plaza,
P.O.B. 101
Woodmere, N.Y., 11598

Printed in Israel

Send for a free copy of the Gefen catalog.

To Chaya With Love

זכרתי לך חסד נעוריך
אהבת כלולתיך
לכתך אחרי במדבר
בארץ לא זרועה.
(ירמיה ב: ב,)

Acknowledgments

There are certain individuals who have helped make this book a reality. My heartfelt gratitude is extended to —

My parents of blessed memory — who brought me into this world and, with great sacrifice, paved my path of life.

Rabbi Joseph B. Soloveitchik — my *rebbe* and mentor, whose genius has profoundly influenced my comprehension and appreciation of Torah. His classes, lectures and writings have been a guiding light of inspiration and humility all my adult life.

Chaya — my beloved wife and friend, whose selfless devotion and persistent encouragement fueled my energies in writing this book. Her astute suggestions, insights and corrections silently pervade every chapter. I thank her too, for the countless hours spent in transforming my handwritten hieroglyphics into a neatly typed manuscript.

My many students who greeted the primordial drafts with countless questions and challenges.

Steve Rosenberg — whose keen eye discovered errors I had overlooked and whose sharp mind demanded clarity and accuracy in places of obscurity.

My dear aunt and uncle, Fanny and Irving Sorkow, who are directly responsible for my early religious education.

My cherished friends who remain in "the old country" but whose friendship and kindness span the ocean: Joan and Bob Arnow, Sheila and Marvin Bernard, Regina and Alan Bisk, Mike Gregor, Harriet and Dan Levitt, Fran and Bob Malina, Anita and Mike Malina, Alex Millman and Hortie and Larry Schur.

Preface

I have had the privilege of teaching Torah for more than twenty-five years. My teaching experiences have been at the James Striar School of Yeshiva University, under the tutelage of the late Rabbi Morris Besdin, of blessed memory, in congregational and yeshiva settings and currently at the Hebrew University in Jerusalem. The challenge set before me as a teacher has been not simply to convey the information of a text, be it Torah, Mishnah, Talmud, or Halachah. A more difficult challenge has been to give meaning and purpose to the lesson, to enable the student to draw valuable conclusions that relate to his/her life.

Much of Torah study appears to be remote and irrelevant to daily life. The study of Mishnah, Talmud and Halachah can be very uninspiring. Talmudic debate and halachic decisions can seem arbitrary, and sometimes even irrational. The subject matter itself may appear cold and dry. But if presented properly, these same subjects can inspire religious and intellectual excitement. They can arouse a student's curiosity and awaken keen interest. Most importantly, they can be sources of profound religious and intellectual growth.

Jewish law grew from the fertile soil of eternal Torah values and ideals. Religious philosophy, ethics and moral values are the ground from which halachah sprouted. One can best understand Jewish values by studying Jewish law. When one may interrupt the recitation of *Sh'mah* in order to greet, or respond to the greeting of, another person, tells us as much about respect for fellow human beings as it does about the importance of *Sh'mah*. Blessings recited upon witnessing natural phenomena tell us as much about the appreciation of the wonders of nature as they do about how to bless. Facing in the direction of Eretz Yisrael while praying tells us as much about the centrality of the Jewish homeland as it does about how to pray.

In writing this commentary on the Mishnah of Tractate Berachot, I have attempted to present the lessons and morals that may be derived from Jewish law. I have prepared for the reader historical and philosophical background. In many instances, I have offered homiletic interpretations of the mishnaic law. Thus, the book brings to the reader not only the letter of the law, but the spirit of the law, as well.

Every effort has been made to present the subject matter in a clear and comprehensible manner. Each chapter contains an introduction that previews the mishnayot in the chapter. Every mishnah is translated in a lucid and concise manner and is accompanied by notes which define technical terms and idioms. Each mishnah is followed by three sections. These are:

THE LETTER OF THE LAW —
A comprehensive explanation of the mishnah based upon the Talmud and the classic commentaries.

THE SPIRIT OF THE LAW —
A commentary that teaches Jewish values, moral lessons, historical background and philosophical perspectives.

THE PRACTICAL LAW —
A review of the law as it is practiced today.

Also included in this work is a comprehensive glossary of Hebrew terms.

In recent years, there has been a renaissance in the study of Judaism. The proliferation of books in English on Jewish subjects is a valid indicator of a growing interest in Judaism. The interest lies not so much in books about Judaism, but in primary, classic texts that, in the

PREFACE

past, were studied only by those who knew Hebrew. There is a growing number of people, young adults and adults, who have not received extensive yeshiva training, but who wish to go back to the original sources. It is my fervent hope that this work will contribute to their knowledge, understanding, and appreciation of Judaism. I believe that advanced students, teachers and rabbis will also find an abundance of material which they may find useful in conveying to others.

Inspiring in the reader a deeper understanding of Torah and a greater love for God is my reward.

Reuven Grodner
Kfar Adumim, Israel
5750 (1989)

Contents Volume 1

Introduction XIX

Chapter One 1

Introduction   3: TEN COMMANDMENTS, *SH'MAH*

Mishnah 1   10: *Letter of Law 11: Spirit of Law 13:* NIGHT AND DAY: Night Precedes Day; Night and Day as Symbols; Jewish History; Redemption; THE TIME THE *KOHANIM* ENTER: WATCHES: TO PREVENT A PERSON FROM TRANSGRESSION: Halacha; Tradition; Interpretation; "Fences"; Torah Fences; Other Communities; Sources of Rabbinic Authority; *Practical Law 27*

Mishnah 2   28: *Letter of Law 29:* WHEN TO RECITE *SH'MAH*: T'CHAYLET: *Spirit of Law 30:* COLORS: NOBILITY: THE CHOSEN PEOPLE: Bible; Talmud; Liturgy; PHILOSOPHY AND *KABBALAH*: R. Judah Halevi; Maimonides; Maharal of Prague; R. Shneur Zalman of Lyady; R. Samson Raphael Hirsch; Samuel David Luzzatto; A PARABLE: *Practical Law 42*

Mishnah 3   43: *Letter of Law 44:* HOW TO RECITE *SH'MAH*: R. TARFON: *Spirit of Law 46:* EXTERNALS AND INTERNALS: BEIT HILLEL AND BEIT SHAMMAI: The Founders; Hillel; The Two Schools; *Practical Law 50*

Mishnah 4   51: *Letter of Law 52:* THE ORDER OF MORNING AND EVENING: THE BLESSINGS OF *SH'MAH*: MORNING BLESSINGS: EVENING BLESSINGS: ON THE NATURE OF BLESSINGS: CONTIGUOUS BLESSINGS: THE FORMULAS OF BLESSINGS: *Spirit of Law 58:* THE BLESSINGS: THEIR HISTORY AND MEANING IN THE HOLY TEMPLE: MORNING BLESSINGS: *Yotzer Ohr; Ahavah Rabah; Emet V'Yatziv;* EVENING BLESSINGS: *Asher Bidvaroh; Ahavat Olam; Emet V'Emunah; Hashkivaynu;* THE THIRD BLESSING: PHILOSOPHY OF THE BLESSINGS OF *SH'MAH: Practical Law 68*

Mishnah 5   70: *Letter of Law 71: Spirit of Law 72:* LIKE A MAN OF SEVENTY: REMEMBERING THE EXODUS AT NIGHT: IN THE DAYS OF THE MESSIAH: *Practical Law 77*

Chapter Two

Introduction **81**

Mishnah 1 **82:** *Letter of Law 83:* DEFINITION OF *KAVANAH*: IN PRAYER: IN PERFORMING MITZVOT: IN RECITING *SH'MAH*: INTERRUPTIONS DURING PRAYER: *Spirit of Law 89:* DO MITZVOT REQUIRE *KAVANAH*?: A KABBALISTIC ANSWER: A PSYCHOLOGICAL ANSWER: PRAYER AND RESPECT FOR PEOPLE: *Practical Law 96*

Mishnah 2 **97:** *Letter of Law 98:* NOT INTERRUPTING BETWEEN "AND THE LORD SPOKE" AND "TRUE AND CERTAIN": THE ORDER OF THE PARAGRAPHS: *Spirit of Law 100:* "THE LORD GOD IS TRUE *(EMET)*": "TRUE" AT BEGINNING AND END: THE YOKE OF THE KINGDOM OF HEAVEN: *KABBALAT OHL MALCHUT SHAMAYIM* IN *SH'MAH*: THREE LEVELS OF FAITH: *Practical Law 110*

Mishnah 3 **111:** *Letter of Law 111:* "HEAR" O ISRAEL: RECITING IN THE WRONG ORDER: *Spirit of Law 113:* VERBALIZATION AND AUDIBILITY: *Practical Law 113*

Mishnah 4 **114:** *Letter of Law 114: KAVANAH DURING SH'MAH* AND THE *AMIDAH:* *Spirit of Law 114:* STEALING TIME: *Practical Law 115*

Mishnah 5 **116:** *Letter of Law 116: Spirit of Law 117:* MARRIAGE IN MISHNAIC TIMES: WEDNESDAY WEDDINGS: PREOCCUPATION WITH A MITZVAH: *Practical Law 120*

Mishnah 6 **121:** *Letter of Law 121: Spirit of Law 122:* MISHNAIC STYLE: THE MOURNING EXPERIENCE: *Practical Law 123*

Mishnah 7 **124:** *Letter of Law 124: Spirit of Law 125:* TABI: *Practical Law 126*

Mishnah 8 **127:** *Letter of Law 127:* WHEN TO GO BEYOND THE LETTER OF THE LAW: *Spirit of Law 130:* ON PIETY AND POMPOSITY: KING SAUL: A WEDDING ON SHABBAT: *KASHRUT*: JACOB'S LADDER: WHEN TO BE *MACHMIR*: THE IMPORTANCE OF STUDY: THE 36: NOT AT OTHERS' EXPENSE: *Practical Law 143*

Chapter Three

Introduction 147

Mishnah 1 **148:** *Letter of Law 149:* THE *ONEN:* WHAT IS THE MEANING OF "EXEMPT?": THE PALLBEARERS: *Spirit of Law 150:* THE MENTAL STATE OF THE *ONEN:* AFTER THE BURIAL: *AHVELUT:* THE *KADDISH* PRAYER: THE *KADDISH* AND *SH'MAH: Practical Law 154*

Mishnah 2 **155:** *Letter of Law 155:* RECITING *SH'MAH* OR COMFORTING THE MOURNER?: *Spirit of Law 156:* "LOVE YOUR NEIGHBOR": BURYING THE DEAD: COMFORTING THE MOURNER: *G'MILUT CHASSADIM: Practical Law 161*

Mishnah 3 **162:** *Letter of Law 162:* WOMEN AND MITZVOT: TIME-ORIENTED MITZVOT: WOMEN AND PRAYER: WOMEN AND *MINYAN:* WOMEN AND THE CONDUCTING OF PRAYER SERVICES: THE SINGLE WOMAN: "WHO HAS MADE ME ACCORDING TO HIS WILL": BONDSMEN: MINORS: *Spirit of Law 171:* SOCIETIES DIFFER: THE STATUS OF WOMEN: TIME-ORIENTED MITZVOT: DIFFERENT ROLES: SLAVERY: EDUCATION: Abraham, The First Educator; *Chinuch;* Universal Education; Goals of Education; Educating Children; Chafetz Chaim's Advice to Parents; *Practical Law 187:* WOMEN AND PRAYER: MINORS

Mishnah 4 **189:** *Letter of Law 189:* HISTORICAL BACKGROUND: TWO INTERPRETATIONS OF THE MISHNAH: *Spirit of Law 191:* SEVERE DECREES: *Practical Law 193*

Mishnah 5 **194:** *Letter of Law 195:* THE *BA'AL KERI* AND PRAYER: *Spirit of Law 196:* "YOUR CAMPS SHALL BE HOLY": CLEANLINESS AND GODLINESS: *Practical Law 200*

Mishnah 6 **201:** *Letter of Law 201: Spirit of Law 202:* TYPES OF PURITY AND IMPURITY: Dead Bodies; *Tzara'at;* Issues from the Sexual Organs; ASSOCIATION WITH DEATH: APPLICATIONS OF THE LAWS OF IMPURITY: LAWS OF IMPURITY TODAY: LESSON OF THE LAWS OF IMPURITY: *Practical Law 206*

Chapter Four

Introduction 209

Mishnah 1 210: *Letter of Law 211:* PRAYER: A BIBLICAL OR A RABBINIC OBLIGATION?: THE TIMES OF PRAYER: *Spirit of Law 214:* THE CONTROVERSY BETWEEN MAIMONIDES AND NACHMANIDES: TWO SOURCES OF PRAYER: THE PATRIARCHS AND TEMPLE SACRIFICE: A THIRD SOURCE FOR DAILY PRAYER: THE TIMES OF PRAYER LINKED TO *SH'MAH*: *Practical Law 218*

Mishnah 2 220: *Letter of Law 220: Spirit of Law 222:* THE IMPORTANCE OF TORAH STUDY: Three Crowns; THE PRACTICAL ASPECT OF TORAH STUDY: TORAH FOR TORAH'S SAKE: REWARDS FOR TORAH STUDY: AN ADMONITION FROM THE THIRTEENTH CENTURY: LOVE FOR TORAH AND HUMANITY: *Practical Law 229*

Mishnah 3 231: *Letter of Law 231:* THE ORIGIN OF THE AMIDAH: WHY EIGHTEEN?: THE NINETEENTH BENEDICTION: THE STRUCTURE OF THE AMIDAH: PSALM 29: THE ABBREVIATED VERSION: *Spirit of Law 237:* PRAYER IN THE PLURAL: THE AMIDAH: PRAYER OF THE ANGELS: *Practical Law 240*

Mishnah 4 241: *Letter of Law 241:* "A FIXED ROUTINE": "AT EVERY DANGEROUS CROSSROAD": R. JOSHUA'S PRAYER: *Spirit of Law 243:* SINCERE AND SPONTANEOUS PRAYER: GOD, THE MERCIFUL PARENT: *Practical Law 246*

Mishnah 5 247: *Letter of Law 247: Spirit of Law 248:* THE CENTRALITY OF ERETZ YISRAEL IN PRAYER: LOFTY FOCAL POINTS: *Practical Law 251*

Mishnah 6 252: *Letter of Law 252: Practical Law 252*

Mishnah 7 253: *Letter of Law 253: Spirit of Law 254: Practical Law 256*

Contents Volume II

Chapter Five 257

Introduction 259

Mishnah 1 **260:** *Letter of Law 260:* KAVANAH: ITS MEANING: AN IN-DEPTH STUDY OF THE FIRST BLESSING OF THE *AMIDAH*: THE NEED FOR *KAVANAH* TODAY: THE EARLY CHASIDIM: PRAYER AND DANGER TO LIFE: *Spirit of Law 272:* THE CHALLENGE OF PRAYER: THE PROBLEM OF PRAYER IN MODERN TIMES: PRESCRIPTIONS FOR *KAVANAH:* Spiritual Preparation; Praying in a Synagogue with a *Minyan*; Knowing the Meaning of the Prayers; Using a Siddur; Arriving at the Synagogue Early; Creativity and Self-Expression; Torah Study; Love; The Place of Prayer; The Reward; THE MOODS OF PRAYER: Prayer and Prophecy; Prayer in Joy; Prayer in Distress; *Practical Law 295*

Mishnah 2 **296:** *Letter of Law 297:* "THE POWERS OF RAIN": ASKING FOR RAIN: "HAVDALAH": *Spirit of Law 299:* RAIN: KNOWING THE DIFFERENCE: *Practical Law 300*

Mishnah 3 **302:** *Letter of Law 303:* THE BIRD'S NEST: "MAY YOUR NAME BE REMEMBERED FOR THE GOOD": "WE GIVE THANKS, WE GIVE THANKS": "IF ONE GOES BEFORE THE HOLY ARK AND MAKES A MISTAKE...": HE SHOULD NOT DECLINE: *Spirit of Law 305:* MERCY ON A BIRD'S NEST: *Practical Law 308*

Mishnah 4 **309:** *Letter of Law 309:* *Spirit of Law 310:* THE PRIESTLY BLESSINGS: *Practical Law 312*

Mishnah 5 **313:** *Letter of Law 314:* *Spirit of Law 315:* R. CHANINAH BEN DOSAH: ON THE EFFICACY OF PRAYER

Chapter Six

Introduction 321: BLESSINGS: "THE EARTH IS THE LORD'S": ADAM'S SIN: THREE KINDS OF BLESSINGS: RABBINIC AND TORAH BLESSINGS: 100 BLESSINGS A DAY; THE VALUE OF A BLESSING: FOOD FORBIDDEN WITHOUT A BLESSING: THE WORLD IS SACRED

Mishnah 1 329: *Letter of Law 330:* WINE: BREAD: RABBI JUDAH'S OPINION: *Spirit of Law 332:* ON WINE: ON BREAD: DIVERSE SPECIES: *Practical Law 338*

Mishnah 2 339: *Letter of Law 339: Spirit of Law 340:* CONSTANT CREATION: *Practical Law 342*

Mishnah 3 343: *Letter of Law 343:* BLESSING ON KINDS OF CURSE: *Spirit of Law 345:* BLESSING AND CURSE: "ON VINEGAR, ON UNRIPE FRUITS, AND ON GRASSHOPPERS": *Practical Law 348*

Mishnah 4 349: *Letter of Law 349: Spirit of Law 350:* THE SEVEN SPECIES: SIZES AND MEASUREMENTS: *Practical Law 353*

Mishnah 5 354: *Letter of Law 355:* TABLE OF MISHNAH: BEIT SHAMMAI: "ALSO ON COOKED GRAIN PRODUCTS": *Spirit of Law 356:* HIERARCHY, DIVERSITY, AND UNITY: *Practical Law 358*

Mishnah 6 360: *Letter of Law 360:* "ALL JEWS ARE RESPONSIBLE FOR EACH OTHER": BLESSING DURING THE MEAL: BLESSING UPON INCENSE: *Spirit of Law 363:* BLESSING OVER SPICES: THE JEWISH TABLE: *Practical Law 366*

Mishnah 7 367: *Letter of Law 367: Spirit of Law 368:* THE FRUITS OF GINNOSAR: THE RISE AND FALL OF BREAD: *Practical Law 369*

Mishnah 8 370: *Letter of Law 371:* THE THREE OPINIONS: GRACE AFTER MEALS: THE THREE-IN-ONE BLESSING: BLESSING OVER WATER: "WHO CREATES MANY SOULS...": *Spirit of Law 374:* THE DESTINY OF ISRAEL: "SEE WHAT PEOPLE DO": *Practical Law 376*

Chapter Seven 377

Introduction 379

Mishnah 1 **381:** *Letter of Law 382:* "...One who ate *d'mai*..."; "*Ma'aser rishon* whose *terumah* has been separated"; "*Ma'aser shaynee* and *hekdesh* that have been redeemed"; "An attendant who ate the volume of an olive"; "The Cuthean"; "One who ate *tevel*"; *Ma'aser rishon* whose *terumah* has not been removed"; "The Gentile"; *Spirit of Law 385: Practical Law 387*

Mishnah 2 **389:** *Letter of Law 389:* WOMEN: SERVANTS: MINORS: AN OLIVE OR AN EGG?: Spirit of Law 392: TWO FAMOUS MINORS: MINIMUM REQUIREMENTS: *Practical Law 394*

Mishnah 3 **395:** *Letter of Law 397: Spirit of Law 398:* THE MINYAN: *Practical Law 400*

Mishnah 4 **401:** *Letter of Law 401: Spirit of Law 402: Practical Law 403*

Mishnah 5 **405:** *Letter of Law 405:* UNDILUTED WINE: *Practical Law 407*

Chapter Eight 409

Introduction 411

Mishnah 1 **413:** *Letter of Law 413:* KIDDUSH: BEIT SHAMMAI AND BEIT HILLEL: *Spirit of Law 416:* HAPPINESS AND HOLINESS: Practical Law 417

Mishnah 2 **418:** *Letter of Law 418:* LAWS OF IMPURITY: CHART OF IMPURITIES: Spirit of Law 421: IMPURITY AND DEATH: WASHING HANDS

Mishnah 3 **425:** *Letter of Law 425*

Mishnah 4 **427:** *Letter of Law 427:* MAHYIM ACHRONIM: *Spirit of Law 430:* "YOU SHALL NOT DESTROY": *Practical Law 431*

Mishnah 5 **432:** *Letter of Law 432:* THE BLESSING ON FIRE: *Spirit of Law 434:* HAVDALAH: BRINGING SHABBAT INTO THE WEEKDAY: *Practical Law 437*

Mishnah 6 **438:** *Letter of Law 438:* UNTIL BENEFIT HAS BEEN DERIVED: *Spirit of Law 439:* THE *HAVDALAH* CANDLE: *Practical Law 440*

Mishnah 7 **441:** *Letter of Law 441:* DIGESTION: Spirit of Law 443: *Practical Law 444*

Mishnah 8 **445:** *Letter of Law 445:* ANSWERING "AMEN": *Spirit of Law 447: Practical Law 448*

Chapter Nine 499

Introduction **451**

Mishnah 1 **452:** *Letter of Law 452:* THE SOURCES FOR BLESSING UPON A MIRACLE: *Spirit of Law 453:* WHAT IS A MIRACLE?: ARE THERE MIRACLES TODAY?: THE SIN OF IDOLATRY: THE ORIGINS OF IDOLATRY: GREEK PAGANISM: MONOTHEISM AND THE TORAH: IDOLATRY AS A BRIDGE: IDOLATRY AND ERETZ YISRAEL: *Practical Law 469*

Mishnah 2 **471:** *Letter of Law 472:* UPON COMETS, EARTHQUAKES, ETC.: LIGHTNING: THUNDER: RIVERS: RAIN: "WHO IS GOOD AND DOES GOOD": *Spirit of Law 474:* NATURE'S WONDERS: JOY IN THE BLESSINGS OF OTHERS: THE TRUE JUDGE: GOOD AND EVIL: *Practical Law 488*

Mishnah 3 **490:** *Letter of Law 491:* SHEH'HEH'CHEE'YAHNU: "ONE BLESSES UPON MISFORTUNE THAT MAY RESULT IN GOOD, ETC...": "HE WHO PRAYS FOR SOMETHING THAT HAS ALREADY OCCURRED": *Spirit of Law 493:* JUDAISM VS. ASCETICISM AND HEDONISM: ACCEPTING REALITY: *Practical Law 496*

Mishnah 4 **498:** *Letter of Law 499: Spirit of Law 499:* GIVING THANKS AND MAKING SUPPLICATION: *Practical Law 500*

Mishnah 5 **501:** *Letter of Law 503:* THE SANCTITY OF THE TEMPLE AND TEMPLE MOUNT: BLESSINGS IN THE TEMPLE: GREETING WITH GOD'S NAME: *Spirit of Law 511:* ...TO BLESS UPON EVIL AS HE WOULD UPON GOOD: BIBLICAL SOURCES FOR BLESSING ON EVIL: "LOVE THE LORD YOUR GOD": "WITH ALL YOUR WEALTH": SHALOM

Glossary 519

Index 523

Introduction

I

Torah incorporates two Laws that are inextricably bound together, *Torah Sheh'bichtav*, the Written Law, and *Torah Sheh'b'al peh*, the Oral Law. The Written Law is contained in the Pentateuch, the Five Books of Moses. The Oral Law has been transmitted, teacher to student, from the time Moses stood on Mt. Sinai.

The Oral Law is a vast body of knowledge that was committed to memory by devoted scholars for many centuries. It contains analysis and interpretation of the Biblical text, legal definitions and precedents, philosophy, homiletics, exegesis, enactments, decrees, and customs. With the passage of time, the Oral Law grew in size and content. It became more and more difficult to preserve this encyclopedic storehouse of legal tradition. A need for order and systematic organization arose. That need was filled by the illustrious scholar of the late second, early third century C.E., R. Judah ha-Nasi (the Prince). His work, second in importance only to the Bible, is called the Mishnah.

R. Judah ha-Nasi, also known as *Rabeynu ha-kadosh* (our holy teacher), or simply as *Rabbi*, completed and perfected the work that was begun by R. Akiva, the leading sage of the previous generation. R.

Akiva lived and died in one of the most turbulent and tragic periods of Jewish history. During the course of his lifetime, he was witness to two Jewish revolts against Rome. The first ended with the decimation of the Jewish population and the destruction of the Second Temple. The second, the Bar Kochba revolt in 132 C.E. (which enjoyed his active support), also ended in dismal failure, with catastrophic consequences. In 135 C.E., R. Akiva, together with many of his colleagues, died a martyr's death.

During that dark era of persecution and destruction, the Torah was in danger of being lost. It became necessary to organize and systematize the enormous *corpus* of law so that the survivors might grasp the torch of Torah knowledge and pass it on to succeeding generations. Several Sages attempted this monumental task. None succeeded like R. Akiva, who laid the foundation for a systematic codification of the Oral Law. R. Judah ha-Nasi acknowledged R. Akiva's contribution and referred to him as "an organized storehouse of knowledge." He said: "R. Akiva may be compared to a worker who takes his basket into the field and fills it with wheat, barley, spelt, beans, and lentils. When he arrives home he organizes each kind separately" (*Avot D'Rabbi Natan* 18). R. Akiva taught his organic structure of law to his student, R. Meir. R. Meir transmitted this knowledge to his student, R. Judah ha-Nasi.

It was R. Judah ha-Nasi who codified the Mishnah and molded its present structure. Sifting through the mountain of laws that he had learned from his teacher R. Meir, and from other Torah scholars of his generation, he methodically extracted and distilled them, and divided them into six sections. These became known as the "Six Orders of the Mishnah" (Heb., *Shishah Sedarim*, or *Shahs*). Whether R. Judah actually wrote the Mishnah or composed it for oral study still remains uncertain. Scholars have debated this issue for centuries. What is clear is that the Mishnah was, and still remains, the cornerstone of Jewish law.

In compiling the Mishnah, R. Judah excluded many teachings and laws. Some were too wordy, others were simply not accepted by him. These teachings and laws are known as baraitot. Many baraitot have been collected in a work that is about four times the size of the Mishnah called the *Toseftah*.

The Six Orders of the Mishnah are:

1. *Zera'im* ("Seeds") — Laws that pertain to agriculture.
2. *Mo'ed* ("Festivals") — Laws concerning Shabbat, Festivals, and fast days.
3. *Nashim* ("Women") — Laws of marriage and divorce.
4. *Nezikin* ("Damages") — Civil and criminal jurisprudence.
5. *Kadashim* ("Holy Things") — Laws of sacrifices, holy objects, and *Kashrut*.
6. *Taharot* ("Purities") — Laws of ritual purity and impurity.

Each Order of the Mishnah is divided into tractates (Heb., *masechtot*, meaning looms on which cloth is woven). In all, there are sixty-three tractates. Each tractate is subdivided into chapters, and each chapter into individual mishnayot. The Mishnah, combined with *Gemarah*, the interpretation and elaboration of the Sages who lived in succeeding centuries, is known as the Talmud.

The academies in Eretz Yisrael developed the Jerusalem Talmud, and the academies in Babylonia, the Babylonian Talmud. The Jerusalem Talmud was redacted in the middle of the fourth century, while the Babylonian Talmud developed for an additional hundred years.

The Sages who lived from the time of Hillel (first century B.C.E.) until the codification of the Mishnah, a period of some 220 years, are known as *Tanna'im*. The Sages who interpreted and explicated the Mishnah until the redaction of the two Talmuds were called *Amora'im*. The teachings of the *Tanna'im* and *Amora'im* form the foundation of Jewish law, known as halachah.

II

Berachot ("Blessings") is the gateway to the Talmud. It is the very first tractate of the first Order, *Zera'im*. Berachot is largely devoted to the laws of prayer. The first three chapters discuss many aspects of *Sh'mah*, a prayer which a Jew is Biblically required to recite twice daily, morning and evening. Chapters 4 and 5 deal mainly with the *Amidah* prayer which is recited three times daily, morning, afternoon, and evening. The laws of blessings upon foods and Grace after Meals are discussed in chapters 6 through 8. Chapter 9 deals mainly with blessings that are recited upon special occasions, such as upon hearing good or bad news and upon witnessing natural phenomena.

Why is Berachot situated in the Order of *Zera'im*? *Zera'im* deals primarily with agricultural laws. Its tractates relate to the portions a farmer must give to the *Kohain*, the *Levi*, and the poor; the Sabbatical year; the seeds that may or may not be sown together, and forbidden fruits. The Order of *Mo'ed* ("Festivals") might have been a more suitable placement for Berachot, as many of the prayers and blessings must be recited at specific times. Indeed, in one Ms. edition (Codex Munich), Berachot is linked with *Mo'ed*. In all standard editions of the Mishnah, *Toseftah* and Talmud, however, Berachot appears as the opening tractate.

The key to understanding the essence of the Order of *Zera'im* and the placement of Berachot at its head may be found in a brief passage in the Talmud: "Reish Lakish said: What is the meaning of the verse: 'He shall be the faith of your times, a storehouse of salvations, wisdom and knowledge; but reverence for the Lord is His treasure' (Isaiah 33:6)? 'Faith' is *Zera'im*, 'your times' is *Mo'ed*, 'storehouse' is *Nashim*, 'salvations' is *Nezikin*, 'wisdom' is *Kadashim* and 'knowledge' is *Taharot*. But 'reverence for the Lord is His treasure' " (Shabbat 31a).

Reish Lakish finds an allusion to the six Orders of Mishnah in the words of Isaiah. Each word in the verse expresses the essence of a particular Order. The essence of *Zera'im* is faith.

Indeed, when a farmer rises at the break of dawn and goes out to sow his field, he expresses his faith in the Almighty that his labor will not be in vain. He works the soil with hope and trust in the Lord that his seeds will grow and one day he will reap a bountiful harvest. But how does the farmer cultivate his faith? How does he sow the seeds of faith in his own heart? The answer lies in tractate Berachot. Before going out to the field, the Jewish farmer dons his *tallit* and *tefillin* and prays fervently to God. He proclaims his faith when he recites *Sh'mah*. He communes with the Lord while quietly whispering the words of the *Amidah*. His early morning meal is preceded with blessings and followed by Grace after Meals. Then, girded with renewed faith, he begins his day's activities with trust in the Lord. These prayers and blessings comprise the subject matter of Tractate Berachot.

We will see that Berachot is much more than a dry list of laws (halachot). It is a fountain of faith that showers all of Jewish law. Berachot is the gateway to the entire Mishnah because the Jewish legal system is a religious system.

Torah addresses all aspects of life. It governs not only our relationship with God but also our relationship with fellow human beings. Property damage, business partnerships, and medical ethics are as much a part of Torah as are the laws of prayer and Shabbat. All human conduct is to be ruled by the divine wisdom that is embodied in halachah. But halachah is meaningful only when it is imbued with piety and faith in God. As the Psalmist writes: "The beginning of wisdom is reverence for the Lord" (Ps. 111:10). King Solomon, in the Book of Proverbs, reiterates this idea with the words: "Reverence for the Lord is the beginning of knowledge" (Proverbs 1:7).

In discussion of the rules and regulations of prayer and blessings, Berachot also points the direction to faith and piety. As the Talmud aptly states: "He who wishes to become pious should study Berachot" (Bava Kamah 30a).

Chapter One

Introduction

Sh'mah Yisrael, Adonai Elohaynu, Adonai Echad, "Hear, O Israel, the Lord is our God, the Lord is One" (Deut. 6:4). This verse contains the most basic and fundamental Jewish belief, i.e., that there is but One God. It is the first verse in the most important prayer in the *Siddur*, the Jewish Prayer Book. The entire prayer consists of three portions from the Torah — Deut. 6:4-9; Deut. 11:13-21; and Num. 15:37-41. The name of the prayer, *Sh'mah*, is taken from the first word, which means "Hear." The translation of the full text reads as follows:

Hear, O Israel, the Lord is our God, the Lord is One.

Blessed be the name of His glorious majesty forever and ever.

You shall love the Lord your God with all your heart, and with all your soul, and with all your might. And these words which I command you today shall be upon your heart. You shall teach them diligently to your children, and you shall speak of them when you are sitting at home and when you go on a journey, when you lie down and when you rise up. You shall bind them for a sign on your hand, and they shall be for frontlets between your eyes. You shall inscribe them on the doorposts of your house and on your gates.

And if you will diligently obey My commandments which I give you today, to love the Lord your God and to serve Him with all your heart and with all your soul, I will give rain for your land in its season, the autumn rains and the spring rains, that you may gather in your grain, your wine and your oil. And I will give grass in your field for your cattle, and you will eat and be satisfied. Take care lest your heart be deceived, and you turn and serve other gods and worship them; for then the Lord's anger will blaze against you, and He will shut up the heaven so that there will be no rain, and the land will not yield its produce, and you will quickly perish from the good land which the Lord gives you. So you shall place these words of Mine upon your heart and upon your soul, and you shall bind them for a sign on your hand, and they shall be for frontlets between your eyes. You shall teach them to your children, speaking of them when you are sitting at home and when you go on a journey, when you lie down and when you rise up. You shall inscribe them on the doorposts of your house and on your gates, so that your life and the life of your children may be prolonged in the land, which the Lord swore He would give to your fathers, for as long as the sky remains over the earth.

The Lord spoke to Moses, saying: Speak to the children of Israel and tell them to make for themselves fringes on the corners of their garments throughout their generations, and they shall put on the fringe of each corner a blue thread. It shall be for you as a fringe, so that when you look upon it you will remember all the commandments of the Lord and do them; and you will not follow your heart and your eyes which lead you astray: that you remember to do all My commandments and be holy for your God. I am the Lord your God who brought you out of the land of Egypt to be your God; I am the Lord your God.

There is a Biblical injunction to recite *Sh'mah* twice every day, once at night and once in the morning. This commandment is based on the phrase in the first paragraph, "when you lie down and when you rise up." Oral tradition interprets the verse in the following manner: "And you shall speak of them (the words of *Sh'mah*) when you are sitting at home and when you go on a journey (wherever you may be), when you lie down and when you rise up (nighttime and morning)." Hence, "when you lie down and when you rise up" is not a continuation of "when you are sitting at home....," but rather a time reference for when *Sh'mah* is to be recited. The first three *mishnayot* of chapter 1 deal with the specific time regulations and body postures that are implied in the words "when you lie down and when you rise up." Mishnah 4 deals

CHAPTER 1: *Introduction* 5

with the blessings of *Sh'mah*. Mishnah 5 speaks of the obligation to remember the Exodus from Egypt at night. This has implications regarding the third paragraph of *Sh'mah*.

Sh'mah is an integral part of the evening and morning services. *Sh'mah*, together with the blessings that precede and follow it, is recited directly before the *Amidah*. When a Jew recites *Sh'mah* in the evening and morning services, he fulfills the Biblical injunction "When you lie down and when you rise up." Because of its importance as a declaration of faith, *Sh'mah* was introduced into other parts of the *Siddur* and is recited on special occasions. It is a bedtime prayer which is said just before retiring. The rabbis based this practice on the verse: "Tremble and do not sin, say in your heart upon your bed and be still" (Ps. 4:5). It is also said in the preliminary morning service. The first verse is recited on Shabbat and Festivals when the Torah is removed from the Holy Ark, in the *Kedushah* of the *Mussaf* service and in the Rosh Hashanah *Mussaf* service. It also marks the conclusion of the *Tachanun* supplicatory prayer said on Mondays and Thursdays, the *Hoshanot* prayers, said on Sukkot, and the *Neilah* service of Yom Kippur. *Sh'mah* is among the first prayers a young child learns to recite. It is the last prayer recited on the deathbed. It is also the prayer of martyrs. The first two paragraphs written on parchment are contained in the *tefillin* and in the *mezuzah*. The Mishnah records that all three paragraphs were recited as part of the daily worship service in the Temple (Tamid 5:1).

"*Baruch shem k'vod malchuto l'olam va'ed*, "Blessed be the name of His glorious majesty forever and ever," is the second line in *Sh'mah*. This sentence is not part of the Torah text. Mishnaic sources tell us that these words were recited in Temple times. On Yom Kippur, the High Priest uttered God's ineffable Name in his confessionals. Each time the multitude heard the Tetragrammaton (God's holiest name, spelled *Yud, hay, vav, hay*) they prostrated themselves and responded "Blessed be the name of His glorious majesty forever and ever." This was done three times (Yoma 3:8; 4:1; 6:2). The basis for responding with praise upon hearing God's name is derived from the verse, "When I call upon the name of the Lord, ascribe greatness to our God" (Deut. 32:3). Moses told the people of Israel, "When I mention the name of the Holy One, blessed be He, you shall ascribe greatness (unto Him)" (Yoma

37a). The people also responded, "Blessed be the name ..." after each of the blessings recited by the *kohanim*, the priests, in the daily worship. It was the ancient counterpart to "Amen" (Ta'anit 16b).

This response was later introduced into *Sh'mah*. The Talmud relates an interesting Aggadah which sheds light on the origin of "Blessed be the name ..." and the reason it is recited in a whisper. "R. Simeon ben Lakish said: And Jacob called unto his sons, and said: 'Gather yourselves together and I will tell you what will befall you in the end of days' (Gen. 49:1). Jacob wished to reveal to his sons the 'end of days', whereupon the Divine Presence departed from him. He said: 'Perhaps, Heaven forbid, there is one unfit among my children, like Abraham, from whom there issued Ishmael, or like my father Isaac, from whom there issued Esau'. But his sons answered him: 'Hear O Israel (our father), the Lord is our God, the Lord is One. Just as there is only One in your heart, so is there only One in our heart'. At that moment, our father Jacob exclaimed: 'Blessed be the Name of His glorious majesty forever and ever'. Said the rabbis, How shall we act? Shall we recite it — although Moses did not say it? Shall we not recite it? — but, Jacob said it? Thus, they enacted that it shall be recited in a whisper" (Pesachim 56a).

"Blessed be the name of His glorious majesty forever and ever" is a prayer of the angels. The Midrash tells us, "When Moses went up to Heaven, he heard the ministering angels saying to the Holy One, blessed be He, 'Blessed be the name of His glorious majesty forever and ever', whereupon he brought the prayer down to the Israelites. Why does Israel not recite it aloud? R. Asi said: To what may this be compared? To one who stole a piece of jewelry from the king's palace. He gave it to his wife and said: 'Don't wear it publicly, only at home'. On Yom Kippur, however, when they are as pure angels, they say it aloud" (*Deut. Rabbah* 2:25).

Sh'mah contains some of the most important tenets of Judaism. It declares the Unity of God and the commandment to love Him. It emphasizes the need to study Torah and teach it to our children. It mentions three great symbols of the Jewish faith: *tefillin, mezuzah*, and *tzitzit*. All of these serve to perpetuate Judaism and emphasize the existence of the One God. Through deep personal love for, and devotion to, God, the knowledge of Torah, the teaching of our

CHAPTER 1: *Introduction* 7

children, and the observance of the daily symbolic *Mitzvot*, we ensure the continuation of Judaism and the belief in God.

The Jerusalem Talmud (Berachot 1:5) reveals that the Ten Commandments are alluded to in *Sh'mah*. In Temple times, the Ten Commandments were recited by the *kohanim* as part of the daily prayer (Tamid 5:1). There was an attempt to introduce the Ten Commandments into prayer outside the Temple, as well. This was discouraged, however, because it might have led to a heretical belief that only the Ten Commandments are divine, whereas the rest of the Torah is not (Berachot 12a). In fact, this became an important doctrine in the early stages of Christianity, and this erroneous belief is still widespread today. Though the Ten Commandments are not included in the liturgy, their message is alluded to in the words of *Sh'mah*.

TEN COMMANDMENTS	*SH'MAH*
1. I am the Lord your God	The Lord is Our God
2. You shall have no other gods	The Lord is One
3. You shall not take the name of the Lord your God in vain	You shall love the Lord your God
4. Remember the Shabbat day	Which I command you today (the Hebrew word *hayom*, today, is reminiscent of the verse "it is Shabbat *hayom* (today)" (Ex. 16:25)
5. Honor your father and mother	You shall teach them diligently to your children
6. You shall not commit murder	When you go on a journey (most murders are committed on the roads)
7. You shall not commit adultery	When you lie down
8. You shall not steal	You shall bind them for a sign on your hand
9. You shall not bear false witness	They shall be for frontlets between your eyes
10. You shall not covet your neighbor's house	You shall inscribe them upon the doorposts of your house (*Abudraham, Siddur* commentary)

The Ten Commandments are only alluded to in the *Sh'mah*, but ten specific commandments are explicitely stated in the first paragraph:

1. Believing in God
2. Believing in the Unity of God
3. Loving God
4. Studying Torah
5. Teaching Torah to children
6. Reciting *Sh'mah* at night
7. Reciting *Sh'mah* in the morning
8. Wearing *tefillin* on the arm
9. Wearing *tefillin* on the head
10. Affixing a *mezuzah* (*ibid.*)

From all of the above, we see that *Sh'mah* is a veritable crown jewel in Jewish prayer. In three brief paragraphs, it outlines the essential elements of faith and the observance of *Mitzvot*. But it is a most unusual prayer. Unlike the *Amidah* which addresses itself to God, the *Sh'mah* addresses itself to the worshipper. "Hear O Israel," "And you shall love the Lord your God ...," speaks not to God but to man. Furthermore, as noted earlier, *Sh'mah* consists of three passages from the Torah. It would seem logical, therefore, to characterize the reading of *Sh'mah* more as Torah study than prayer.

In point of fact, *Sh'mah* is both prayer and Torah study. Prayer and Torah study are the two key elements of worship. Together they form the essence of communication between man and God. In prayer, man speaks to God. In Torah study, God speaks to man. Prayer alone is a monologue. Prayer combined with Torah study is a dialogue. When a Jew studies Torah he hears the voice of God addressing him. God's words inspire him to respond in prayer. This is why *Sh'mah* immediately precedes the *Amidah*.

Sh'mah is not the only Torah study contained in the *Siddur*. In fact, the morning service is replete with passages and verses from the Bible and from the Talmud. Both the Written Law and the Oral Law are well represented in the morning prayers. In the preliminary prayers three blessings upon the Torah are recited. These are immediately followed with a passage from the Torah (the Priestly Blessing, Num. 6:24-26), a passage from the Mishnah (Peah 1:1), and a passage from the Talmud (Shabbat 127a, Kiddushin 39b). A major part of the service consists of Psalms. In addition, there are quotes and passages from other books of the Bible and from the Mishnah and the Talmud. Even the brief *Mincha* service is preceded by verses from the Book of Psalms. On Monday and Thursday mornings, on the mornings of Shabbat, Festivals, and fast days, and on the afternoons of Shabbat and fast days, the Torah scroll

CHAPTER 1: *Introduction*

is removed from the Holy Ark and a passage is read for the congregation. The Torah reading is an additional form of Torah study that is linked to prayer.

Though *Sh'mah* is but one in a wide selection of Torah learning experiences included in the prayers, it holds a very special place. There is an obligation for a Jew to study Torah every day, as it is written: "This book of Torah shall not depart from your mouth, and you shall meditate therein day and night" (Joshua 1:8). The verse states that the obligation is for both day and night. The Talmud says: "If a person recites *Sh'mah* in the morning and evening he has fulfilled 'This book shall not depart.' " One opinion forbids publicizing this law to unlearned people, as it would discourage them from learning and teaching Torah to their children. Another opinion, however, encourages publicizing this law to unlearned people. Rashi explains the reasoning of the second opinion as follows: the above verse promises prosperity for the person who studies Torah daily. "For then your ways will prosper" continues the verse. If prosperity is granted to someone who merely recites *Sh'mah* twice a day, how much more so will there be prosperity for someone who studies Torah all day long and sets a good example for his children (Menachot 99b). We see, then, that reciting *Sh'mah* fulfills the mitzvah of Torah study.

It is no surprise that R. Judah ha-Nasi, the codifier of the Mishnah, chose *Sh'mah* as the first topic in Tractate Berachot. *Sh'mah* is the foundation of faith, religious observance, and Torah study. When a Jew declares "Hear O Israel, the Lord is our God, the Lord is One," he affirms his readiness to make a total commitment to God. The observance of the *Mitzvot* and the study of the Torah are natural consequences of a complete and perfect faith. Similarly, the Ten Commandments begin with a declaration of God's existence: "I am the Lord your God." Maimonides followed the example of the Ten Commandments and the Mishnah by beginning his *magnum opus, Mishneh Torah*, with the words, "The foundation of all foundations and the pillar of all wisdom is to know that there is a Prime Being who has created all of creation." When a person knows that there is a God, he is inspired to communicate with Him through prayer and blessings.

Mishnah 1

From what time do we read *Sh'mah* in the evening? From the time the *Kohanim*[1] enter to eat their *Terumah*,[2] until the end of the first watch.[3] This is the opinion of R. Eliezer. The Sages say: Until midnight.[4] Rabban Gamliel says: Until dawn.[5] Once, his sons

משנה א

מֵאֵימָתַי קוֹרִין אֶת שְׁמַע בְּעַרְבִית? מִשָּׁעָה שֶׁהַכֹּהֲנִים נִכְנָסִים לֶאֱכֹל בִּתְרוּמָתָן עַד סוֹף הָאַשְׁמוּרָה הָרִאשׁוֹנָה; דִּבְרֵי רַבִּי אֱלִיעֶזֶר. וַחֲכָמִים אוֹמְרִים: עַד חֲצוֹת. רַבָּן גַּמְלִיאֵל אוֹמֵר: עַד שֶׁיַּעֲלֶה

1. *KOHANIM* — Priests, descendants of Aaron, Moses' brother, who received certain offerings and portions of the sacrifices from the people. These foods were forbidden to other Israelites because they were sacred. The *kohanim* played an important role as officiants in the Temple and as judges and teachers.

2. *TERUMAH* — Heave-offering. This refers to the portion of produce the farmer gave to the *kohanim* as part of his religious agricultural obligations. The Torah does not prescribe a specific amount to be given. Rabbinic law requires about two percent.

A *kohain* who was rendered impure, either by contacting an impure substance or by contracting certain diseases, was forbidden to eat the sacred offerings. The process of purification entailed immersion in a *mikveh* (ritual bath). Though a *kohain* had immersed in a *mikveh*, he was prohibited from eating the heave-offering until nightfall, i.e., when the stars appear. This is derived from the verse "And when the sun goes down, he shall be pure, and afterwards, he may eat from the holy for it is his bread" (Lev. 22:7). Even though, in certain cases, the *kohain* must also bring a sacrifice the next day, this does not prevent him from eating his heave-offering directly after nightfall.

3. THE FIRST WATCH — i.e., one third of the night. In ancient times, soldiers stood guard during the night in three shifts. Each "watch" was one third of the night. "And Gideon, and the hundred men who were with him, came to the edge of the camp at the beginning of the middle watch" (Judges 7:19).

4. MIDNIGHT — The middle of the night, relative to its length. "Midnight" does not mean 12:00 o'clock.

5. DAWN — Heb., *amud hashachar*. According to many authorities, 72 minutes before sunrise. Another view is that *amud hashachar* is determined by latitude and season of the year.

CHAPTER 1: *Mishnah 1*

returned from a festivity and they said to him: "We have not (yet) recited *Sh'mah*." He said to them: "If it is not yet dawn, you are obligated to recite it. And not only in this case, but wherever the Sages said 'until midnight,' the obligation lasts until dawn." The burning of the (sacrificial) fats and pieces may be done until dawn. Whichever sacrifices[6] are supposed to be eaten on the same day, their times are until dawn. If so, why did the Sages say "until midnight"? In order to prevent a person from transgression.[7]

עַמוּד הַשַּׁחַר. מַעֲשֶׂה שֶׁבָּאוּ בָנָיו מִבֵּית הַמִּשְׁתֶּה, אָמְרוּ לוֹ: לֹא קָרִינוּ אֶת שְׁמַע. אָמַר לָהֶם: אִם לֹא עָלָה עַמּוּד הַשַּׁחַר, חַיָּבִין אַתֶּם לִקְרוֹת. וְלֹא זוֹ בִלְבַד, אֶלָּא כָּל מַה שֶּׁאָמְרוּ חֲכָמִים "עַד חֲצוֹת" מִצְוָתָן עַד שֶׁיַּעֲלֶה עַמּוּד הַשָּׁחַר; הֶקְטֵר חֲלָבִים וְאֵיבָרִים — מִצְוָתָן עַד שֶׁיַּעֲלֶה עַמּוּד הַשַּׁחַר; וְכָל הַנֶּאֱכָלִין לְיוֹם אֶחָד — מִצְוָתָן עַד שֶׁיַּעֲלֶה עַמּוּד הַשַּׁחַר. אִם כֵּן לָמָּה אָמְרוּ חֲכָמִים "עַד חֲצוֹת"? כְּדֵי לְהַרְחִיק אֶת הָאָדָם מִן הָעֲבֵרָה:

---

6. SACRIFICES — Such as the Thanksgiving, Sin and Guilt offerings which were eaten on the day they were sacrificed and the following night.
7. TRANSGRESSION — He is liable to fall asleep and thereby lose the opportunity to fulfill the mitzvah of reciting *Sh'mah* at night. This would be a violation of a positive commandment.

The Letter of The Law

The commandment to recite *Sh'mah* at night and the time frame in which this commandment is to be performed are expressed by the single word, *u'v'shach'bechah*, "and when you lie down." There is unanimous agreement in the mishnah that the time frame begins

"From the time the *kohanim* enter to eat their tithe," i.e., when the stars appear. In the Talmud, however, there are differing opinions, some stating an earlier time, others a later one. One opinion is: "When people arrive home on Friday evening to eat their bread." Another opinion is: "When the poor person arrives home to eat his bread and salt." The variety of opinions is a result of the undefined term "When you lie down" (Berachot 2b).

There are, basically, two interpretations of "when you lie down" insofar as the time limit is concerned. R. Eliezer understands the term to mean "When you prepare yourself to lie down." It is during the first third of the night that most people retire to bed. Rabban Gamliel, on the other hand, views the term to mean "When you are lying down," viz., all night long when people are in bed. The Sages agree in principle with Rabban Gamliel's interpretation as attested to by Rabban Gamliel himself. They superimposed, however, an earlier time limit "in order to prevent a person from transgressing." This is in keeping with the vital role played by the Sages of building "fences" in order to safeguard the Torah.

Other examples are cited in the mishnah where the Sages imposed a midnight deadline. According to the Torah, sacrifices that are supposed to be eaten on the same day must be eaten before the following dawn. "He shall not leave of it until the morning" (Lev. 7:15). The Sages, however, decreed that the sacrifices may be eaten only until midnight. It would appear from the mishnah that the burning of the sacrificial fats and limbs is also rabbinically limited to midnight. Rabban Gamliel's statement: "Wherever the Sages said until midnight ....," is immediately followed by the example of the burning of the sacrificial fats and limbs. Maimonides, in fact, understands the mishnah this way. He writes: "In order to prevent transgression, the Sages said that the portions of the sacrifices and the limbs of the burnt offering must be burnt before midnight" (*Mishneh Torah*, Laws of Sacrifices 4:2).

Rashi, however, says that the midnight deadline does not apply to the burning of the sacrificial fats and limbs. If it did, our mishnah would contradict a mishnah in tractate Megillah that specifically says that the burning may take place until dawn (Megillah 2:6). The reason for mentioning the burning of the sacrificial fats and limbs is not to include it in the midnight deadline, but instead to emphasize that it may be done all night long, until dawn. Why, in fact, did the Sages not put a time limit on the burning? Perhaps because the *kohanim*, who are responsible for this procedure, can be trusted to perform the mitzvah in its appropriate time. All Jews, however, participated in the eating of the sacrifices, even children. Here, there is a greater likelihood of the meat not being consumed before dawn. Therefore, the Sages applied the midnight deadline (*Tiferet Yisrael*). As far as the contradiction of mishnayot is concerned, Maimonides probably understood the mishnah in tractate Megillah as referring to the essential Torah law which allows the burning all night long, and not with the practical time limit imposed by the Sages.

The Spirit of The Law

NIGHT AND DAY
Night Precedes Day

The first mishnah teaches the laws of *Sh'mah* in the evening. The second mishnah teaches the laws of *Sh'mah* in the morning. The Talmud asks: "Why this specific order? Why not begin with the morning, instead of the evening?" (Berachot 2a) Two answers are given. Firstly, the mishnah is guided by the order of the words — "When you lie down and when you rise up." Secondly, in the first chapter of Genesis we find night preceding day, as it says: "And there was evening and there was morning, one day" (1:5). The same phrase "and there was evening and there was morning" is repeated on each of the six days of creation. Thus, we have two Biblical sources for the order of evening and then morning.

There is a general rule in Talmudic study. Whenever two or more answers are given to a single question, we must assume that either the first answer is insufficient or the second answer includes a concept that is not contained in the first. A student of Talmud should ask, "Why did the Talmud deem it necessary to give a second answer? What does the second answer teach us that the first did not?"

In our case, the answer is quite simple. "When you lie down and when you rise up" is limited specifically to *Sh'mah*. The order of night preceding day as indicated in this verse only applies to *Sh'mah*. "And there was evening and there was morning," on the other hand, is written in the context of the creation of the universe. Thus, the order of night preceding day is a universal principle. It applies not only to *Sh'mah*, but also to all laws in which night and day are concerned. We see a clear application of this principle in references to Shabbat and festivals, all of which begin at sundown and conclude the following night.

Night and Day as Symbols
Aside from the legal aspect of this principle, there is a philosophical aspect, as well. Night is a symbol of suffering, fear, and exile. Many verses in the Bible associate night with human tribulation and tragedy, e.g., "Every man has his sword upon his thigh because of fear in the nights" (Song of Songs 3:8); "She weeps sorely at night, and her tears are upon her cheeks" (Lamentations 1:2). Morning, on the other hand, is a symbol of redemption and happiness, e.g., "Weeping will endure in the evening, but there is joy in the morning" (Ps. 30:6); "Satisfy us in the morning with your kindness" (Ps. 90:14).

Nighttime is shrouded in mystery and darkness. It is a time of stillness and shadows. The surrounding environment is veiled from our eyes. We feel the helplessness of the blind even as we walk. We hope that an unseen danger is not lurking in our path. It is a time when work and productive activity cease. The daily labors that give man a sense of worth and accomplishment come to an end. Man retreats from this inhospitable environment. Feeling tired and fatigued from his daytime toil, he closes his eyes and welcomes sleep.

Morning is rebirth. With every rising sun a new day is born. The sun's bright rays chase away the obscure and the unseen. Morning brings new hope, new challenges, new life. It is a time of optimism and renewed confidence. Man arises from his bed with renewed strength and vigor. He feels redeemed from night's whisper of death. He goes out to master his environment. He experiences, once again, the joy of living.

Jewish History
Jews, as a nation, have experienced nights and days in their long and vicissitudinous history. First, there was a night of slavery in Egypt. For

CHAPTER 1: *Mishnah 1*

two hundred and ten years Jewish backs were broken by their masters' rods and Jewish babies were drowned in the Nile River or entombed in mortar used for making bricks. Then the long night ended on the fifteenth of Nisan (c. 1280 B.C.E.). A new day of redemption and freedom was born. The sun shone brightly upon the Jewish people when they finally reached their destination, the Promised Land. King Solomon's reign was the noontime of that day. The Temple was built and there was peace and tranquility throughout the land.

But, night returned. On the ninth of Av, 586 B.C.E., Nebuchadnezzar, King of Babylonia, destroyed the Temple and the Jewish people was cast into exile. It was a relatively short night. Under the protection of Cyrus' edict, the Jews were allowed to return to their homeland. Seventy years after its destruction, the Temple was rebuilt and a Second Commonwealth began. Another day, and then, another night. This time, it was Titus of Rome who razed the Temple, decimated the population, and cast countless numbers into slavery. This was to be the beginning of a very long and painful night of exile. Nineteen centuries passed, in which the Jewish people suffered every form of persecution and extermination known to mankind. This tragic period climaxed in the Holocaust, which began on January 30, 1933, when the Nazis rose to power, and ended on May 8, 1945, with the unconditional surrender of Nazi Germany. Three years and six days later, on May 14, 1948, Israel was declared an independent state. A new day was born.

All of Jewish history is capsulized in an event in the life of Jacob, the Patriarch. Jacob, too, experienced a long night of exile and suffering. Fleeing from Esau who wished to kill him, Jacob sought refuge in the house of Laban. There he was a victim of perpetual deceit. And then, after twenty years, it was time to go home. One night, on his return journey, Jacob found himself all alone. He encountered a stranger who wrestled with him. They struggled all night until dawn. The mysterious foe had wounded Jacob in the thigh. Now, he begged to be released "for day is breaking." But Jacob held on to his opponent and said: "I will not let you go unless you bless me." The mysterious stranger said: "Your name shall no longer be Jacob, but Israel, for you have contended with God and with men and have prevailed" (Gen. 32:25-29).

The Sages saw in this incident a precursor to the destiny of Jacob's descendants. Jacob experienced in one night what his children were to experience for two millenia. The spirit of Esau will do everything in its power to destroy the Jewish people during a long period of exile. The Jewish people will not escape unscathed. They will suffer a wound to the thigh. But a new dawn will appear. The angel of destruction will want to flee. But he will not be free to do so until he blesses the Jewish people with the name "Israel." The Midrash says: " 'And a man wrestled with him until dawn' — until the sun will rise for Israel. Israel's salvation is like dawn, because exile is like night. The nations of the world and the evil kingdom of Edom (Esau) will wrestle with Israel in order to turn them away from the path of God" (*Midrash Lekach Tov*).

Redemption
Night and day in the halachic sense are two components of a twenty-four-hour period. In a philosophical sense, however, they represent periods of the human condition that, at times, is dark, and at other times, bright. This being the case, the question of sequence takes on universal significance. If night precedes day, as cosmogony indicates, mankind can look forward to a bright future. The law of the universe dictates that there is a light at the end of every dark tunnel. When the individual, or mankind as a whole, is thrown into an abyss of despair, there ever remains a glimmer of hope. It is this optimistic outlook that has sustained the Jewish people throughout its history. No matter how bleak the situation, the Jew hangs on to a resolute belief that there are better times ahead. This explains the almost incomprehensible phenomenon of Jews walking into the gas chambers singing, "I believe with perfect faith in the coming of the Messiah."

The Jerusalem Talmud expresses the eschatological implications of night and day. Each dawn holds a promise of the future redemption of the Jewish people. "R. Chiya Rabbah and R. Simeon ben Chalaftah were walking through the Valley of Arbel at dawn when they saw the morning star. R. Chiya said to R. Simeon: "Rabbi, so shall the redemption of Israel be. It will flicker, at first, little by little. But the more it twinkles, the faster it will come" (Berachot 1:1). Redemption will not occur in a cataclysmic fashion. It will be a process. At first, it

CHAPTER 1: *Mishnah 1* 17

will appear no brighter than the twinkle of the morning star. Slowly, the light on the horizon will shine more brightly. More and more darkness will be dispelled. Fiery rays will ignite the east. The sun will peep above the horizon. And then, with what will seem as the blink of an eye, the world will be filled with light. Redemption is born.

THE TIME THE *KOHANIM* ENTER
The Talmud asks: "If the time that the *kohanim* enter to eat their heave-offering is "when the stars appear," why didn't the mishnah simply state "when the stars appear?" The answer — "In order to teach an additional point with regard to *kohanim*" viz., a *kohain* who is rendered impure may eat his heave-offering on the day of immersion, after nightfall, even though his atonement sacrifice will not be brought until the following day. In other words, the only prerequisites for eating the heave-offering are immersion and nightfall, and not the sacrifice (Berachot 2a).

This answer is problematic. Tosafot raises the point that there are other sources that state quite clearly that the *kohain* does not have to bring his sacrifice before eating the heave-offering (Mishnah, Nega'im 14:3; Yevamot 74b). Why is it necessary for our mishnah to allude to this law? Furthermore, the mishnah usually aims for clarity. "When the stars appear" is certainly a more direct and understandable time frame than "When the *kohanim* enter." Why then, did the mishnah not employ the simpler "when the stars appear?"

Apparently, the mishnah wishes to make an association between reciting *Sh'mah* and the *kohanim* eating their heave-offering. There is a Talmudic principle that states, "*Kohanim* are diligent" (Shabbat 20a; *ibid.*, 114b; Eruvin 103a, *et al.*). This means that *kohanim* have the distinction of being very meticulous about religious observance. They are careful in carrying out all the details of the law. They are also diligent in the sense of fulfilling their religious obligations promptly, without delay or procrastination. "The diligent perform *Mitzvot* promptly" (Yomah 28b). Rashi describes *kohanim* as "All are Torah observant and God-fearing" (Shabbat 20a). *Kohanim*, then, are excellent role models for the average Jew. They set an example for all Jews as to the manner in which *Mitzvot* are to be performed.
(See note no. 2., above)

Thus, the association between *Sh'mah* and *kohanim* is designed to teach us not only when to say *Sh'mah* but also how to say *Sh'mah*. A Jew should make every effort to recite *Sh'mah* with the diligence of a *kohain*. *Sh'mah* should be recited carefully, with understanding and concentration. Every word should be pronounced properly. Its recitation should not be delayed. Every attempt should be made to recite it as soon after nightfall as possible. This is the message of the mishnah. *Sh'mah* is recited not only "when the *kohanim* enter" but, "as when the *kohanim* enter."

WATCHES

Eliezer says that the time limit for *Sh'mah* in the evening is "until the end of the first watch." This term is ambiguous, because there is a dispute in the Talmud (Berachot 3b) as to how many watches there are each night. Rabbi says there are four watches and R. Nathan says there are three. According to Rabbi, each watch is three hours long; and according to R. Nathan, four hours long. Does R. Eliezer mean that *Sh'mah* may be recited until three hours into the night or four? Furthermore, why didn't R. Eliezer simply state "until the third hour" or "until the fourth hour"? Why did he find it necessary to refer to the watches?

The Talmud asks these questions and answers that R. Eliezer is of the opinion that there are three watches in the night. And the reason why he makes reference to watches is to teach us, "Just as there are watches on earth, there are watches in heaven... and with each and every watch the Almighty roars like a lion... as it is written: 'The Lord roars from on high and from His holy dwelling place He shall shout; He shall mightily roar because of His habitation' (Jer. 25:30)....There are signs (on earth that reflect the heavenly watches): In the first watch the donkeys bray; in the second watch the dogs bark; and in the third watch infants are nursing from their mothers and wives are talking with their husbands....R. Yitzchak ben Samuel said in the name of Rav: There are three watches in the night and with each and every watch the Almighty roars like a lion and says: 'Woe unto My children; because of their sins I have destroyed My Temple, burned My Sanctuary, and exiled them amongst the nations of the world' " (Berachot 3a).

From time immemorial, soldiers have been assigned guard duty to

CHAPTER 1: *Mishnah 1*

protect army camps and civilian populations. Each shift of guard duty is called "a watch" (Heb. *ashmurah* or *mishmar*). The Bible mentions the watches in the Midianite army camp in the time of Gideon (Judges 7:19). Rabbi Adin Steinsaltz, in his commentary on the Talmud, notes that Greek armies had three watches each night, while the Roman armies had four. The watch means protection. Watches in heaven mean divine protection. God roars like a lion three times every night as He guards and protects His people. He mourns for the suffering of His children whose sins resulted in a long, dark night of exile.

The night of exile will hear donkeys bray, dogs bark and, finally, infants nursing and women talking to their husbands. This Aggadic statement may be interpreted as symbolic of the exile experience. The Hebrew word *chamor*, donkey, is related to the word *chamriyut*, materialism. In many of his commentaries and writings, the Maharal of Prague consistently interprets Biblical references to "donkey" as meaning materialism. For example, when Abraham tells his servants "remain here with the donkey," he was saying, in effect, "You remain in a world of materialism. My son Isaac and I will climb the mountain of God."

One of the characteristics of exile is a disintegration of spiritual values and an emphasis upon materialism. Jews in exile forget their role as "a kingdom of priests and a holy people." They pursue the physical comforts and material wealth enjoyed by their neighbors, often at the expense of their religion. They quickly become acculturated and lose their Jewish identity. Precious time that should be used for Torah study and prayer is squandered on the pursuit of riches. God in heaven sees and roars like a lion.

But "golden eras" do not last very long. The mood of the host country changes and Jews are no longer welcome. Their once friendly neighbors grow resentful and envious. The ills of society are heaped upon Jewish heads. Jews become convenient scapegoats. Rabid anti-Semites bark at the Jews as dogs bark at an unwelcome stranger. They seek to rid themselves of the foreign "parasites" in their midst. Before long, the Jewish community finds itself fearful of its enemies. Dark clouds appear that threaten physical violence. In the end, the Jewish community is either expelled or slaughtered. This story has been repeated many times over: Alexandria in the first century, England in the 13th century, France and Germany at the beginning of the 14th century, Spain at the end of the 15th century, Russia at the end of the 19th century, and Germany in the 20th century. Once again, God in heaven sees the affliction of His children and roars like a lion.

But night will come to an end. Jews will no longer drown in the sweet waters of materialism, or the murky depths of anti-Semitism. As the dark exile draws to an end, the Jewish people will be nourished by the Torah as an infant is nourished by his mother's breast. The Jewish people will turn to God as a wife turns lovingly to her husband in the early morning. The night shall pass and a new day of redemption shall begin. "Therefore, behold, I will allure her, and bring her into the wilderness and speak tenderly to her. I shall give her her vineyards from there and the Valley of Suffering will be a Gate of Hope; and she will respond there as in the days of her youth, as on the day she came up out of the land of Egypt. And it shall be on that day, says the Lord, that you will call Me 'My husband' and you will no longer call Me 'My Master'....And I will betroth you to Me forever; I will betroth you to Me in righteousness and justice, in kindness and mercy. I will betroth you to me in faithfulness and you will know the Lord" (Hosea 2:16-22).

TO PREVENT A PERSON FROM TRANSGRESSION
Halachah

The very first mishnah of the Six Orders of the Mishnah lays the cornerstone of rabbinic law. Jewish law may be divided into two categories: 1) Torah law, and 2) Rabbinic law. Torah law is God-given. It consists of the 613 commandments, a body of laws given to Moses by God on Mount Sinai, and a host of other laws that are derived from the Torah text. Rabbinic law consists of a vast body of rabbinic decrees and enactments that cover every facet of religious observance. Together, they make up what is called halachah, or Jewish law.

It is important to understand the nature and the authority of rabbinic law. Many Jews erroneously minimize its importance. Because they are "man-made," they are often viewed as being of lesser importance than Torah law. The nature of rabbinic law is so widely misunderstood that it would be useful to explain its essence and character.

CHAPTER 1: *Mishnah 1*

Tradition
There is a long, unbroken chain of tradition that extends from Moses to this very day. In every generation there have been Sages and scholars who served as keepers of the tradition. They are sometimes referred to as the *chachmay ha'mesorah*, the Sages of the tradition. In his introduction to *Mishneh Torah*, Maimonides lists by name the *chachmay ha'Mesorah* of the forty generations between Moses and Rav Ashi, the redactor of the Babylonian Talmud. Generation after generation, an Oral Law was transmitted from teacher to student. This Law contained a storehouse of wisdom and knowledge. Each generation accumulated and absorbed the Torah of its predecessors and then handed it down, intact, to the next generation. The *chachmay ha'mesorah* understood that to them was entrusted the essence of Judaism and the Jewish way of life. This ancient treasure was treated with awe and reverence. Each detail of law, each concept, and each interpretation was a priceless jewel. These were studied, memorized, and taught to the next generation of willing students.

Interpretation
Contained in the vast body of Jewish law are principles and rules by which the Torah is to be interpreted. These principles, known as the hermeneutic rules, enabled the *chachmay ha'mesorah* to plumb the infinite depths of Torah and discover laws and concepts that lay hidden in a word or a phrase. Other rules and principles were used to uncover additional knowledge. The interpretive powers of the Sages and scholars were very great. But interpretation was never viewed as an invention of the law. Rather it was viewed as a discovery of what lay hidden in the Torah that had been revealed to Moses by God Almighty Himself at Mt. Sinai. An Aggadic passage conveys this very idea. "When Moses went up to heaven, he found God sitting and tying crownlets on the letters of the Torah. Moses asked: 'Why are you doing this?' God replied: 'Many generations from now there will be a man named Akiva ben Joseph who will interpret heaps upon heaps of laws on each jot.' Moses said: 'Show him to me.' God said: 'Turn about.' (Moses found himself in R. Akiva's classroom) and he sat at the end of the eighth row. When he could not understand the lesson he felt faint, until a student asked (R. Akiva): 'Rabbi, from where do you know

this?' He answered: 'It is a law that was given to Moses at Mt. Sinai' " (Menachot 29b). At first, Moses thought that R. Akiva was inventing new laws that had no basis in Torah. This grieved Moses. But when R. Akiva told his students that all laws are derived from a tradition that originated at Mt. Sinai, he felt relieved.

The genius of the *chachmay ha'mesorah* is exemplified in their ability to apply the law to new situations. Working within the framework of tradition, they used the rules of interpretation to meet the never-ending social and economic changes of society. Halachah was never a frozen body of law. It is a living, dynamic system that is capable of meeting new challenges. Were it not for halachah's adaptibility in the hands of the Sages, it would have fallen into disuse as an archaic legal system long ago. An example of the dynamic approach of halachah is the institution of *Prosbul*. According to Torah law, all outstanding debts are nullified by the Sabbatical year. Thus, if a debtor did not pay his creditor by the end of the Sabbatical year, the debt was cancelled and the creditor lost his money. This situation presented a serious problem not only to creditors, but also to all would-be debtors. The poor found it impossible to acquire a loan with the approach of the Sabbatical year. This created a severe hardship for them. The great sage Hillel confronted the problem with an ingenious solution. The Torah states: "But that which is yours with your brother, your hand shall release" (Deut. 15:3). This is interpreted to mean that no individual has the right to collect debts from "his brother" once the Sabbatical year has elapsed. The court, however, as a corporate body, does have the right to collect debts if the bonds have been delivered to the court by the creditors. Hillel extended this ruling to allow the collection of debts, even if no bond had been delivered to the court (Sheve'eet 10:3-4). In this manner, Hillel upheld the letter of the law, and at the same time, adapted the spirit of the law to the pressing economic needs of the time.

"Fences"
The *chachmay ha'mesorah* are responsible for yet another form of legislation that is designed to safeguard the integrity of the Torah. Again, working within the guidelines that were established on Mt.

CHAPTER 1: *Mishnah 1*

Sinai, they "built fences around the Torah." The first mishnah in Ethics of the Fathers states: "Moses received the Torah at Sinai and handed it down to Joshua; Joshua to the elders; the elders to the prophets; and the prophets handed it down to the Men of the Great Assembly. They said three things: Be patient in the administration of justice; raise up many students; and make a fence for the Torah."

The Torah may be compared to a flower garden containing 613 beautiful, precious flowers. There is an ever-present danger that people may inadvertently or maliciously trample the flowers and destroy them. Thus, a fence is needed to protect the Torah garden. It is the Sages who have built that fence. Wherever the Sages felt that a Torah law was endangered, they established laws to protect it. Their decrees and rulings have far-reaching implications and applications as far as the observance of halachah is concerned. For example, the Torah prohibits carrying articles in a public domain on Shabbat. In order to protect the law of "carrying," the Sages decreed that it is forbidden to take up a *lulav* or blow a *shofar* on Shabbat for fear that some people may forget that it is Shabbat and carry the *lulav* or *shofar* in a public domain.

Our mishnah provides us with the very first Mishnaic example of a rabbinic "fence." Torah law allows *Sh'mah* to be recited all night long. The Sages, however, understood human nature very well. Most people are procrastinators, especially when it comes to religious observance. At the end of a day's work there is a strong temptation to eat dinner and relax with some good music, a book, or a television program. Before long, drowsiness sets in and the individual is overcome by sleep. It isn't until the next morning that he realizes that he had failed to recite *Sh'mah* the night before. Thus, the Sages set a midnight deadline for reciting *Sh'mah*. This way, a person is less likely to forget to say *Sh'mah*. The Talmud puts it as follows: "The Sages made a fence so that a person would not come from the field in the evening and say: 'I will go home, eat a little, drink a little, sleep a little, and then recite *Sh'mah* and pray.' Sleep will overtake him and he will sleep all night long. A person should rather come from the field in the evening and go the the synagogue. If he is accustomed to study Scripture, let him study Scripture; to study Mishnah, let him study Mishnah. Then, let him recite *Sh'mah* and pray, eat his bread and bless" (Berachot 4b).

Torah Fences

The concept of a "fence around the Torah" is not a rabbinic invention. The Torah itself provides us with examples of "fences" that are designed to protect its own laws. For example, the *Nazir* is one who makes a vow of abstinence in order to raise himself to a higher spiritual level. The Nazirite vow entails three restrictions: not coming in contact with a corpse, not cutting his hair, and abstaining from wine. In order to reinforce the prohibition of drinking wine, the Torah forbids all grape products, such as grape juice, grapes, and even the pits and skins of grapes (Num. 6:2-4). As a logical extension of Biblical law, the Sages forbade the *Nazir* from even entering a vineyard, lest he momentarily forget his status and eat some grapes. This gave rise to an often quoted saying in the Talmud: "Go away, we say to the *Nazir*, go around and don't come near the vineyard" (Shabbat 13a, Pesachim 40b, Bava Metziah 92a, *et al.*). (This rule explains an enigmatic Biblical passage. Judges 14:5-6 tells of Samson and his parents going to Timnah. When they came to the vineyards of Timnah, Samson came upon a roaring lion, whereupon he tore the lion apart with his bare hands. It then states: "He did not tell his father and mother what he had done." But if they were walking together, wouldn't they have seen the lion and Samson's heroic act? Apparently, when they reached the vineyards they parted company. Samson walked around the vineyards because he was a *Nazir*. His parents walked through. Thus, they were not aware of his encounter with the lion [*Ha'amek Davar*, Num. 6:3]).

Another example of a Biblical "fence" pertains to the law of leaven that is forbidden on Passover. Not only does the Torah prohibit eating leaven, it also prohibits its ownership. Furthermore, there is a positive commandment to eliminate all traces of leaven from our possession. The reason why the Torah heaped prohibitions on leaven is because, unlike most other forbidden foods, leaven is eaten all year. It is very likely for a person to forget the law and eat leaven on Passover if it is in his posession and ownership. Again, the Sages extended the Torah law to include the requirement of searching for leaven and burning it, even if it is legally no longer in one's possession through nullification.

Other Communities

There are religious communities today that have not embraced the teachings and rulings of the *chachmay ha'mesorah*. The Samaritans and the Karaites, for example, have adopted a literal interpretation of the Torah. Their practices differ widely from traditional Judaism. The Jewish Ethiopian community, until recently, had been cut off from the mainstream of Judaism for twenty-five centuries. Their religious practices did not develop under the guidance and leadership of the *chachmay ha'mesorah*. As a result, those who miraculously have been brought home to Eretz Yisrael face an enormous challenge. Fortunately, most are willing to make a giant leap of 2,500 years and integrate themselves into the halachic Judaism of their brethren.

Sources of Rabbinic Authority
From where do the Sages derive their authority to legislate ordinances and decrees? Who gives them the right to interpret the Torah? Who says that rabbinic law is as binding as Torah law? The answer is — the Torah itself!

1) "And you shall come to the *kohanim*, the Levites, and to the judge that shall be in those days, and you shall inquire; and they will tell you the sentence of the judgment.... According to the law which they shall teach you and the judgment that they shall tell you shall you do; you shall not deviate from the word which they shall tell you, neither to the right nor to the left" (Deut. 17:9-11). The Talmud comments: "All rabbinic laws are based on the verse: 'you shall not deviate' "(Berachot 19b).

2) "Ask your father and he will tell you; your elders, and they will say to you" (Deut. 32:7).

One opinion in the Talmud derives from this verse that it is fitting to recite the words "who has sanctified us with His commandments" even on rabbinic commandments such as reading the *Megillah* and lighting Chanukah lights (Shabbat 23a).

Nachmanides, in his glosses on Maimonides' *Sefer Hamitzvot*, derives from this verse the rabbinic authority to establish enactments such as *Megillah* reading on Purim and the lighting of candles on Chanukah (Principle One).

3) "And you shall keep my ordinance" (Lev. 18:30). This verse is found in the context of forbidden sexual relations. From here the Talmud derives that the Sages shall extend the number of relations

included in the laws of incest. For example, the Torah prohibits sexual relations with one's mother. Rabbinic law extends the prohibition to one's grandmother (Yevamot 21a).

4) "Six days you shall do your work and on the seventh day you shall rest... and everything that I have said to you, shall be kept" (Ex. 23:12-13). The Midrash infers from "shall be kept" that the Sages are authorized to enact rabbinic laws that will protect the Shabbat (*Mechiltah*).

All the above verses underscore the authority that is vested in the rabbinic leadership of every generation to legislate and promulgate laws, decrees, and ordinances. As *chachmay ha'mesorah*, it is their duty to preserve and protect the tradition that emanated from Mt. Sinai when God revealed the Law, in its entirety, to Moses. With a careful and deliberate use of this authority, the Sages erected a magnificent legal structure that encompasses every aspect of Jewish life. They have given to the Jewish people a halachah (from the Hebrew *holech*, go), a way in which to go, at all times, in every place. They have given Judaism a body in which to house the soul of the God-given law. It is this edifice, this body, that has given life and endurance to the Torah for more than three thousand years.

There is a story told in the Talmud that poignantly conveys the supreme authority of the Sages. There was once a dispute on a point of law between R. Eliezer and the Sages. R. Eliezer was unsuccessful in persuading the Sages of the validity of his opinion. Unwilling to relinquish his position, R. Eliezer resorted to enlisting divine support. He said to them: "Let this carob tree prove that I am right." Miraculously, the carob tree moved from its place. The Sages responded: "You cannot bring proof from a carob tree."

He then said: "Let this channel of water prove that I am right." Suddenly, the water in the channel began to flow backwards. The Sages said: "You cannot bring proof from a channel of water."

R. Eliezer persevered. He looked at the walls of the study hall and declared: "Let the walls of the study hall prove that I am right!" Slowly, the walls of the study hall began to totter until R. Joshua ordered them to stay in place.

Finally, in one last desperate attempt to win his argument, R. Eliezer shouted: "Let heaven prove that I am right!" The Sages listened. Suddenly, a voice from heaven was heard: "Why do you argue with R. Eliezer? The halachah is in accordance with his opinion!" But, the Sages were still not intimidated. R. Joshua stood on his feet and firmly declared: "It (the Torah) is not in heaven!" (Deut. 30:12). The matter was settled. R. Eliezer was overruled by the majority opinion. The halachah is in accordance with the Sages.

The story has a fascinating postscript. Shortly after this incident, R. Nathan met the prophet Elijah and asked him: "What was the Almighty's reaction to all this?" Elijah replied: "He smiled and said: '*Nitzchunee banai, nitzchunee banai*, My children have defeated Me, My children have defeated Me' " (Bava Metziah 59b).

The message is clear. Rabbinic legal authority is unquestioned. Not even divine intervention can overturn rabbinic rule. God Almighty Himself granted legal power to the Sages at Mt. Sinai when He said: "You shall not deviate from the word which they shall tell you, neither to the right nor to the left."

R. Tzvi Hirsch Chajes (1805-1855) in his annotations on the Talmud offers a novel interpretation of God's words: "*Nitzchunee banai, nitzchunee banai.*" "*Nitzchunee*" is related to the Hebrew word "*netzach*" which means "eternal." God smiled and said: "My children have eternalized Me, My children have eternalized Me." God was saying, in effect: "By their steadfast determination to interpret the law as they saw fit, by their not being persuaded by supernatural feats — My children have demonstrated the inviolability of their authority and have thereby ensured the eternity of My Torah."

The Practical Law

1. The time for reciting *Sh'mah* at night begins at nightfall when three small stars are visible. If one recited *Sh'mah* before nightfall, he must recite it again, without the blessings, after nightfall (*Orach Chaim* 235:1).

2. One should try to recite *Sh'mah* as soon after nightfall as possible. He should certainly make every effort to recite before midnight. If, due to circumstances, midnight elapsed, he may recite until dawn (*ibid.*, 235:3). (See Note No. 5 on mishnah).

3. If one recites nighttime *Sh'mah* after dawn, but before sunrise, he has not fulfilled his obligation unless it was due to circumstances beyond his control, as in the case of illness or intoxication (*ibid.*, 235:4).

Mishnah 2

From what time do we read *Sh'mah* in the morning? When a person can distinguish between blue[1] and white. R. Eliezer says: between blue and green.[2] The time limit is until sunrise. R. Joshua says: Until three hours,[3] because it is the manner of nobility[4] to arise in the third hour. Whoever recites *Sh'mah* after the time limit has not (totally) forfeited (reward) because he is as a person who reads in the Torah.[5]

משנה ב

מֵאֵימָתַי קוֹרִין אֶת שְׁמַע בְּשַׁחֲרִית? מִשֶּׁיַּכִּיר בֵּין תְּכֵלֶת לְלָבָן. רַבִּי אֱלִיעֶזֶר אוֹמֵר: בֵּין תְּכֵלֶת לְכַרְתִי; וְגוֹמְרָהּ עַד הָנֵץ הַחַמָּה. רַבִּי יְהוֹשֻׁעַ אוֹמֵר: עַד שָׁלשׁ שָׁעוֹת, שֶׁכֵּן דֶּרֶךְ בְּנֵי מְלָכִים לַעֲמֹד בְּשָׁלשׁ שָׁעוֹת. הַקּוֹרֵא מִכָּאן וְאֵילָךְ, לֹא הִפְסִיד, כְּאָדָם הַקּוֹרֵא בַּתּוֹרָה:

---

1. BLUE — Heb. *t'chaylet*. Maimonides describes the color as: "The color of the sky when the sun is at its zenith," i.e., light blue. Rashi, however, says *t'chaylet* is green "similar to the color of leeks." The Babylonian Talmud states that *t'chaylet* "resembles the sea, the sea resembles the sky, the sky resembles the sapphire, the sapphire resembles the Throne of Glory" (Menachot 43b). The Jerusalem Talmud states that it "resembles the sea, the sea resembles grass, and grass resembles the heavens" (Berachot 1:2).
2. GREEN — The color of leeks.
3. THREE HOURS — One quarter of the length of the day. There are two opinions as to the definition of the length of the day: 1) from dawn until the stars appear (*Magen Avraham*). 2) from sunrise to sunset (*Vilna Gaon*).
4. NOBILITY — Nobility are presumed to sleep late. As long as there are even a few people still arising in the morning, one is within the time period of "when you rise up".
5. WHO READS IN THE TORAH — Though he does not receive the reward of reciting *Sh'mah* in the appropriate time, he earns the reward of studying Torah. (See the Introduction for the Torah study aspect of *Sh'mah*.) The Talmud adds that he has, also, not forfeited the opportunity of reciting the accompanying blessings even though the time for saying *Sh'mah* has elapsed.

The Letter of the Law

WHEN TO RECITE *SH'MAH*

The time to recite *Sh'mah* in the morning begins "when you rise up." The Rabbis interpreted this to mean, not when each individual arises, but when people generally arise. The two opinions in the mishnah offer empirical time frames. The *Tannah Kamah* (the first opinion which is that of the Sages) says this time begins when a person can distinguish between blue and white. In Mishnaic times, one of the *tzitzit* strings was dyed blue (*t'chaylet*) in accordance with the scriptural injunction "and they shall place on the corners of their garment a blue thread" (Num. 15:38). As a practical matter, a person can tell if it is time to recite *Sh'mah* by looking at his *tzitzit* and seeing if he can distinguish between the blue thread and the white threads. R. Eliezer disagrees. He says that *Sh'mah* may not be recited until it is possible to distinguish between blue and green. This would require that a person be able to differentiate between the blueness of the sky and the greenness of the field. This, of course, is somewhat later than the time determined by the Sages.

T'CHAYLET

T'chaylet is a dye that was extracted from a certain sea snail, called *chilazon*, that inhabited the coastline between Tyre and Haifa. This portion of Eretz Yisrael was allocated to the tribe of Zevulun, who received in its blessing "the hidden treasures of the sands" (Deut. 33:19). From the discrepancies in its description in the Babylonian and Jerusalem Talmuds, it was apparently a bluish-green color.

T'chaylet was very rare and expensive because the snails only reached shore infrequently and even then it was very difficult to extract their dye. A counterfeit tint made from the indigo plant, *kela ilan*, found its way to the marketplace, making it even more difficult to obtain authentic *t'chaylet*. For these reasons it fell into disuse and only white *tzitzit* were used. The Midrash notes: "Nowadays we have only white *tzitzit*, the *t'chaylet* has been concealed" (*Num. Rabbah* 17:7). The *tzitzit* that were discovered in the Bar Kochba caves were dyed with indigo.

In the late nineteenth century, R. Gershon Hanoch Leiner, the

Chasidic rabbi of Radzin, tried to reintroduce the use of *t'chaylet*. His investigations led him to believe that the *chilazon* was a cuttlefish, *Sepia officinalis (Vulgaris)*, which secretes a blue-black dye. His opinion was not adopted by other Torah authorities. To this day, however, Radziner and some Breslav Chasidim wear the blue thread on their *tzitzit*.

The Spirit of the Law

COLORS

The Sages and R. Eliezer each suggest a practical method for determining the point at which *Sh'mah* may be recited in the morning. By looking at *tzitzit*, according to the Sages, or by looking out the window, according to R. Eliezer, a person knows if it is time to recite *Sh'mah*. But their choice of colors has other implications, as well. As noted above, both the Babylonian and Jerusalem Talmuds attribute symbolic significance to the thread of *t'chaylet*. Blue is associated with heaven and the "Throne of Glory." It is a color that reminds us of God's glorious majesty. In ancient times, blue was a color of royalty and princes (Ezekiel 23:6, Esther 1:6). White is a symbol of purity and innocence. The prophet declares: "If your sins shall be as scarlet, they shall turn white as snow" (Isaiah 1:18). This is one of the reasons why it is customary to wear a white robe, a *kittel*, on Yom Kippur. It is also customary to hang a white curtain on the Holy Ark and to cover the Reading Table with a white cloth during the High Holy Days. Thus, the time frame for *Sh'mah*, according to the Sages, is a daily reminder of the purity of the human soul and the majesty of God from whom the soul derives. This concept is beautifully expressed in our morning prayers: "My God, the soul which You have placed in me is pure. You created it, You formed it, You breathed it into me, and You preserve it within me."

R. Eliezer believes that *Sh'mah* should evoke another awareness, viz., the difference between heaven and earth as symbolized by the colors blue and green. The human being is a composite of spirituality and earthly matter. The Torah's description of the creation of Adam highlights man's duality. "And the Lord God formed man from the dust of the earth and breathed into his nostrils the breath of life, and man became a living soul" (Gen. 2:7). The human being is governed by two complementary forces, the physical and the spiritual. There is a part of man that is subject to biological law and driven by material needs and physical impulses. The human being shares with the animal kingdom the need to eat, drink, sleep, and procreate. At the same time, however, he is singularly endowed with a spiritual dimension, a divine "breath of life." This unique human quality is expressed through the universal quest for the Higher Being, the Source of life. Man's unquenchable religious thirst may take many forms and directions, from the most primitive idolatry to enlightened monotheism. Yet, almost all religions share the common goal of seeking a relationship with the Creator. The spiritual dimension is also manifest in man's self-awareness and his search for meaning in life. The cow is content to munch on grass in the pasture. Man, on the other hand, be he hungry or well-fed, is painfully aware of his frailty and mortality. He questions why he was put on earth and seeks purpose to his existence. At times, he is driven to reject his spirituality and to submit to the pleasures and delights of the flesh. And at times, he fights off his bodily appetites and immerses himself in a life of asceticsism and self-denial.

R. Eliezer sees in the *Sh'mah* a reminder of the distinction between blue and green, the spiritual and the earthly. But rather than reject one, or choose one at the expense of the other, he sees the need to create a harmonious balance, so that the human being can develop both aspects of his personality to their fullest potential. Indeed, the balance of physical and spiritual is epitomized by a promise found in *Sh'mah* itself: "It shall be, if you shall surely hearken to my commandments which I command you this day, to love the Lord your God and to serve Him with all your heart and with all your soul... you shall gather in your grain, your wine and your oil... and you shall eat and be satisfied" (Deut. 11:13-15).

There is a third time frame for *Sh'mah* which is recorded in the Talmud: "When a person can recognize his fellow from a distance of four cubits" (approximately seven feet) (Berachot 9b). The Jerusalem Talmud clarifies the word "fellow" to mean an acquaintance, because a close friend can be recognized even at a greater distance, while a stranger cannot be identified even at close range. This third opinion suggests another significance to the recitation of *Sh'mah*. Love for God should be integrated with a recognition of our fellow human being. If we are unable to "see" our neighbor, our love for God is incomplete. True love for the Almighty should manifest itself in love and care for our fellow human beings. The commandment "Love thy neighbor as thyself" is followed by the words "I am the Lord" (Lev. 19:18), meaning, that love for one's neighbor is a natural extension of love for the Lord. We all share the same divine spark. Failure to see the divinity within our fellow human being is a failure to see the true greatness of God. Thus, our day should begin not only with an affirmation of our belief in God, but with a recognition of our neighbor, as well.

NOBILITY
Centuries of persecution have inflicted an inferiority complex on the Jewish nation. For nearly two thousand years, Jews were a people without a homeland. The "wandering Jew" was a stranger in foreign lands. At times, he was a welcomed guest, treated with respect. But more often, he was scorned by his host country. When Emancipation swept through Western Europe in the beginning of the eighteenth century, the Jew dreamed of equality and full acceptance. It did not take long for the dream to be shattered. The Dreyfus trial in Paris in 1894 brought to light the latent anti-Semitism of the masses of the French people. Even in the United States, where the Jew is legally protected by the Bill of Rights and the Constitution, he is constantly reminded of the fact that many Americans view him as an alien and an undesirable citizen. No nation can undergo such experiences without suffering damaging effects on its collective psyche.

R. Joshua permits the recitation of the morning *Sh'mah* until three hours "because it is the manner of nobility (lit. princes) to arise in the third hour." In effect, R. Joshua's statement is a reminder that every Jew possesses nobility and dignity. Every Jew is granted the privilege of reciting *Sh'mah* during the rising time of princes. Even the poor Jewish laborer who must awaken at the crack of dawn to eke out a living is a nobleman.

This is not an isolated example of an halachic opinion shaped by Jewish nobility. For example, the Jewish laborer is granted certain rights and privileges. Workers are entitled to free meals and coffee breaks if such is the local custom. The working hours, as well, are determined by local custom. Once, R. Yochanan ben Matya sent his son to hire some laborers. The son returned and told his father that he had hired workers and had promised them full meals though the local custom only required their receiving bread and beans. R. Yochanan ben Matya said: "My son, even if you were to prepare the feasts of King Solomon, you still would not be keeping your word because they are the children of Abraham, Isaac, and Jacob. Before they begin working you had better tell them that all they will receive is bread and beans" (Bava Metziah 7:1). What R. Yochanan was saying to his son was, if you do not guide yourself by the standards of local custom, you will never be able to do enough for them. They are princes, descendants of the royal patriarchs. They deserve nothing less than royal banquets.

Another example of Jewish nobility in halachah is found in the prohibition of taking medicines on Shabbat. Only a person whose life is or may be in danger, or someone who is bedridden by his illness or pain, is permitted to take medicines. Foods and oils that are generally used for medicinal purposes are also forbidden. If, however, they are also used for nonmedicinal purposes, they may be used as medicines, as well. For example, it is permitted to eat oranges to fight a cold, or to eat hard candies to soothe a sore throat. Aspirins and cough medicine, however, are forbidden. It is permitted to put oil on a rash or irritation so long as people use that oil for nonmedicinal reasons, as well. The Mishnah says that princes and nobility may place rose oil on their wounds because they also use rose oil for nonmedicinal purposes. R. Simeon ben Gamliel, however, argues that every Jew may use rose oil on wounds because "All Jews are nobility" (Shabbat 14:4).

THE CHOSEN PEOPLE

The phrase "all Jews are nobility" stems from the concept that the Jews are the Chosen People, which is a central belief in Jewish thought. This concept is deeply rooted in the Bible, the Talmud, the liturgy, and in philosophical and Kabbalistic writings. The following is a sampling of sources on the Chosen People:

Bible

1. "And you shall say to Pharaoh: So said the Lord, Israel is My son, My firstborn" (Ex. 4:22).

2. "And now, if you will surely listen to My voice and keep My

covenant, you shall be unto Me a treasure from among all the nations, for all the earth is Mine. And you shall be unto Me a kingdom of priests and a holy nation... " (Ex. 19:5-6).

3. "And you shall be holy unto Me, for I the Lord am holy, and I will separate you from the nations to be Mine" (Lev. 20:26).

4. "And yet for all that, when they will be in the land of their enemies I will not abhor them or loathe them to destroy them utterly, to break My covenant with them, because I am the Lord their God" (Lev. 26:44).

5. "For you are a holy nation to the Lord, your God; the Lord God has chosen you to be a treasured people to Him from all the nations that are upon the face of the earth. It is not because you are more in number than the nations that the Lord desires you, for you are the fewest of all nations. But rather, because of the Lord's love for you and his keeping of the oath which He swore unto your forefathers... " (Deut. 7:6-8).

6. "You are the children of the Lord, your God... For you are a holy nation to the Lord your God; and the Lord has chosen you to be a treasured people to Him from all the nations that are upon the face of the earth" (Deut. 14:1-2).

7. "And I shall give you for a light to the nations, that My salvation be to the end of the earth" (Isaiah 49:6).

8. "Only you have I known of all the families of the earth; therefore, I will punish you for all your sins" (Amos 3:2).

9. "And who is like Thy people Israel, a singular nation on the earth... ? " (I Chron. 17:21)

Talmud

We have cited above three Mishnaic references to the Jewish people as being "children of kings" and "children of Abraham, Isaac, and Jacob." The following are several additional Mishnaic and Talmudic sources:

1. "He (R. Akiva) used to say ... Beloved are Israel for they are called the children of God; it is with special love that it was made known to them that they are called the children of God, as it is written: 'You are the children of the Lord your God.' "

"Beloved are Israel that a precious instrument was given to them. It

CHAPTER 1: *Mishnah 2*

is with special love that it was made known to them that a special instrument with which the world was created was given to them, as it is written: 'For I have given you good doctrine, do not forsake My Torah' (Proverbs 4:2)" (Ethics of the Fathers 3:14).

2. "R. Meir said: Even though they are filled with blemishes they are called 'children,' as it is written: 'Not His is the corruption, but the blemish is of His children' (Deut.32:5)" (*Sifre* 308).

3. "What is written in God's *tefillin*? 'And who is like Thy people Israel, a singular nation on the earth' (I Chron. 17:21)" (Berachot 6a).

Liturgy
1. "Blessed are You ... Who has chosen us from all the nations and has given us His Torah. Blessed are You, O Lord, Giver of the Torah" (blessing on the Torah).

2. "Blessed are You ... Who has not made me a Gentile" (morning blessing).

3. "With great love You have loved us Lord, our God, great and abundant mercy You have bestowed upon us... Blessed are You, O Lord who chooses His nation Israel with love" (blessing before morning *Sh'mah*).

4. "It is our duty to praise the Master of all, to exalt the Creator of the universe, Who has not made us like the nations of the world... " (*Aleynu*).

5. "For You have chosen us and sanctified us from all the nations..." (*Shabbat Kiddush*).

6. "Blessed are You... Who has chosen us from every nation and exalted us above every tongue and sanctified us with His commandments" (Festival *Amidah* and *Kiddush*).

PHILOSOPHY AND KABBALAH
R. Judah Halevi
"The Rabbi said: Bear with me a little until I explain to you the greatness of this nation. It is sufficient for me that God chose them as a nation and a people amongst the peoples of the world. He placed His divine influence upon their masses until they all reached the level of prophecy. This divine influence rested upon the women, too, some of

whom were prophetesses. Until that time, the divine influence rested only upon individuals from the time of Adam....

"Abraham's special quality was passed on to Isaac to the exclusion of all his other children whom he removed from the special land, so that it became designated for Isaac. Isaac's special quality was passed on to Jacob, and Esau, his brother, was excluded because Jacob was entitled to that land. Jacob's children were all special, all were worthy of the divine influence and the country unique with divine influence was theirs. This was the first time the divine influence rested upon a group, because, until then, it was only found amongst individuals" (*Kuzari* 1:95).

Maimonides

"It is by virtue of the Torah that we are distinguished from the rest of humanity, as is written: 'Only your forefathers did the Lord desire, to love them, and He chose their children after them, you, from all the nations, as it is this day' (Deut. 10:15). It is not because we were worthy of this, rather the Creator's kindness and goodness that He dealt kindly with us and benefitted us is for the sake of our forefathers who previously had displayed good deeds and knowledge of the Creator and how to worship Him. And because the Creator singled us out with His commandments and statutes, and our status amongst others became apparent because of His rules and laws... all the nations became terribly jealous of our religion... " (*Letter to Yemen*).

In a letter to a convert named Obadiah who questioned his status as a Jew because he did not descend from Abraham, Isaac, and Jacob -

"Do not consider your origin as inferior. While we are the descendants of Abraham, Isaac and Jacob, you derive from Him through whose word the world was created. As it is said by Isaiah: 'One shall say, I am the Lord's, and another shall call himself by the name of Jacob' (Isaiah 44:5)" (Quoted in *Letters of Maimonides*, Leon D. Stitskin, Y.U. Press, p. 189).

Maharal of Prague

"The difference between Israel and the nations is that God chose Israel for themselves, not because of their good deeds. Do not say He chooses them only when they do God's will, and not when they do not do His will.... Do not say that He chose Abraham and his children after him for the sake of their deeds.... This is called 'general election.' With regard to the nations, however, only when their deeds are good and righteous, does the Almighty draw them near. His nearness to them is of a specific nature, it is not a 'general election ' " (*Netzach Yisrael* Chap. 11).

R. Shneur Zalman of Lyady
" 'The soul of man is a candle of the Lord' (Proverbs 20:27) means that Israel, who is called 'man,' is like the light of a candle that constantly flickers upward because it is the nature of fire to want to separate from the wick and cleave to its source above which is the element of fire.... Even though this would cause the candle to be extinguished and there will be no light below, and it will disappear above in the light of its source, even so, this is what it naturally desires. So, too, the soul of man... has a natural desire and yearning to separate and leave the body and cleave to its source which is the Living God. Even though it will become nonexistent entirely, and nothing of its original essence will remain, even so, this is its natural will and desire.... This is a principle with everything that comes from 'the Holy Side'... and it is the opposite of the 'shell' and 'the Other Side' from which the souls of Gentiles are derived..." (*Tanya*, chap. 19).

R. Samson Raphael Hirsch
"In no wise does Jewish thought look on the choice of Israel as a rejection of the rest of humanity. It regards the choice of Israel to be only a beginning, only a restarting of the spiritual and moral rebuilding of mankind, only the first step to that future where many nations will attach themselves to God, and become His people, and Israel's Sanctuary will not be the central heart of Israel, but the center of mankind who will have found their way to God " (*Commentary on Lev.* 20:26).

Samuel David Luzzatto
"The Jewish belief about the difference between Jews and Gentiles is that the Jew sees all mankind as the children of one Father, all are in the image of God and no person is judged for his beliefs, only for his

deeds. But he also believes that because all the nations were idolators and Abraham cleaved to the One God, Creator of heaven and earth, that God made a covenant with him to multiply his children and be a God to them... and to give them the Land of Canaan. As a sign of this covenant He commanded him and his descendants to circumcise themselves. When God came to give them the Torah through Moses, he affirmed and strengthened this faith and said to them: 'If you will surely listen to My voice and keep My covenant, you shall be unto Me a treasure from among all the nations, for the earth is Mine (and all of humanity is precious to Me). And you shall be unto Me a kingdom of priests and a holy nation.' And with this intention, to strengthen this belief in their hearts, He gave them the Torah and many mitzvot, so that the masses of the Jewish people should be on the level of priests in relation to other nations and that they be separated from the multitudes by special commandments and statutes, to sanctify them to their God " (*Principles of Torah*, Chapter 16).

A careful study of the sources that deal with the Chosen People concept reveals two schools of thought. R. Judah Halevi and Kabbalistic-Chasidic philosophers maintain that there is an essential spiritual difference between the Jew and the Gentile. R. Judah Halevi sees the difference in the Jews' unique capacity to receive divine influence and reach a level of prophecy. Just as Israel is the land of prophecy, Jews are the people of prophecy. A unique sanctity sets the land and the people apart from the rest of the world. Maharal stresses the concept of "general election." Israel's chosenness is unconditional. Worthy or not, the Jewish people are a Chosen People. R. Shneur Zalman focuses on the Jewish soul whose origin differs from the Gentile soul. The Jewish soul derives from "the Holy Side." It is a divine spark that is compared to the light of a candle. The Gentile soul derives from "the Other Side" and is a "Shell." (These concepts are derived from the mystical work, the Zohar, and are beyond the scope of this work.)

The second school of thought maintains that the Jew does not differ intrinsically from the non-Jew. All human beings are the children of one Father. What sets Israel apart is the Torah. The uniqueness and chosenness of the Jew is manifest in his God-given rules and laws. In his letter to Obadiah the proselyte, Maimonides stresses the equality of mankind. R. Samson Raphael Hirsch sees the chosenness of Israel in the special mission of being a spiritual guide and mentor for other nations. The Jewish people have a unique responsibility for "the spiritual and moral rebuilding of mankind." According to Luzzatto, Abraham earned a special covenant with God because of his belief in the One God at a time when the rest of the world practiced idolatry. God is the Father of all mankind, but He set Israel apart with the laws of the Torah so that they should be a nation of priests in relation to the nations of the world.

Are Jews the Chosen People or the Choosing People? In other words, which came first — God's election of Israel or Israel's election of God? The first school of thought supports the doctrine that the chosenness of Israel preceded Israel's choosing of God. R. Judah Halevi sees chosenness as a hereditary quality that was transmitted in a direct line from Adam to Abraham. Jacob was successful in bequeathing this quality to all of his twelve sons. At Mt. Sinai, the divine quality was bestowed upon the entire Jewish people. Maharal and R. Shneur Zalman of Lyady also see the chosenness of Israel as a spiritual quality that is inborn. Maimonides, however, maintains that the election of Israel was earned by the "forefathers who previously had displayed good deeds and knowledge of the Creator." It is not heredity, but Torah, that distinguishes the Jew from the Gentile. R. Samson Raphael Hirsch and Samuel David Luzzatto also see the Torah with its ethical and moral laws as the distinguishing factor between Jew and Gentile. Israel is chosen with a specific mission and purpose. Israel's acceptance of the Torah at Mt. Sinai earned it the title "Chosen People." *Noblesse oblige.* Being chosen means being responsible for the spiritual development of all of mankind. This second school of thought would respond to Hilaire Belloc's poem: "How odd of God to choose the Jews." with: "It was not odd, the Jews chose God."

A PARABLE
There was once a king in a distant land who was blessed with many children. The king loved all his children dearly. In his eyes each one was talented and gifted. The wise king saw the unique qualities of each child

and decided to hire special tutors to educate them. He instructed the tutors to teach his children in such a manner that their full potentials would be realized. One child received a music teacher, another an art teacher. One child studied law, another studied philosphy. There was one child, however, who did not manifest special skills or talents. He was not interested in the arts and sciences. Nothing seemed to interest him. This child, however, was very attached to his father. When the king took long walks, he would follow behind. The child constantly ran to his father with questions. He excitedly shared new experiences and insights. He was affectionate. He loved to hold his father and to be held by him.

The king contemplated his young child. He asked himself — "What special instruction shall I give my son?" After much serious thought and deliberation, the king decided that he would not hire a tutor to teach this special son. He, himself, will be his teacher. He will not teach him music or art or dance. He will not educate him to become a brilliant scientist or philosopher. Instead, he will take the child under his personal care and guidance and teach him to forever be a loving, loyal son. He would develop the child's great capacity to love his father to its fullest potential. By doing this, the king hoped that his other children would learn from their brother's example. He feared that someday they will not only grow up, but also grow away from him. He foresaw the day when his children will take their skills and professions out into the world and forget their father. "Let this son remain here with me," he thought. "Let him be a reminder to his brothers and sisters that they, too, have a father who loves them dearly, who awaits their visits, who seeks their love."

Years passed and the children grew older. One by one they left the palace and traveled to distant places. They took with them the special skills and knowledge they had learned from early childhood. Each one was outstanding in his respective profession. Each one made a major contribution to the community in which he lived. They developed centers of learning and schools of higher education. Their reputations spread far and wide. But, they were so deeply occupied with their fields of endeavor that they neglected to give any thought to their father, the king.

The young son, Ephraim, as he was called, also grew older. As he matured, he was better able to understand what his father had intended for him. Loving his father was not simply a privilege. It became a responsibility. The king was loving, but he could be very stern. When Ephraim was neglectful of his studies or his duties, he was punished. At times, he would lie in bed late at night and think about his brothers and sisters. He, too, had not heard from them for a long time. He missed them and sometimes felt jealous of their freedom and accomplishments. He sometimes yearned to leave the palace and be with them. At times, he even desired to be like them, away from the awesome presence of the king. Nighttime thoughts soon became daydreams. Ephraim was no longer the obedient, loving child. He spent less time with his father and often ignored his instructions. Slowly and insidiously, devoted Ephraim became rebellious and defiant. He began to challenge his father's authority. He began to mock his father's rules.

The king saw the changes in his son's attitude and behavior. His heart was broken. All the years of tender love and caring seemed fruitless. Ephraim was no longer his sweet, affectionate child. He had become openly hostile. The king cried silently when he saw Ephraim debase himself in debauchery with courtesans. Visitors to the royal court, ministers and noblemen, were shocked by the transformation. They still remembered Ephraim as the favored child tucked in his father's arms. They recalled him as a young lad tagging after his father, asking to be held. Now, they saw only the king's shattered dream.

The situation was intolerable. One day, the king called Ephraim into his chamber. With tears in his eyes he said: "My son, perhaps you will never know how much I love you. I do know how much you loved me. You were always special to me because of that love. You were, and still are, the apple of my eye. But you have changed. You are no longer the little Ephraim I once knew. I had hoped that someday you would be an example of loyalty and devotion to your brothers and sisters. I prayed that you would influence them to remain devoted to me. But, instead, you disgrace me and disgrace yourself. I can no longer tolerate your insolence and your behavior. I am ashamed of you. This can no longer continue. I want you to pack your bags and leave my palace at once. You wanted freedom. Now you have it. You envy your brothers and sisters. Go to them. See if they will accept you. See if they are not jealous of you. See how they will pour out their wrath on their father's spoiled favorite.

"But remember one thing. I still love you. I will always love you. A piece of my love will follow you wherever you go. And I make one promise. Someday, after you have wandered and suffered for a long time, when your tears will flow like streams of water, when your body is bruised and wounded like a beaten olive and you will call 'Father, Father,' I will come to you and take you home."

The Practical Law

1. The time for reciting *Sh'mah* in the morning is when one is able to recognize an acquaintance at a distance of four cubits. (Opinions as to the size of a cubit vary from approximately 19 to 24 inches. Four cubits is anywhere from 6′4″ to 8 feet.) This time frame is the equivalent of when one is able to distinguish between blue and white. (*Orach Chaim* 58:1, *Mishnah B'rurah, ad loc.*)

2. Ideally, one should make an effort to recite *Sh'mah* a few moments before sunrise so that the *Amidah* will coincide with the moment of sunrise. This was the practice of the *vatikin* (devout and humble Jews, who lived in Talmudic times) (*ibid.*)

3. The time limit for the morning *Sh'mah* is three hours, which is one quarter of the length of the day, measured from sunrise to sunset (*Vilna Gaon*) or from dawn to nightfall (*Magen Avraham*) (*ibid.*)

4. One must be careful not to delay reciting *Sh'mah* until after the time limit, not even for the purposes of donning *tallit* and *tefillin*, or praying with a *minyan. Sh'mah* must be recited in its proper time (*Orach Chaim* 58:1, *Mishnah B'rurah, ad loc.*). This is especially important on Shabbat and festivals when many congregations begin morning services later than weekdays.

5. If three hours elapsed and *Sh'mah* has not been recited, it may yet be recited during the fourth hour with its blessings. After the fourth hour, *Sh'mah* should still be recited for the purpose of fulfilling the mitzvot of *Kabbalat Ohl Malachut Shamayim* (accepting the yoke of the Kingdom of Heaven) and remembering the Exodus from Egypt. These mitzvot have no time limit and may be performed any time during the day. Beyond the fourth hour, however, the blessings of *Sh'mah* may not be recited (*Orach Chaim* 58:6, *Mishnah B'rurah, ad loc.*).

Mishnah 3

Beit Shammai[1] says: In the evening everyone must recite *Sh'mah* while reclining, and in the morning, while standing, as it is written, "When you lie down and when you rise up" (Deut. 6:7). Beit Hillel[2] says: Everyone may recite in any position, as it is written, "And when you go on the way" (*ibid.*). If so, why is it written "When you lie down and when you rise up"? This means, during the time period in which people are lying down and during the time period in which people are arising. R. Tarfon said: I was once travelling on the road and I reclined to recite *Sh'mah* in accordance with the opinion of Beit Shammai. In so doing, I endangered my

משנה ג

בֵּית שַׁמַּאי אוֹמְרִים: בָּעֶרֶב כָּל אָדָם יַטּוּ וְיִקְרְאוּ, וּבַבֹּקֶר יַעֲמֹדוּ, שֶׁנֶּאֱמַר (דברים ו) "וּבְשָׁכְבְּךָ וּבְקוּמֶךָ". וּבֵית הִלֵּל אוֹמְרִים: כָּל אָדָם קוֹרֵא כְדַרְכּוֹ, שֶׁנֶּאֱמַר (שם) "וּבְלֶכְתְּךָ בַדֶּרֶךְ". אִם כֵּן, לָמָּה נֶאֱמַר "וּבְשָׁכְבְּךָ וּבְקוּמֶךָ"? בְּשָׁעָה שֶׁבְּנֵי אָדָם שׁוֹכְבִים וּבְשָׁעָה שֶׁבְּנֵי אָדָם עוֹמְדִים. אָמַר רַבִּי טַרְפוֹן: אֲנִי הָיִיתִי בָא בַדֶּרֶךְ, וְהִטֵּיתִי לִקְרוֹת, כְּדִבְרֵי בֵית שַׁמַּאי, וְסִכַּנְתִּי בְעַצְמִי מִפְּנֵי הַלִּסְטִים. אָמְרוּ לוֹ: כְּדַי הָיִיתָ לָחוּב

---

1. BEIT SHAMMAI — The school named after the great scholar Shammai who lived in Eretz Yisrael at the end of the first century B.C.E. and the beginning of the first century C.E.
2. BEIT HILLEL — The school named after Shammai's colleague, Hillel. Beit Hillel and Beit Shammai existed from the time of their founders until the beginning of the second century C.E.

life because of highway robbers. They[3] said to him: You had forfeited your life because you violated the words of Beit Hillel.

3. THEY — i.e., the Sages.

The Letter of The Law

HOW TO RECITE SH'MAH

Beit Shammai takes the words "when you lie down and when you rise up" literally; not only do these phrases teach us when to say *Sh'mah*, they tell us how to say it, as well. Thus, in the evening, *Sh'mah* must be recited in a reclining position. In the morning, it must be recited while standing.

Beit Hillel, on the other hand, interprets the phrase as applying only to the time frame for reciting *Sh'mah* and not to how it is to be recited. The posture of the body is irrelevant. This interpretation is based on the context of the previous phrase "And when you go on the way." When a person is going (walking), he is neither lying down nor standing.

R. TARFON

R. Tarfon was severely rebuked for adopting Beit Shammai's point of view by lying down to recite *Sh'mah*. At that point in time, the dispute between Beit Shammai and Beit Hillel had been resolved in favor of Beit Hillel. R. Tarfon had thus violated Rabbinic authority. Such a violation is viewed very harshly because Rabbinic authority is the cornerstone of Torah. (See "Spirit of the Law" on mishnah 1 for a comprehensive discussion on the subject of Rabbinic authority.) Though R. Tarfon was one of the outstanding sages of his time, he was obliged to accept the halachic decision which favored Beit Hillel.

This is not the only instance in which R. Tarfon put himself in danger by accepting the opinion of Beit Shammai. Once, R. Tarfon went to one of his fields to pick figs during the Sabbatical year. This was permissible according to Beit Shammai, but forbidden according to Beit Hillel. The guards did not recognize R. Tarfon as the owner. Thinking that he was a robber, they quickly grabbed him, threw him to the ground and began beating him with their sticks. Seeing that his life was in danger, he said to them: "Please go to my house and tell them to prepare shrouds for Tarfon." When the guards heard the name "Tarfon," they suddenly realized whom they were hitting. They quickly dropped their sticks and begged R. Tarfon's forgiveness. R. Tarfon replied: "Don't worry, I have already forgiven you with every blow" (Jerusalem Talmud, Sh'vee'it 4:2).

There was a period of time in which the disputes between Beit Shammai and Beit Hillel were unresolved. During that time, a person was free to choose either school of thought provided he was consistent. In the generation after the destruction of the Temple, however, when the seat of Rabbinic authority rested in Yavne, the law was decided in favor of Beit Hillel. Once the halachah was decided in favor of Beit Hillel, it was forbidden to accept the opinion of Beit Shammai. The decision, says the Talmud, was determined by a "heavenly voice." "Before the heavenly voice, whoever wished to adopt the strict decisions of both the School of Hillel and the School of Shammai, to him the verse is applied: 'The fool walks in darkness' (Eccl. 2:14). Whoever adopted the lenient decisions of both is called 'wicked.' Rather, adopt the view of one or the other consistently. When the heavenly voice decided, however, in favor of the School of Hillel, whoever violates their decision is liable the death penalty. The heavenly voice went forth and said: 'These and these are the words of the living God, but the halachah follows the School of Hillel' " (Jerusalem Talmud, Berachot 1:4).

It is ironic, notes the Talmud, that if R. Tarfon would have refrained from reciting *Sh'mah* altogether, he would have been better off. If he had not recited *Sh'mah* at all, at worst he would have violated the positive commandment to recite *Sh'mah*. Such a violation does not carry a harsh punishment. By reciting *Sh'mah* in accordance with the opinion of Beit Shammai, however, he deserved to forfeit his life (*ibid.*).

It is puzzling that the halachah should be determined by a voice from heaven. As we have already seen (page no. 27), R. Eliezer's opinion was not accepted, even though he had the support of a heavenly voice. R. Joshua declared "It is not in heaven." Here, however, we find that the heavenly voice did, in fact, sway the decision in favor of Beit Hillel.

In point of fact, it was not a voice from heaven that decided the halachah in favor of Beit Hillel. The Talmud says that Beit Hillel's opinions were adopted in most cases because they were in the majority. It is a fundamental principle in Jewish law that where there is a divided opinion, the majority rules. This principle is based on the verse "Decide the law in favor of the majority" (Ex. 23:2). Because the scholars of Beit Hillel outnumbered the scholars of Beit Shammai, the law is in their favor. The heavenly voice did not determine the law. It merely gave divine sanction to a law that was already established. R. Eliezer's opinion, however, was in the minority. Not even a heavenly voice could make his judgment prevail. God's law and its Rabbinic interpretation "is not in heaven" (*Tosafot*, Yevamot 14a, Bava Metziah 59b).

The Spirit of The Law

EXTERNALS AND INTERNALS

Beit Shammai is overruled. *Sh'mah* may be recited while walking, riding, sitting, standing, or lying down. The Torah places no restrictions or limitations on how *Sh'mah* may be recited. (The rabbis insisted, however, that a person should not be moving about while reciting the first verse, because it requires special attention and concentration.) As long as it is said properly, with the words pronounced correctly and understood, posture is of no consequence. What is important is that *Sh'mah* be recited in devotion and sincerity.

There is an important lesson to be learned from this law. All too many Jews measure the religiosity of others by external manifestations. External criteria, however, are often misleading. There are all too many examples of individuals who parade their piety in religious garb. Their personal lives, their business affairs, and the manner in which they treat other people, reflect neither religiosity nor piety. In such cases, a religious mode of dress is merely an indication of sociological pressure or misplaced priorities. It is certainly not an indication of genuine godliness.

There is a Talmudic dictum: "*Hakadosh baruch hu libah ba'ee*," "The holy One, blessed be He, desires the heart" (Sanhedrin 106b). It is crucial for the religious Jew to be sincere in his religious observance. Every *mitzvah* should be performed with love and devotion. A Jew should be humbled by a sense of awe and reverence for the Almighty. Humility should permeate every aspect of his life. Honesty and sensitivity should be extended to everyone with whom he comes in contact — loved ones, friends, acquaintances, business associates, colleagues, etc. His religious faith should reach the innermost recesses of the heart. He should feel that faith not only when he prays and performs *mitzvot*, but when he sits at home and when he goes on a journey, when he lies down and when he rises up. If such a Jew wishes to outwardly express his inner feelings and faith with a religious mode of dress, then there is no contradiction. On the contrary, his mode of dress will enhance his religious feelings and be a true expression of piety and faith.

BEIT HILLEL AND BEIT SHAMMAI
The Founders

Two Torah giants dominated the religious stage of Eretz Yisrael two thousand years ago — Hillel and Shammai. They lived in an era that bore the yoke of Roman rule. Dark clouds of pending doom gathered on the horizon. The authority of the Great Sanhedrin in Jerusalem had diminished. Roman procurators treated the population with contempt. Political and economic pressures caused a decline in scholarship. Jews prayed for a savior. There was talk of rebellion in the air. The destruction of the Holy Temple was only decades away.

In that dark era, the light of these two luminaries shone brightly. Together they carried the torch of tradition and Rabbinic learning. Students flocked to their academies. There they learned law and methodology in interpreting the law. The impact of Hillel and Shammai, the influence of their knowledge and personalities, continued long after their demise. Each bequeathed a school of learning that dominated the world of halachah for more than a century. These were Beit Hillel and Beit Shammai.

Hillel

Hillel the Elder was born into a wealthy family in Babylonia. When he moved to Eretz Yisrael he brought no wealth with him, only the pride of being a descendant of King David and an unquenchable thirst for Torah knowledge. He found a job and worked for meager wages, using half his income to support himself and the other half to pay tuition for study in the *Beit Midrash* (study hall). Once he was unable to pay the entry fee for the *Beit Midrash* and the guard at the door refused to let him enter. So Hillel climbed up on the roof and put his ear to the skylight in order to hear the lessons. It was a cold winter night and snow began to fall. In the morning, the rabbis noticed the figure of a person shading the skylight. They quickly climbed to the roof and pulled the nearly-frozen Hillel from the snow. From that time on, Hillel was a welcome student in the *Beit Midrash*.

Hillel was a man of extraordinary patience. His title *Nasi*, Head of the High Court, a title which he carried for forty years, did not diminish his humility. A person once made a wager that he could cause Hillel to lose his temper. He approached Hillel with a series of ridiculous questions. "Why are the heads of Babylonians round?" he asked. "Why are the feet of Africans wide? Why are Tadmoreans nearsighted?" To increase his chances of winning the bet, the questioner chose a late Friday afternoon, while Hillel was making his Shabbat preparations, to ask these questions. But Hillel did not lose his composure. He provided answers that were appropriate to the questions. The bettor, on the other hand, did lose his patience when he realized that his wager had cost him four hundred *zuz*.

Some of the popular anecdotes that portray Hillel's humility and patience are about Gentiles who were interested in converting to Judaism. A Gentile once approached Shammai and asked him "How many laws do you have?" Shammai replied: "Two. A Written Law and an Oral Law." The Gentile said, "I will accept the Written Law but not the Oral Law. Will you convert me by teaching me only the Written Law?" Shammai responded in anger. He scolded the stranger and chased him away. The Gentile then came to Hillel with the same proposal and Hillel converted him. The first lesson was the Hebrew alphabet, "*Aleph, Bet, Gimmel, Dalet.*" In the second lesson Hillel reversed the order of the letters: "*Dalet, Gimmel, Bet, Aleph.*" "But yesterday you taught me differently?" the convert asked. Hillel replied: "If you trust me with teaching you the Written Law, then trust me with teaching you the Oral Law, as well."

Perhaps the most famous story is the one about the Gentile who said, "Teach me the whole Torah while I stand on one leg." Shammai chased him away, but Hillel responded: "That which is hateful unto you, do not do to your neighbor. This is the essence of the Torah. The rest is commentary. Go and study."

When a certain Gentile had illusions about converting and becoming a High Priest, Shammai chased him away. Hillel accepted him and said: "Can someone be appointed as king without knowing the protocols of royalty? Go and study." When the convert came across the verse "The stranger who draws near shall be put to death" (Num. 1:51) he questioned Hillel, "To whom does this refer?" Hillel replied: "Even King David (whose great-grandmother was a convert) may not usurp the rights of the tribe of Levi. Only a member of the tribe of Levi may carry the Tabernacle." The convert realized that he was not being discriminated against. He returned to Shammai and said: "Of course I cannot become a High Priest. Doesn't it say 'The stranger who draws near shall be put to death'?" To Hillel he said: "Humble Hillel, may you be blessed for bringing me under God's wings." The moral lesson of all these stories is clearly stated in the Talmud, "A person should be patient like Hillel and not intolerant like Shammai" (Shabbat 30b, 31a).

There is an interesting postscript to these anecdotes. Hillel's teachers, Sh'mayah and Avtalyon, were both converts!

The Two Schools
More than three hundred and fifty controversies between Beit Hillel and Beit Shammai are recorded in the Talmud. The disputes run the gamut of religious law, ethics, and philosophy. In the vast majority of cases Beit Shammai is stricter than Beit Hillel. The two schools applied different methodologies in interpreting the Torah. Beit Shammai usually opted for the more literal interpretation. Notwithstanding their differences, the students of both schools respected each other's opinions. "Although these prohibited what the others permitted, nonetheless Beit Shammai did not refrain from marrying women from

the families of Beit Hillel, and Beit Hillel did not refrain from marrying women from the families of Beit Shammai.... Although these considered impure what the others considered pure, nonetheless they borrowed utensils from one another" (Yevamot 14a).

The disparate personalities of Hillel and Shammai were reflected in their students. Notwithstanding their differences, "They (the students) treated each other with love and friendship and fulfilled the verse: 'Love truth and peace' (Zechariah 8:19)" (*ibid.* 14b). Shammai's intolerance, however, led to extremism on the part of some of his students, who acted violently against students of Hillel (Jerusalem Talmud, Shabbat 1:4). Even the moderate ones never acquired the patience and humility of Hillel's students. The Talmud passes moral judgment on the two schools when it asks: "Why was Beit Hillel privileged to have the halachah decided in its favor? Because they were gentle and temperate, they analyzed Beit Shammai's point of view as well as their own, and they always quoted Beit Shammai's opinion before their own.... From this we learn, whoever lowers himself will be lifted up by the Almighty, and whoever raises himself will be lowered by the Almighty" (Eruvin 13b). Beit Hillel, whose ways were ways of pleasantness and whose paths were paths of peace, won a moral victory that helped shape the destiny of halachah and the Jewish way of life.

The Practical Law

1. *Sh'mah* may be recited in any position: walking, standing, sitting, lying, and even while riding an animal. When lying, one should be lying on the side and not prone or supine (*Orach Chaim* 63:1).

2. One who is sitting may not stand up to recite *Sh'mah* in the morning. Also, one may not sit down or lie down from a standing position to recite the evening *Sh'mah*. The latter two cases give the appearance of following the opinion of Beit Shammai (*Orach Chaim* 63:2, *Mishnah B'rurah, ad loc.*).

Mishnah 4

In the morning a person recites two blessings[1] before and one blessing[2] after (*Sh'mah*); in the evening, two before[3] and two after[4] (*Sh'mah*). One is long[5] and one is short.[6] Where they[7] said a blessing is to be long, it

משנה ד

בַּשַּׁחַר מְבָרֵךְ שְׁתַּיִם לְפָנֶיהָ וְאַחַת לְאַחֲרֶיהָ; וּבָעֶרֶב שְׁתַּיִם לְפָנֶיהָ וּשְׁתַּיִם לְאַחֲרֶיהָ. אַחַת אֲרֻכָּה וְאַחַת קְצָרָה. מָקוֹם שֶׁאָמְרוּ לְהַאֲרִיךְ, אֵינוֹ רַשַּׁאי לְקַצֵּר;

1. TWO BLESSINGS — *Yotzer ohr*, "Who creates light" and *Ahavah rabah*, "A great love."
2. ONE BLESSING — *Emet v'yatziv*, "True and certain."
3. TWO BEFORE — *Asher bidvaroh ma'ariv aravim*, "Who with His Word brings on the evenings" and *Ahavat olam*, "An everlasting love."
4. TWO AFTER — *Emet v'emunah*, "True and trustworthy" and *Hashkivaynu*, "Cause us to lie down."
5. LONG
a) According to Rashi, *Emet V'emunah*. It is called a "long" blessing because it contains several ideas.
b) According to Maimonides, *Yotzer ohr* and *Asher bidvaroh*. These are called "long" blessings because they both begin and conclude with the words: "Blessed are You, O Lord."
6. SHORT
a) According to Rashi, *Hashkivaynu*. It is called a "short" blessing because it has one central idea.
b) According to Maimonides, *Ahavah rabah* and *Ahavat olam*. They are called "short" blessings because they only conclude with "Blessed are You, O Lord" but do not begin with "Blessed...."
c) Rabaynu Tam suggests a totally different interpretation of the words "one is long and one is short." He interprets the phrase to mean that the aforementioned blessing, i.e., *Emet v'emunah* may be either short or long. In other words, one may recite either a long version or a short version. The Gemara on this mishnah mentions the short version on page 14b.
7. THEY — The Sages.

is not permitted to make it short. (Where they said a blessing is to be) short, it is not permitted to make it long. (Where they said) to conclude,[8] it is forbidden not to conclude. (And where they said) not to conclude, it is forbidden to conclude.

לְקַצֵּר, אֵינוֹ רַשַּׁאי לְהַאֲרִיךְ. לַחְתֹּם — אֵינוֹ רַשַּׁאי שֶׁלֹּא לַחְתֹּם; וְשֶׁלֹּא לַחְתֹּם, אֵינוֹ רַשַּׁאי לַחְתֹּם:

8. TO CONCLUDE — The blessing with "Blessed are You, O Lord."

The Letter of the Law

THE ORDER OF MORNING AND EVENING
In the first two *mishnayot*, evening precedes morning (see above, "Spirit of the Law" on mishnah 1). Here the order is reversed. The Talmud explains that the reason is stylistic. Since the second mishnah dealt with *Sh'mah* in the morning, it continued with the blessings of *Sh'mah* in the morning and then returned to the blessings of *Sh'mah* in the evening (Berachot 2a).

THE BLESSINGS OF *SH'MAH*
There are seven blessings that accompany *Sh'mah*. In the morning there are two blessings that precede and one that follows *Sh'mah*. In the evening there are two that precede and two that follow *Sh'mah*. The fact that there are seven blessings is significant. Several reasons are given:

1. The Sages found a source for seven blessings in the verse: "Seven times a day I praise You for your righteous laws" (Ps. 119:164). "Righteous laws" alludes to *Sh'mah* which is found in the Torah (*Rashi*, in the name of the Jerusalem Talmud).

2. Seven symbolic mitzvot are mentioned in *Sh'mah*, i.e., *tefillin* on the hand, *tefillin* on the head, *mezuzah*, and the four fringes (*Bach* 236). The blessings correspond in number to these seven mitzvot.

Several reasons are also given for the division of three blessings in the morning and four blessings in the evening:

1. During the Mishnaic period, the third paragraph of *Sh'mah* was not recited in the evening (See the next mishnah). Thus, the sum total of blessings and paragraphs of morning and evening *Sh'mah* is equal. In the morning there are three blessings and three paragraphs of *Sh'mah*, which number six, and in the evening there are four blessings and two paragraphs of *Sh'mah*, which number six (*Vilna Gaon*).

2. The evening *Sh'mah* precedes the morning *Sh'mah*, therefore, the larger number was assigned to the first *Sh'mah* in order to recite more blessings sooner (*L'vush* 58).

MORNING BLESSINGS
1. *Yotzer ohr*
The first blessing before *Sh'mah* emphasizes the role of God as the Creator. He creates light and darkness. All the universe is His. Even the angels in heaven proclaim God's sovereignty and sanctity. Creation is not an event of the past, but a continuous process. And someday, a spiritual light will shine over Zion.

2. *Ahavah rabah*
The second blessing before *Sh'mah* emphasizes God's infinite love. As an expression of love, the Almighty gave the Torah and its commandments to the Jewish people. He has enabled us to serve Him so that we may be able to reciprocate His love. The blessing makes a request that all Jews return back to Eretz Yisrael, the Jewish national homeland.

3. *Emet v'yatziv*
The blessing that immediately follows *Sh'mah* is known as the "Blessing of Redemption." It recalls God's saving power from the time He brought the Jewish people out of the Egyptian bondage. His redemption and protection continue in each and every generation.

EVENING BLESSINGS
1. *Asher bidvaroh ma'ariv aravim*
The first blessing before the evening *Sh'mah* also speaks of God as the Creator. His wisdom causes the changes of night and day and the seasons. He is the sovereign Lord who brings on the evenings.

2. *Ahavat olam*
The second blessing before the evening *Sh'mah* speaks of God's love for the Jewish people, as does its morning counterpart. It also emphasizes the importance of the Torah and its laws, which are the very life of the Jew.

3. *Emet v'emunah*
This blessing immediately follows *Sh'mah* in the evening, and is also similar to its morning counterpart. It recalls the miracles and wonders that the Almighty performed for the Jewish people when He redeemed them from Egypt. Throughout the ages, God has saved the Jewish people in times of oppression and punished its enemies. God is the perpetual Redeemer.

4. *Hashkivaynu*
This fourth blessing of the evening *Sh'mah* is a plea for divine protection from all possible dangers. It is a blessing that is appropriate to the nighttime, when fear and danger are more prevalent. On Shabbat and festivals, the concluding words change the mood of the blessing from anxiety to peace. On these holy days a Jew feels less anxious and more serene.

ON THE NATURE OF BLESSINGS

There are three types of blessings: 1) *Birchot Ha'nehenin*, recited on the pleasure derived from food, drink and fragrances; 2) *Birchot Hamitzvot*, recited before performing a religious obligation (mitzvah); and 3) *Birchot Shevach, Hoda'ah, u'Vakashah*, praises, thanksgiving, and requests (*Mishneh Torah*, Laws of Blessings 1:4). The first two types are characteristically short blessings that begin with the words: "Blessed are You, Lord our God, King of the universe." *Birchot Hamitzvot* contain the additional phrase: "Who has sanctified us with His commandments and commanded us to... (e.g., light the Shabbat lights)." The third type is often more lengthy and descriptive. At times, it begins and concludes with the words: "Blessed are You, O Lord."

All blessings are of Rabbinic origin with the exception of Grace after Meals, which is of Torah origin, as it is written, "And you shall eat and be satisfied and bless the Lord your God" (Deut. 8:10). Some say that the Abridged Grace which is said after eating of one or more of the seven species of food with which Israel is blessed (wheat, barley, grapes, figs, pomegranates, olives, and dates) is also ordained by the Torah. There are some who suggest that the blessing recited on the Torah is also of Torah origin.

A blessing, by definition, must include the Name of God and His Kingship (*Adonai* and *Melech Ha'olam*). This requirement is derived from the verse: "I will exalt You my God the King" (Ps. 145:1). This applies, however, only to the beginning of a blessing. A blessing may conclude with "Blessed are You, O Lord" without mentioning "King of the Universe." Why doesn't the first blessing of the *Amidah* contain the words" King of the Universe"? One of the answers given to this question is that the words "the great God" signifies Kingship.

Some blessings begin with *Baruch atah Adonai*, "Blessed are You, O Lord," some only conclude with *Baruch*, and others both begin and conclude with *Baruch*. The following are some examples of the guidelines for determining the structure of a blessing:

1. Short blessings that have a single theme only begin with *Baruch*, e.g., blessings on foods and blessings on mitzvot.

2. Blessings that contain more than one theme both begin and conclude with *Baruch*, e.g., *Kiddush*, which thanks God for sanctifying the Jewish people with the Shabbat and extols the importance of Shabbat; *Yotzer ohr*, which praises God as the Creator and petitions His mercy.

3. When there are two contiguous blessings the first of which concludes with *Baruch*, the second blessing does not open with *Baruch*. For example, the first blessing of the *Amidah* concludes: *Baruch atah Adonai, Magen Avraham*. Thus, the second blessing begins: *Atah Gibor*, without the words, *Baruch atah Adonai*. This rule follows the logic that when a blessing ends with *Baruch* it is simply unnecessary to repeat *Baruch* in the blessing that immediately follows. This is in keeping with the law of not uttering God's Name in vain.

4. There are several isolated blessings that are lengthy, and are not contiguous with a previous blessing, yet do not begin with *Baruch*, e.g., the blessing for rain, the blessing for travellers, the Abridged *Amidah* that is said in time of emergency. These are exceptions to the rule because they are said infrequently.

CONTIGUOUS BLESSINGS

Let us analyze the concept of contiguous blessings more carefully. As explained earlier, a concluding *Baruch* serves a dual purpose. It is the conclusion of the first blessing, as well as the introduction to the following blessing. This results in a "domino effect" on all successive blessings in the series:

 Blessing One — *Baruch atah Adonai ... Baruch atah Adonai*
 Blessing Two — *... Baruch atah Adonai*
 Blessing Three — *... Baruch atah Adonai*, and so on.

In the *Amidah*, only the first blessing has an introductory and concluding *Baruch*. The following eighteen blessings simply conclude with *Baruch*. Similarly, only the first blessing of Grace after Meals has an introductory and concluding *Baruch*. The successive two blessings have no introductory *Baruch*.

There seems to be a striking exception to the rule in the fourth blessing of Grace after Meals. In this instance, the blessing begins with *Baruch*, even though it immediately follows the third blessing, which concludes, "Blessed are You, O Lord, who builds Jerusalem in His mercy, Amen." The reason for this exception is that the fourth blessing of Grace after Meals is qualitatively different from the first three. The first three blessings are of Torah origin, whereas the fourth blessing is of Rabbinic origin. In order to demonstrate this differentiation, the fourth blessing was set apart with its own introductory "Blessed are You, Lord our God." It is for this very reason that "Amen" is said at the conclusion of the third blessing.

THE FORMULAS OF BLESSINGS

It is forbidden to change the formulas of blessings. The mishnah is quite explicit about the prohibition of lengthening or shortening blessings. Each blessing was carefully composed by Ezra and the Men of the Great Assembly. Each word was selected because of its special meaning. The order and arrangement of the blessings were also very well planned. Therefore, what may appear as a minor revision or change may have dramatic consequences on the essence of a blessing. This ruling also has a pragmatic function. The *Siddur* is one of the most potent binding forces that the Jewish people possesses. A Jew can travel to remote parts of the world and feel comfortable with the prayerbook that is used there despite minor variations and differences. The Ashkenazic ritual is not the same as the Sephardic. The Sephardic is not the same as the Eastern communities. The Yemenites have their own version. The marvel of Jewish liturgy is not, however, in its differences, but in its uniformity. The basic structure of all the services, prayers, and blessings is predominantly the same. This, despite a history of some 2,500 years and a geographical distance that spans the ends of the globe. Because the *Siddur* was treated with reverence, and every prayer and blessing was treasured in its original form, Jewish prayer has an inherent and immutable unity. Attempts to "modernize" the *Siddur* by amputating individual prayers and, sometimes, even entire sections, does harm not only to Jewish prayer but to the very unity of the Jewish people.

Professor Joseph Heinemann, in an essay on R. Saadya Gaon's attitude toward changing the formulas of prayers, writes that R. Saadya Gaon was guided by three basic principles with regard to preserving the integrity of prayer. 1) He forbids any change that damages the formal structure of the prayer. In other words, the *Baruch* at the beginning and/or end, and the words *Adonai Elohaynu* may not be tampered with. 2) The basic concept of a blessing may not be altered, added to, or deleted. For instance, he opposes the introduction of the words " O cause a new light to shine upon Zion" into the first blessing of *Sh'mah* in the morning, because this changes the basic meaning of "light" in the blessing, i.e., from physical to spiritual light. His opinion on this matter was adopted by Sephardic Jewry. 3) As a general rule, blessings that are not found in the Talmud are not allowed to be introduced at a later period. He does allow certain exceptions which were well entrenched in the *Siddur* such as *Baruch she'amar* and *Yishtabach* in the morning service (*Iyunay Tefillah*, Magnes Press, Hebrew University, 1983, pp. 110-113).

A serious debate was waged with regard to the addition of *piyutim*, liturgical poetry, in the prayers. The addition of *piyutim* seems to defy the Mishnaic ruling about not lengthening blessings. Many authorities, in fact, banned them from the liturgy (*Orach Chaim* 68). Most authorities, however, viewed the addition of *piyutim* as permissible because they conform to the content and meaning of the blessings in which they are found (*Ramah, ibid.*).

The Spirit of the Law

THE BLESSINGS: THEIR HISTORY AND MEANING IN THE HOLY TEMPLE

The blessings of *Sh'mah* and *Sh'mah* itself were part of the daily prayer service in the Temple. Early in the morning, before sunrise, the *kohanim* would enter the Chamber of Hewn Stones which was located in the southeast corner of the Temple Courtyard. The Chamber of Hewn Stones served as the seat of the Great Sanhedrin, as well as a synagogue for prayer. The *kohanim* would recite the following prayers: the blessing *Ahavah rabah*, the Ten Commandments, the three paragraphs of *Sh'mah*, the blessing *Emet v'yatziv*, a blessing for the Temple service and the Priestly Blessing (Tamid 5:1). The blessing *Yotzer ohr* was not recited until later in the day, after the sun rose (Berachot 12a). The people stood in the Temple Courtyard and listened attentively to the prayers of the *kohanim*. At the conclusion of each blessing they responded, "Blessed is the Name of His glorious majesty forever and ever" (*ibid.* 63a). They did not recite *Sh'mah* until after the sun had risen (Yoma 37b).

MORNING BLESSINGS

Yotzer Ohr (Who Creates Light)

The blessing *Yotzer ohr* was composed by the Men of the Great Assembly, a legislative body that consisted of one hundred and twenty Sages and prophets, in the fifth century B.C.E. The Persian Empire dominated the world scene at that time. Zoroastrianism was the prevalent religion amongst the Gentiles. This religion practiced the doctrines taught by its founder Zoroaster, or Zarathusthra (c. 630-541 B.C.E.). The basic tenet of Zoroastrianism is that there is a divine dualism. Two gods dominated the universe and were in constant struggle with each other. Ahura-Mazda was the god of light. All that is good in the world derived from this god. He had seven qualities: light, logos, right, dominion, piety, well-being, and immortality. Angro-Mainyus, or Ahriman, was the god of darkness. All evil in the world emanated from him. Though Zoroastrianism was a great step forward towards monotheism when compared with the polytheism of the time, it still did not approach the pure monotheism of Judaism. The blessing

CHAPTER 1: *Mishnah 4*

Yotzer ohr was formulated and introduced into daily prayer in order to negate the dominant belief of the time. R. Samson Raphael Hirsch in his *Siddur* commentary writes:

"The blessing *Yotzer ohr* pays tribute to the glory of God as demonstrated by the rays of the rising morning sun. The very first sentence of this blessing refutes one of the oldest fallacies to be devised by human thought; namely, that the contrasts found in the phenomena of nature and the world indicate the existence of more than one Deity; that is two separate and opposing divinities — a god of day, life, and prosperity on one hand, and one of night, death, and evil on the other. Our blessing, however, opposes this view by avowing that light and darkness were created by one and the same God, that day and night and all other phenomena which appear to us to be antitheses of one another, actually serve, under the Providence of One God, solely to advance one and the same purpose; the welfare of both man and nature. It is this Divine Providence which shapes this world of apparent conflicting phenomena into a unified world of perfect harmony. Therefore, when we recite this blessing in the morning, we add that God Who made light is also the creator of darkness, and when we say it in the evening, we remember that the same God Who created night is also the maker of the light of day."

The opening of the blessing is derived from the Book of Isaiah, 45:7. There is, however, one important distinction. Isaiah uses the term: "Who creates evil." The blessings reads: "Who creates everything." This change in wording, according to the Talmud, is because the Sages did not want to introduce the word "evil" into the blessing (Berachot 11b). It might also have been made to further emphasize the Unity of God.

The angels in heaven sanctify the Name of God as man does here on earth. They say to each other: "Holy, holy, holy is the Lord of Hosts, the world is filled with His glory." The angels and the heavenly bodies join in acknowledging the Supreme Creator. R. Judah Halevi writes in his *Kuzari*: "The pious person thinks about the meaning of each blessing and understands its purpose and the principle from which it is derived. The blessing 'Who creates lights' describes the order of the upper world, the greatness of the heavenly bodies, the importance of their usefulness. Yet, they are as small as worms compared to Him"

(3:17). The reason for introducing the prayer of the angels is to negate the notion that angels are independent beings who do not depend upon the Will of God.

"O cause a new light to shine upon Zion, and may we all be worthy soon to enjoy its brightness."

This passage is omitted in Sephardic liturgy because the blessing *Yotzer ohr* has no bearing on the spiritual light of redemption, only on the physical light of the sun, moon, and stars. Ashkenazic tradition, however, includes this passage, because it sees a meaningful connection between the light of creation and the light that will shine in the days of the Messiah. Rashi's comment on the verse: "And God saw the light, that it was good; and He divided..." (Gen. 1:4) reads: "He saw that evildoers are not worthy of it so he separated (assigned) it for the righteous in the World to Come." Rashi's Midrashic statement also associates the light of creation with spiritual light.

Ahavah Rabah (With a Great Love)

According to Ashkenazic tradition, the second blessing in the morning begins with the words: "With a great love You have loved us," and that in the evening begins with the words: "You have loved the house of Israel with everlasting love." In the Sephardic and Chasidic version, the latter phrase is used morning and evening. The source for these two texts is found in a Talmudic dispute. Samuel says "With a great love..." and the Sages say "You have loved..."(Berachot 11b). The Sephardim adopt the view of the Sages, while the Ashkenazim accomodate both opinions.

Ahavah rabah appropriately follows *Yotzer ohr*. *Yotzer ohr* describes God's love for mankind which is manifest in the creation of light. "In mercy You give light to the earth and to those who dwell on it; in Your constant goodness You renew the work of Creation every day constantly." *Ahavah rabah* is also a beautiful expression of God's love. This love for the Jewish people is manifest in the gift of Torah and mitzvot. The Jewish people are privileged with God's Law and the Holy Land.

Rabbi Samson Raphael Hirsch expresses another insight into the juxtaposition of the two blessings: "In the blessing immediately preceding this paragraph, our contemplation of the physical luminaries created by God led us to consider the spiritual and moral light of revelation which God has prepared in Zion and as whose bearer He has appointed Israel. The blessing beginning with *Ahava rabah* is a continuation of this thought. It is founded upon our awareness of the infinite love which God has shown us by our spiritual election, and of how utterly desolate we would be, if we were to become estranged from this spiritual heritage, and if we were to fail to derive from it the proper understanding and conviction to guide us in the fulfillment of our God-given mission in life. We therefore call upon Divine compassion to protect us from such spiritual desolation and to guide us to the joyous study, teaching, and observance of His Law. It is only once, with the help of God, we will have redeemed ourselves from this spiritual desolation, that our deliverance from political misfortune will have value for us. Hence we hopefully look forward to our return, as one united people, to our homeland which is dedicated to the full observance of the Law of God, and where the Abode of God at Zion, which was destined to afford enlightenment to all of mankind, awaits our coming " (Commentary on the *Siddur*).

Ahavah rabah is immediately followed by the first paragraph of *Sh'mah*, which contains the commandment: "And you shall love the Lord your God with all your heart, with all your soul, and with all your might." The question is, how can love be commanded? A person can be commanded to perform a deed or an action. Love, however, is an emotion. How can a person be commanded to feel an emotion?

The answer lies in the blessing *Ahavah rabah*. This blessing is a beautiful expression of God's unbounded love for the Jewish people. "With a great love You have loved us, O Lord our God... You have chosen us from all people and nations... Blessed are You, O Lord, who has graciously chosen Your people Israel." When a Jew contemplates God's love, when he opens his heart to that love and feels the radiant glow of divine caring and mercy, he will naturally respond with a deep feeling of love for God. Who teaches the child to love his parents? A child grows up loving his parents in natural response to the love they have showered upon him from birth. Long before the child has cognitive understanding, parents pour love upon their child. The child does not have to be taught how to love. If he is given love, he will instinctively respond with love.

In the Book of Proverbs it is written: "As water reflects the face, so does the heart reflect the heart" (27:19). When a person looks into a pond of water he sees his own reflection. If he is smiling, he will see a smiling face. If he is frowning, he will see a frown. So too, does the heart reflect the heart. When a person feels the love of another person, his heart will reflect that love. The reverse is also true. If a person feels disliked by another, he instinctively responds with dislike.

Love for God is, in fact, not commanded. No commandment is necessary when a person is aware of God's love for him. It comes instinctively, automatically. What the Torah does command, however, is that a person make every effort to increase his natural love for God, which is essentially the love of a child towards a parent, to the extent that it will be "with all your heart, with all your soul, and with all your might." This is a difficult, but not unobtainable, goal. It requires a great deal of thought and contemplation. It requires a serious commitment to Torah study and the observance of mitzvot. But it is a goal whose reward is a life enriched by faith and love (R. Baruch Epstein, *Baruch She'amar*, Publ. Am Olam, p. 101).

Emet V'Yatziv (True and Certain)

The blessing after *Sh'mah* contains some of Judaism's most important and fundamental principles. It holds a very special place in the order of the prayers by serving as a bridge betwen *Sh'mah* and the *Amidah*. Let us explore some of the highlights of *Emet v'yatziv*.

1. It is a mitzvah for a Jew to remember the Exodus from Egypt every day (see the next mishnah). The Torah states: "So that you will remember the day of your departure from the Land of Egypt all the days of your life" (Deut. 16:3). The commandment to remember the Exodus is usually fulfilled by reciting the third paragraph of *Sh'mah*. The last verse of the paragraph recalls the Exodus from Egypt. If, however, a person did not recite the third paragraph of the *Sh'mah*, the commandment may be fulfilled by saying the blessing *Emet v'yatziv* (Berachot 21a).

2. The themes of each of the three paragraphs of *Sh'mah* are found in the blessing:

"True it is that the eternal God is our King" corresponds with the first paragraph of *Sh'mah*.

"Happy is the man who obeys Your commands" corresponds with the second paragraph.

"From Egypt You did redeem us, O Lord our God" corresponds with the third paragraph.

3. R. Judah Halevi notes that the blessing contains five tenets of Judaism:
a) belief in God
b) belief in God as an eternal Being
c) belief in divine providence
d) belief that the Torah is God-given
e) belief in the Exodus from Egypt (*Kuzari* 3:17)

4. The blessing concludes with "Blessed are You, O Lord, who has redeemed Israel." Upon concluding the blessing, the worshipper immediately begins the *Amidah*. The Talmud requires that there be no interruption between "Redemption" and "*Tefillah (Amidah)*" (Berachot 4b, 9b, 42a). It is forbidden to answer "Amen" upon hearing the blessing from the reader. One who is careful about not interrupting between "Redemption" and "*Tefillah*" will be rewarded with a share in the World to Come (*ibid.*, 4b) and no harm will befall him that day (*ibid.*, 9b).

The Talmud's insistence upon joining the two prayers has several reasons. Rashi (*ibid.*, 4b) bases this law upon the juxtaposition of the verses "The Lord is my Rock and my Redeemer" (Ps. 19:15) and "The Lord will answer you in time of trouble" (Ps. 20:2). He also quotes the Jerusalem Talmud's analogy: Whoever does not immediately precede *Tefillah* with Redemption may be compared to a king's friend who knocks on the door of the palace. When the king answers the door to see who is knocking, there is nobody there. In other words, *Tefillah* should not be an abrupt "knock on the door," but rather should be gradually introduced with the praise of God the Redeemer.

There is another reason for joining the two prayers. The first blessing of the *Amidah* also contains the theme of redemption, as it says: "...Who will bring a redeemer to their children's children for His Name's sake." There is, however, a difference between the two. *Emet v'yatziv* refers to the past, while the first blessing of the *Amidah* refers to the future. By connecting the two blessings, we indicate that Israel's past is inextricably connected with its future.

5. Following the word "True," there are fifteen adjectives that describe the divine Word. The number fifteen corresponds with: a) the fifteen Songs of Ascent in the Book of Psalms (120-134); b) the fifteen miracles God performed for the Jewish people at the time of the Exodus as described in the Passover Haggadah; and c) the fifteen steps that connected the Women's Courtyard with the Israelite Courtyard in the Temple (*Abudraham*).

6. The phrase *Tzur Yisrael*, "Stronghold (Rock) of Israel," is a Biblical term found in the Book of Isaiah: "To come to the mountain of the Lord, to the Rock of Israel" (30:29).

The themes of the three morning blessings of *Sh'mah*, i.e., the creation of the heavenly bodies, the gift of Torah, and the redemption of Israel, are rooted in Psalm 19. There we find the following statements: "The heavens declare the glory of God and the firmament tells His handiwork "(v. 2), "He has set a tent for the sun" (v. 5) (first blessing); "The Lord's Torah is perfect" (v. 8), "The statutes of the Lord are right... the commandment of the Lord is pure" (v. 9) (second blessing); "O Lord, my Rock and my Redeemer" (v. 15) (third blessing). (*Netiv Binah*, vol. 1, p. 229.)

EVENING BLESSINGS
Asher Bidvaroh (Who at Your Word)
The Talmud points out that there is a reference to night in the first blessing of *Sh'mah* in the morning ("and creates darkness") and there is a reference to day in the first blessing of *Sh'mah* in the evening ("You create day and night")(Berachot 12a). This is to emphasize, once again, the Unity of God, the Creator of everything. R. Samson Raphael Hirsch writes: "This is repeated testimony of the truth of the oneness and unique nature of God in His world of contrasts and opposites. Day and night are created by one and the same Almighty Power, and day and night alike serve the unified, harmonious purposes of the One God."

Ahavat Olam (With Everlasting Love)
The parallel blessing in the morning contains many requests. This evening blessing simply says, "May You never take away Your love from us." Rabbi Issachar Jacobson explains that, at the end of a long hard day, it is sufficient to make a general request for God's endless

love. In the morning, however, as the worshipper prepares himself to meet the challenges of a new day, he is more eager to enlist specific manifestations of God's love and mercy (*Netiv Binah*, vol. 1, pp. 237, 238).

The term "House of Israel" applies not simply to the Jewish people as a whole, but to each and every individual. In the words of R. Samson Raphael Hirsch: "The Torah and the teachings and commandments it contains are the inalienable, blessed heritage, not simply of our nation, as such, but of each and every individual member of this entity which comprises the House of Israel." These words are reminiscent of Maimonides' ruling: "Every Jew is obligated to study Torah, whether rich or poor, healthy or in pain, young or very old. Even a beggar and a person who must support a family are obligated to set aside time to study Torah both by day and by night, as it says: 'And you shall meditate therein day and night'" (Joshua 1:8) (*Mishneh Torah*, Laws of Studying Torah 1:8).

As noted earlier (p. 60), Ashkenazic practice is to say "With a great love" in the morning and "With everlasting love" in the evening. Rabbi Haim Donin offers a marvelous explanation of these two phrases: "The difference in the wording may seem trivial, yet enormous meaning lies embedded in it. Picture two young people declaring their great love for one another, when they first marry in the morning of their lives. The test of their relationship is whether that great love becomes an enduring, abiding love that will also bind them in the evening of their lives. Early love, no matter how great or passionate, can be short-lived. God's great love for Israel, we proclaim, is not short-lived. It is everlasting!" (*To Pray as a Jew*, H. Donin, Basic Books, 1980.)

Emet V'Emunah (True and Trustworthy)

The Talmud says: "Whoever does not say '*Emet v'yatziv*' in the morning and '*Emet v'emunah*' in the evening has not fulfilled his obligation, as it is written, 'To tell of your kindness in the morning and your faithfulness at night' (Ps. 92:3)" (Berachot 12a). Rashi (*ad loc.*) explains that *Emet v'yatziv* speaks of the many kindnesses and wonders that God has performed for the Jewish people in the past, whereas *Emet v'emunah* is a prayer for future redemption, as well. It is important for a Jew to recall his past and keep faith in his future.

Nighttime evokes fears and doubts. The lesson of the Exodus should give a feeling of confidence and trust in God who will deliver the Jewish people in the dark moments of the future.

Hashkivaynu **(That we Lie Down)**

Hashkivaynu is an extension of the theme of redemption. Though *Emet v'emunah* and *Hashkivaynu* are two separate blessings, they are referred to in the Talmud as "an extended redemption" (Berachot 4b). R. Yonah explains that this blessing is reminiscent of the prayer uttered by the Jewish people in Egypt during the Tenth Plague. All about them the Egyptian firstborn were dying. The Jews prayed that no evil should befall them or their children (*ad loc.*).

Reference to "the adversary" (Heb. Satan) alludes to the evil impulse that exists within the human being. We pray that the evil impulse be removed from before us and from behind us. R. Isaac Elijah Landau explains that there are times when a human being causes his own downfall by choosing a harmful path. There are other times when a person is pursued by evil that chases after him. This is the meaning of the words: "Remove the adversary from before us and from behind us" (*Dover Shalom, Otzar Hat'fillot*).

There is another interpretation. "Adversary" may literally mean "enemy." Many people have enemies who wish to do them harm. It is difficult enough to deal with known enemies. It is almost impossible to deal with supposed friends who are enemies behind one's back. Thus, the prayer: "remove the adversary from before us (the ones we know about) and from behind us (the ones we do not know about)."

THE THIRD BLESSING

In Ashkenazic communities outside of Eretz Yisrael there is a custom to include a third blessing after *Sh'mah* in the weekday evening service. The prayer consists of eighteen verses which contain eighteen references to God's name and a concluding blessing: "Blessed are You, O Lord, glorious King Who will reign over us and over Your entire creation for ever and ever." This prayer was unknown in Mishnaic times and is therefore not mentioned in the mishnah. The origins of the prayer are obscure. Several theories have been advanced:

1. The eighteen verses with their eighteen references to God's name were introduced as a substitute for the *Amidah* at a time when

synagogues were located in fields and it was dangerous to return home in the dark (*Abudraham*).

2. The prayer was instituted as a response to the decrees of the non-Jewish civil authorities forbidding Jews to pray the evening service. This abridged prayer was substituted instead (*Ba'al Minhagot*).

3. The prayer was instituted for the purpose of prolonging the evening service for the sake of the latecomers who would have a chance to catch up to the congregation and therefore would not have to return home alone from the fields in the dark (*Tosafot*, Berachot 4b).

It is likely that the above circumstances did not exist in Eretz Yisrael at the time this prayer was formulated. It therefore never was adopted there, neither in the Ashkenazic nor the Sephardic liturgy.

PHILOSOPHY OF THE BLESSINGS OF *SH'MAH*

Our survey of the blessings of *Sh'mah* leads us to conclude that they contain three fundamental tenets of Judaism: Creation, Revelation, and Redemption. These mark three distinct stages in God's relationship with the world and man's relationship with God. All three events are motivated by divine love. In a deeper sense, however, the three principles do not imply one-time events. Each is an ongoing process that is realized in the human experience. Creation continuously happens. As the blessing states: "He renews the creation every day, constantly." Revelation took place at Mt. Sinai, but continues daily through the study of Torah, which reveals the infinite divine wisdom contained in it. Redemption from Egypt is a starting point. Redemption continues, however, through the course of history for the nation of Israel as a whole, and for each individual who is confronted with danger and oppression. The redemptive process will continue until the world in its entirety is redeemed of all fear, pain, and suffering.

These fundamental concepts pose a challenge to man. If man is destined to be a partner with God, if he is enjoined to "walk in His ways," then he, too, must be actively involved in creation, revelation, and redemption. Man possesses a divine calling to be a creator, to build and shape the world and to make it a better place in which to live. He also has a responsibility to be a revealer. His conduct, his values, and his aspirations should make manifest that he is a veritable "image of

God." The Torah is his guidebook which shows him how to live life in relation to God and in relation to fellow human beings. The mitzvot are the rules by which the human being is afforded the opportunity to reveal the Divine Word in daily action and deed. And man is to be redeemer, as well. Life presents ample opportunities to redeem others from suffering and sorrow. The world with all its negative qualities — poverty, illness, unemployment, marital strife, emotional disturbances, etc. — challenges us to take an active role in being helpers and supporters to those less privileged than ourselves. We not only can, but should, be redeemers in a world that needs much redemption. Praising God as Creator-Revealer-Redeemer is not enough. We should draw conclusions from that praise and apply those qualities to ourselves.

Creation, Revelation, and Redemption are the cornerstones of Franz Rosenzweig's philosophy. In his *magnum opus*, The Star of Redemption, Rosenzweig portrays the world as consisting of three elements — man, world, and God. These elements interact with each other through the processes of Creation, Revelation, and Redemption. Creation is a continuous process and the first point of contact between God and world. The second step is revelation in which God reveals His love for man. Love is the essence of revelation. When man translates God's love into love for fellow man, the redemptive process begins. Pictorially, man, world, and God form one triangle. Creation, revelation, and redemption form another. When superimposed one upon the other, they form the six-pointed Star of David from which the title of Rosenzweig's book is derived.

The Practical Law

1. In the morning, two blessings are recited before *Sh'mah* and one after. In the evening, two blessings are recited before *Sh'mah* and two after (*Tur, Orach Chaim* 58).
2. In the Diaspora, most Ashkenazic congregations add the verses of *Baruch Adonai* and the blessing *Yiru eineinu*. These are not recited in Sephardic congregations. The custom in Eretz Yisrael in both Sephardic and Ashkenazic congregations is to omit these prayers.
3. *Emet v'yatziv* is said in the morning and *Emet v'emunah* is said in the evening (*Orach Chaim* 66:10).

4. The first blessing of *Sh'mah* begins and concludes with *Baruch*. The subsequent blessings only conclude with *Baruch* (*Mishneh Torah*, Laws of *Sh'mah* 1:7).
5. It is forbidden to change the formulation of any blessing, or to add or subtract blessings (*ibid.*).

Mishnah 5

The Exodus from Egypt[1] is to be mentioned at night. R. Elazar ben[2] Azariah said: I am like a man of seventy,[3] yet I was never able to convince my colleagues[4] that the Exodus from Egypt must be said at night until Ben Zoma interpreted it. It is written, "So that you will remember the day of your departure from the Land of Egypt all the days of your life" (Deut. 16:3); "The days of your life" refers to the days; "*all* the days of your life" refers to the nights. The Sages say: "the days of your life" refers to this world; "*all* the days of your life" refers to the days of the Messiah.

משנה ה.

מַזְכִּירִין יְצִיאַת מִצְרַיִם בַּלֵּילוֹת. אָמַר רַבִּי אֶלְעָזָר בֶּן עֲזַרְיָה: הֲרֵי אֲנִי כְּבֶן שִׁבְעִים שָׁנָה, וְלֹא זָכִיתִי שֶׁתֵּאָמֵר יְצִיאַת מִצְרַיִם בַּלֵּילוֹת, עַד שֶׁדְּרָשָׁהּ בֶּן זוֹמָא, שֶׁנֶּאֱמַר (דברים טז) "לְמַעַן תִּזְכֹּר אֶת יוֹם צֵאתְךָ מֵאֶרֶץ מִצְרַיִם כֹּל יְמֵי חַיֶּיךָ", "יְמֵי חַיֶּיךָ" — הַיָּמִים, "כֹּל יְמֵי חַיֶּיךָ" — הַלֵּילוֹת. וַחֲכָמִים אוֹמְרִים: "יְמֵי חַיֶּיךָ" — הָעוֹלָם הַזֶּה, "כֹּל יְמֵי חַיֶּיךָ" — לְהָבִיא לִימוֹת הַמָּשִׁיחַ:

---

1. EXODUS FROM EGYPT — The third paragraph of *Sh'mah* which mentions the Exodus: "I am the Lord your God who brought you out of the Land of Egypt to be your God."
2. BEN — Son of.
3. LIKE A MAN OF SEVENTY — Though he was only eighteen years old, he was prematurely gray and appeared like a man of seventy.
4. TO CONVINCE MY COLLEAGUES — This is R. Obadiah Bertinoro's interpretation. Another rendering is: "I was not privileged to understand why the Exodus from Egypt must be said at night" (Maimonides).

CHAPTER 1: *Mishnah 5*

The Letter of the Law

The key issue in the mishnah is whether or not a person must include the third paragraph of *Sh'mah* in the evening prayer. The central theme of the paragraph is the mitzvah of *tzitzit* (a fringed garment). *Tzitzit* are not required to be worn at night because the phrase "and you shall see them" implies that they are to be worn at a time when they can be seen, i.e., during the day. It would therefore seem that the paragraph is not appropriate for the evening. On the other hand, there is another theme in the paragraph, namely, the Exodus from Egypt. If it can be proven that the Exodus must be mentioned in the evening, as well as in the morning, then including the third paragraph at night is justifiable. This is precisely what Ben Zoma explained. His interpretation of the words "All the days of your life" to include nights, provided R. Elazar b. Azariah with the convincing argument that the third paragraph of *Sh'mah* should be recited in the evening.

The matter was not settled for a long time, at least as far as Eretz Yisrael was concerned. The Talmud records that in the fourth century, some two hundred years after Ben Zoma, the custom in Eretz Yisrael was to recite a shortened version of the third paragraph. All that was said was: "Speak unto the children of Israel and say to them — I am the Lord your God, true." Neither *tzitzit* nor the Exodus were mentioned. The Exodus was mentioned, however, in the blessing that follows *Sh'mah*. In Babylonia, there was also a difference of opinion as to whether the paragraph should be recited. Abaye was of the opinion that it should be said. R. Kahana said in the name of Rav that it should not be said. But, if said, it should not be in an abbreviated form, but in its entirety. A special prayer to remember the Exodus was recited when the third paragraph was not said: "We thank You, O Lord our God, for taking us out of the land of Egypt and for redeeming us from the house of bondage and for performing miracles and wonders for us upon the Sea where we sang to You" (Berachot 14b).

The custom of Eretz Yisrael persisted for at least another four or five hundred years. The *Halachot G'dolot*, an eighth or ninth century Geonic work, writes: "Several communities in Eretz Yisrael to this day say: 'Speak unto the children of Israel and say to them — I am the Lord your God'" (Eliezer Levi, *Yesodot Ha'tfillah* Tel Aviv:1958, p. 141).

The Spirit of the Law

LIKE A MAN OF SEVENTY

R. Elazar ben Azariah's premature graying occurred as a result of an unfortunate political dispute. Rabban Gamliel was the *Nasi*, or head of the Sanhedrin. It seems that he was intolerant of opinions that opposed his own. On several occasions, R. Joshua disagreed with him and Rabban Gamliel used his authority to publicly embarrass R. Joshua. Once they disputed over a calendrical reckoning as to when Yom Kippur falls. To prove his point, Rabban Gamliel ordered R. Joshua to appear before him carrying his walking stick and money on the day which, according to R. Joshua's calculation, was Yom Kippur. R. Joshua submitted in deference to Rabban Gamliel's position as *Nasi*. Another time, the two disputed over whether the *Arvit*, evening service, was obligatory or voluntary. Rabban Gamliel exercised his authority and ordered R. Joshua to remain standing during a class that Rabban Gamliel was teaching. The scholars present were appalled by the treatment R. Joshua was receiving and stopped the lesson.

Rabban Gamliel was finally impeached by his colleagues and steps were taken to depose him. But, who would replace Rabban Gamliel? Several names were suggested — R. Joshua, R. Akiva - but these were turned down. Finally a consensus was reached. R. Elazar ben Azariah was the most suitable candidate. He was a brilliant scholar. He was a man of great wealth who could deal with the rapacious Roman authorities. Also, as a tenth generation descendent of Ezra the Scribe, he possessed an enviable ancestry. R. Elazar ben Azariah had but one handicap. He was only eighteen years old! This, however, could be overlooked. The fact that he had outstanding qualifications and was politically neutral made him an excellent choice.

R. Elazar ben Azariah had apprehensions about accepting the offer. He said: "Let me first go home and discuss it with my wife." His wife was a perceptive woman. She recognized the political battle at hand and predicted that as soon as things calmed down, Rabban Gamliel would be restored to his position. R. Elazar ben Azariah, however, did not want to miss the glorious opportunity to hold the highest seat in the court, even if it were to be short-lived. "Let a man drink from a precious goblet even one day, though tomorrow it will break," he said. His wife reminded him of his youth. "Do you expect to preside over a group of scholars whose beards are gray?" she asked. Then a miracle occurred. R. Elazar ben Azariah awoke the next morning to find his beard had turned gray. That is why he said: "I am like a man of seventy" (Berachot 27a, 28b).

Maimonides had difficulty in accepting the story of the miracle literally. In his Commentary on the Mishnah he writes: "He devoted so much of his energies studying Torah day and night that he aged prematurely."

The Jerusalem Talmud interprets "like a man of seventy" differently. It explains the phrase to mean "almost seventy." R. Elazar b. Azariah's youthful appointment (age 16 according to this source) is unrelated to his statement in the mishnah. He wishes to emphasize that it wasn't until his advanced age that he learned of Ben Zoma's interpretation.

REMEMBERING THE EXODUS AT NIGHT

The Exodus from Egypt consisted of two stages. The first was the termination of slavery and the Israelites becoming a free nation. The second was the actual departure from the land of Egypt. The status of slavery was officially terminated on the night before the departure from Egypt. On that fateful night the Jewish people acquired freedom. "And it was at midnight that the Lord smote all the firstborn in the land of Egypt.... And Pharaoh arose on that night... and he called to Moses and Aaron at night and said: 'Arise, go out from the midst of my people, you and the Children of Israel; go and serve the Lord as you have spoken' " (Ex. 12:29-31). With these words Pharaoh uttered Israel's declaration of independence. This is why the Torah later states: "The Lord your God took you out of the Land of Egypt at night" (Deut. 16:1). It is on the basis of this verse that the Talmud states: "Everyone agrees that when Israel was redeemed from Egypt, they were redeemed at night" (Berachot 9a).

The physical departure from Egypt, however, did not take place until the following morning. During the night, the Jewish people celebrated its freedom with the first Passover Seder. They ate the meat of the Paschal lamb together with matzah and bitter herbs. It was a night of joy and thanksgiving. In the morning, they hurriedly gathered their possessions, assembled together, and began their march to freedom. "On the fifteenth day of the first month, on the morrow of the Passover offering, the Children of Israel went out with a high hand before the eyes of all of Egypt" (Num. 33:3).

The controversy between R. Elazar ben Azariah and the Sages hinges on these two stages of redemption. According to R. Elazar ben Azariah, both stages of redemption are to be remembered daily — the redemption at night which was *de jure* and the redemption by day which was *de facto*. The Sages, on the other hand, maintain that only the *de facto* redemption should be remembered. So long as the Children of Israel remained in Egypt, surrounded by hostile neighbors and a pagan culture, the redemption was incomplete. They were truly liberated only when they began their trek into the wilderness following the lead of God's glory.

The halachah requires that the Exodus be remembered by day and by night. At night we remember the magnificent moment when the shackles of slavery were broken, when the might of Pharaoh and his master race was shattered. We remember God's awesome power and His ability to cast down the arrogant, and at the same time, to raise up the downfallen. We also remember the Exodus of the day. We recall the hope and faith of a newly freed people as they begin their long journey into a vast wilderness. They leave behind dark memories and an empire in ruin. They carry with them a profound trust in a loving God who will guide them through the barren desert and lead them to the Promised Land. "So said the Lord, I remember unto you the kindness of your youth, your bridal love, when you followed after Me into the wilderness, into a land that was not sown" (Jeremiah 2:2).

Memories of the past are an inspiration for the future. The Exodus is a living memory for the Jewish people. An event that occurred more than three millenia ago is recalled every day, twice a day. And on Passover, the Exodus is not simply remembered, it is relived in the Seder. On dark nights of national despair and on bright days of national glory, the Jew remembers the Exodus. And on somber nights of personal grief, and on sunny days of personal joy, the Jew remembers the Exodus. The indelible impact of the Exodus experience remains with the Jewish people until the ultimate Redemption.

IN THE DAYS OF THE MESSIAH

Two miraculous events mark the beginning and ultimate stages of Jewish history: the Exodus from Egypt and the days of the Messiah. The Exodus was the birth of the Jewish nation. The days of the Messiah will be its spiritual flowering. The Exodus is meaningful only insofar as the Jewish people is concerned. The Messianic era will usher in an age of peace and harmony for all the nations of the world. The Messiah himself will not be a miracle worker. He will be an exceptional leader, endowed with charisma and wisdom. He will successfully preach and teach the Word of God to all mankind. His crowning achievements will be the construction of the Holy Temple in Jerusalem and the ingathering of Jews from all parts of the Diaspora to their national homeland. Maimonides concludes his *Mishneh Torah* with a description of the Days of the Messiah: "At that time there will be neither hunger nor war, neither jealousy nor strife. Goodness will be bountiful. Delicacies will be as available as dust. The world's only preoccupation will be to know the Lord. Jews will be looked upon as great scholars who know the hidden secrets and comprehend the Creator's knowledge, as much as is humanly possible, as it is written: 'For the world shall be filled with the knowledge of the Lord as the waters fill the sea' (Isaiah 11:9)" (Laws of Kings 12:5).

Will the Exodus be eclipsed by the Days of the Messiah? Will the memory of the Exodus vanish as does the moon when it is drowned in sunlight, or will the Exodus remain permanently fixed in Jewish consciousness? This is the debate between Ben Zoma and the Sages. Ben Zoma says that the Messianic era will so greatly exceed the Exodus experience that the Exodus will be all but forgotten. He supports his argument with a quote from Scripture: "Behold, the days will come, says the Lord, and they will no longer say, 'By the life of the Lord who raised the children of Israel from the Land of Egypt,' but rather, 'By the life of the Lord who has raised and who has brought the children of the House of Israel from the land of the north and from all the lands where I dispersed them' " (Jeremiah 23:7-8). The Sages, on the other hand, believe that the Exodus will not, nor should not, ever be forgotten. Jeremiah prophesied that the Messianic redemption will supersede the Exodus only insofar as the Exodus will be of secondary importance. But the ancient miracles and redemption that took place in Egypt will never be forgotten. They are to be remembered "all the days of your life," in this world and in the Days of the Messiah.

The future redemption will outshine the redemption of the past. The Messianic era will be a time when God will balance the scales of reward and punishment. Until that time, evil is allowed to flourish and righteousness is not fully rewarded. Redemption, however, will bring equity into the world. The Jewish people who, for millenia, suffered persecution and oppression, who tenaciously held on to their faith in God and His Torah, will receive their ultimate reward. The divine Hand will restore justice to a world that is unjust. The Exodus serves as a model for the future redemption. The evil perpetrated by the Egyptians and the harsh cruelty inflicted upon their Jewish slaves were ultimately punished. The Children of Israel who endured more than two centuries of inhumane treatment finally left the House of Bondage in dignity and pride and with great riches.

The Exodus gives assurance to Jews of every age that there is a God of justice and that justice will eventually prevail. The Exodus offers hope and consolation. It offers a promise for the future. R. Saadya Gaon, in his eighth treatise on the Redemption of Israel in his *Emunot V'dayot* writes: "Our eyes have seen the things which He performed for us in dividing the Sea, in feeding us with Manna and the quails, in giving us the Law at Sinai, in causing the sun to stand still and similar things. For the future, He promised us wonderful and immeasurable bliss and happiness, and that honor, glory and distinction which He will bestow upon us will be a double reward for all the humiliation and misery which He brought upon us, as it says, 'For your shame which was double... therefore in their land they shall possess double' (Isaiah 61:7)... For the trials and ordeals of the past He will give us the double of our double share, which is over and above that which He promised, an amount of bliss not quickly or easily to be measured. Thus, it is said, 'and He will do thee good, and multiply thee above thy fathers' (Deuteronomy 30:5). For this reason He mentions to us the Exodus from Egypt so frequently and in so many places. He wants us to remember the things we experienced. If anything He did for us in the course of the redemption from Egypt is not explicitly included in the promise of the Final Redemption, it is implied in the statement 'As in the days of thy coming forth out of the land of Egypt, will I show unto him marvelous things' (Micah 7:15)" (Quoted from *The Perfect Faith*, J. David Bleich, Ktav Publishers, 1983, pp. 599-600).

The Practical Law

1. Even though the mitzvah of *tzitzit* does not apply at nighttime, we do say the third paragraph of *Sh'mah* because it contains mention of the Exodus from Egypt. One must remember the Exodus both by day and night, as it says: "So that you will remember the day of your departure from the Land of Egypt all the days of your life" (*Mishneh Torah*, Laws of *Sh'mah* 1:3).

Chapter Two

Introduction

Chapter 1 deals mainly with the structure of *Sh'mah* and its blessings and the regulations of time and posture. The time frames of evening and morning, the positioning of the body, the number and placement of the blessings, and the importance of the third paragraph, are all stated and debated. Chapter 2 deals primarily with the degree of concentration and attention that must be devoted while reciting *Sh'mah*. The focus of this chapter is not so much on the *Sh'mah* itself, but on the individual who is praying. Clearly, reciting *Sh'mah* in a perfunctory manner, without knowing what one is saying, is purposeless. How can a person give testimony to the Oneness of God and the majesty of His Name without being aware of what he is saying? On the other hand, the Torah says that *Sh'mah* is to be recited "When you sit at home, and when you go on a journey." This implies that normal activities may be performed even while reciting *Sh'mah*. Thus, the Mishnah attempts to define the degree of concentration required, using various examples and situations.

Mishnah 2 delineates the paragraphs of *Sh'mah* and its blessings. It is a continuation of mishnah 1, which discusses the distinction between interrupting between the paragraphs and in the middle of a paragraph. Mishnah 3 draws our attention to the proper reading and pronunciation of the words. Mishnayot 4, 5 and 8 deal with the unique situations of the laborer, the bridegroom, and the mourner. These three are either occupied or preoccupied, and the degree of concentration they can give to *Sh'mah* is diminished. Mishnayot 6 and 7 are a continuation of mishnah 5, in which Rabban Gamliel conducted himself in an unusual manner.

Mishnah 1

If one was reading in the Torah[1] and the time to recite *Sh'mah* arrived: If he had intent,[2] he has fulfilled his obligation.[3] If not, he has not fulfilled his obligation.[4]

Between the paragraphs[5] it is permitted to greet (another person) out of respect[6] and to respond (to a greeting out of respect). And in the middle (of the paragraphs), it is permitted to greet out of fear[7] and to respond (out of fear); this is the opinion of R. Meir. R. Judah says: In the middle (of the paragraphs) it is

משנה א

הָיָה קוֹרֵא בַתּוֹרָה וְהִגִּיעַ זְמַן הַמִּקְרָא; אִם כִּוֵּן לִבּוֹ — יָצָא. וְאִם לָאו — לֹא יָצָא. בַּפְּרָקִים שׁוֹאֵל מִפְּנֵי הַכָּבוֹד וּמֵשִׁיב, וּבָאֶמְצַע שׁוֹאֵל מִפְּנֵי הַיִּרְאָה וּמֵשִׁיב; דִּבְרֵי רַבִּי מֵאִיר. רַבִּי יְהוּדָה אוֹמֵר: בָּאֶמְצַע שׁוֹאֵל מִפְּנֵי הַיִּרְאָה וּמֵשִׁיב מִפְּנֵי הַכָּבוֹד; בַּפְּרָקִים שׁוֹאֵל מִפְּנֵי הַכָּבוֹד וּמֵשִׁיב שָׁלוֹם לְכָל אָדָם.

---

1. READING IN THE TORAH — The portions that contain the paragraphs of *Sh'mah*.
2. INTENT — To fulfill the mitzvah of reciting *Sh'mah* (see "Letter of the Law" for detailed explanation).
3. FULFILLED HIS OBLIGATION — He need not recite *Sh'mah* a second time.
4. NOT FULFILLED HIS OBLIGATION — He must, therefore, recite *Sh'mah* a second time with proper intent.
5. BETWEEN THE PARAGRAPHS — I.e., the paragraphs of *Sh'mah* and its blessings as delineated in the next mishnah.
6. RESPECT — I.e., someone to whom he is required to show respect such as a parent, a teacher, or a Torah scholar (Maimonides). Another interpretation: a respected member of the community, and not necessarily a parent, teacher, or Torah scholar (Rashi).
7. FEAR — Of someone who may kill him (Rashi), or of someone who may harm him physically or financially (Maimonides), or of his parent or teacher (Rosh).

permitted to greet out of fear and to respond out of respect. Between the paragraphs it is permitted to greet out of respect and to respond "Shalom" to everybody.

The Letter of the Law

DEFINITION OF *KAVANAH*
The Hebrew word *kivun* means direction. *Kavanah*, a word related to *kivun*, means intention, attention, and premeditation. *Kavanah* may be defined as a purposeful direction of one's thoughts towards a specific goal.

IN PRAYER
Kavanah is a word closely associated with prayer. The time spent in prayer should be an awesome experience in which the worshipper feels that he is in the presence of God. His thoughts should be concentrated upon the meaning of the words he is saying and to Whom he is saying them. If a person prays in a perfunctory, mechanical manner, his prayer is like a body without a soul. It is merely a cold, lifeless soliloquy addressed to no one, neither to God, nor to the worshipper himself. Prayer with *kavanah*, on the other hand, is a profound religious experience that links mortal man with the Infinite God. *Kavanah* lifts man from his terrestial dwelling place and carries him to the celestial portals of the King's palace.

    The Talmud places great importance upon *kavanah* in prayer. For example, the first mishnah of Chapter 5 reads: "One may not stand up to pray unless he is in a reverent state of mind. The early Chasidim used to wait one hour before praying in order to direct their thoughts to the Omnipresent." *Kavanah* is not meant only for Chasidim. Every Jew is required to pray with *kavanah*. "He who prays must direct his mind to heaven" (Berachot 31a). When the students of R. Eliezer came to visit him while he lay on his deathbed, they asked him to teach them the way of life that would make them worthy of life in the World to Come. Included in his words of advice was the admonition: "When you pray, know before Whom you are standing" (*ibid.*, 28b).

IN PERFORMING MITZVOT

The word *kavanah* is often used in the Talmud in a different context and with a different meaning. In these cases, *kavanah* means directing one's thoughts towards the fulfillment of a mitzvah while performing a mitzvah. For example, a Jew is commanded to hear the blowing of the *Shofar* on Rosh Hashanah. While listening to the blowing, he should have *kavanah*, intent, to fulfill his obligation. This is true of all mitzvot: donning *tallit* and *tefillin*, eating in a *Sukkah*, lifting the Four Species, reciting *Kiddush*, eating matzah at the Passover Seder, etc. A mitzvah should not be performed in a perfunctory manner, but should be performed with specific intention to fulfill one's obligation.

What if a person performed a mitzvah without *kavanah*? For example, what if a person blew a *Shofar* on Rosh Hashanah as a musical instrument, or as practice for blowing the *Shofar* in the synagogue? Has he or has he not fulfilled his obligation? If he has fulfilled his obligation, he need not hear the *Shofar* a second time. If he has not fulfilled his obligation, he must hear the *Shofar* again, this time with *kavanah*. This question — do mitzvot require *kavanah* — is the subject of debate in the Talmud (Berachot 13a, Eruvin 95b, Pesachim 114b, Rosh Hashanah 28b). No clear-cut answer is given. A full discussion of the details of this subject is beyond the scope of this work. Several key opinions proffered by halachic authorities do, however, deserve mention.

a) Several authorities distinguish between mitzvot that are performed through action and mitzvot that are verbal (e.g., reciting *Sh'mah* or *Kiddush* on Friday night) or auditory (e.g., hearing the *Shofar*). A mitzvah that is performed through action, such as eating matzah at the Passover Seder or lifting a *Lulav* and *Etrog* on Sukkot, does not require *kavanah*. The reason is because the action speaks for itself. The very act of lifting the *Lulav* and *Etrog* or the eating of matzah expresses the fact that the deed is being performed for the sake of fulfilling the mitzvah. Where, however, there is no visible action, as in the case of hearing the *Shofar*, or, reciting *Sh'mah*, *Kiddush*, or Grace after Meals, *kavanah* is required (students of R. Jonah, Berachot, end of chap. 1).

The distinction between an action mitzvah and a non-action mitzvah is used to explain a glaring contradiction in Maimonides'

CHAPTER 2: *Mishnah 1*   85

Mishneh Torah. In Laws of Leaven and Matzah it states: "If a person ate matzah (on Passover night) without *kavanah*, for example, if idolaters or thieves forced him to eat, he has fulfilled his obligation" (6:3). But, in Laws of *Shofar* it states: "If a person was practicing *Shofar* blowing he has not fulfilled his obligation... Both the one blowing *Shofar* and the one who hears must have *kavanah*"(2:4). (The mitzvah of *Shofar* is to hear the sound. Blowing the *Shofar* is simply the means by which the sound is produced. Therefore, blowing the *Shofar* is considered an audial mitzvah and not an action mitzvah.) The *Maggid Mishneh*, a commentary on *Mishneh Torah* written by Vidal Yom Tov of Tolosa, Spain, in the fourteenth century, states that Maimonides is of the opinion that an action mitzvah such as eating matzah does not require *kavanah*, whereas an audial mitzvah such as hearing the *Shofar* does. The author himself, however, is not quite satisfied with his answer and writes that perhaps the text in Laws of Leaven and Matzah is inaccurate and the law should read "has not fulfilled his obligation" (*Maggid Mishneh*, glosses on Laws of *Shofar* 2:4).

Another attempt to distinguish between matzah and *Shofar* is ventured with the idea that eating differs from hearing or reciting. When a person eats matzah, his body derives the benefit of the ingested matzah and the mitzvah is fulfilled. Hearing a *Shofar* or reciting *Sh'mah*, however, has no physical effect upon the body; thus, *kavanah* is necessary (*Tosafot,* Pesachim 115a).

b) Some authorities distinguish between mitzvot that are ordained by the Torah, such as *Lulav* and *Etrog, Shofar, Matzah, Sh'mah*, etc., and mitzvot that are ordained by the Rabbis, such as washing the hands, reciting blessings, etc. The former require *kavanah* because of their special status as Torah mitzvot. Rabbinic laws are fulfilled even if a person fails to perform them with *kavanah (Magen Avraham* in the name of R. David ben Zimri). The Vilna Gaon, however, disagrees and says no distinction should be made between Torah and Rabbinic laws.

c) Even according to those authorities who say that mitzvot do not require kavanah, if a person expressly has in mind not to fulfill his obligation, the mitzvah is not fulfilled. This principal has practical applications. For example, a teacher who is reciting Grace after Meals with his pupils may wish to recite the Grace afterwards, privately, when he can pray with more concentration. In such a case, he should have in mind not to fulfill his obligation while reciting with the pupils. Or, another example, the counting of the *Omer* which takes place during the seven weeks between the second day of Passover and Shavuot should be done after nightfall. Some congregations pray *Arvit* early and count the Omer before nightfall. In such a case, a person may count with the congregation, having in mind not to fulfill his obligation, and later, after nightfall, count again with a blessing. Because he had specific intent not to fulfill his obligation, the first counting is not a fulfillment of the mitzvah.

d) The *Shulchan Aruch* presents the following succinct statement: "Some say mitzvot do not require *kavanah*, and some say mitzvot do require *kavanah* to fulfill one's obligation while performing a mitzvah. The halachah is according to the latter opinion" (*Orach Chaim* 60:4).

IN RECITING *SH'MAH*

The mishnah says that if one had *kavanah* while reciting *Sh'mah*, he has fulfilled his obligation. The question is: To what type of *kavanah* is the mishnah referring? Does it mean the *kavanah* that is usually associated with prayer, i.e., removing all distractions and concentrating on the meaning of the words, or, does it mean *kavanah* in the more general sense, i.e., intent to fulfill one's obligation? The Talmud notes that there is even a third possibility. Perhaps the *kavanah* referred to in the mishnah is simply focusing attention upon reading the words accurately. In other words, the mishnah may be interpreted to mean that if a person paid attention to accurate pronunciation and vowelization, he has fulfilled his obligation. According to this interpretation, neither intent to fulfill the mitzvah of reciting *Sh'mah*, nor concentration on the meaning of the words, is necessary for the obligation to be fulfilled.

Maimonides makes the following statement: "A person who recites *Sh'mah* and does not have *kavanah* in the first verse, i.e., *Sh'mah Yisrael*, has not fulfilled his obligation. As far as the rest of *Sh'mah* is concerned, if he did not have *kavanah*, even if he were reading in the Torah in his usual manner or proofreading the texts of these paragraphs — and it was time to recite *Sh'mah* — he has fulfilled his obligation, so long as he had *kavanah* for the first verse" (*Mishneh*

CHAPTER 2: *Mishnah 1*

Torah, Laws of Reciting *Sh'mah* 2:1). Maimonides reached this conclusion on the basis of the following Talmudic statement: "'Hear O Israel, the Lord is our God, the Lord is One' — until here *kavanah* is necessary, this is the opinion of R. Meir. Raba said: The halachah is according to R. Meir" (Berachot 13b). Thus, we have a Talmudic decision which Maimonides adopts, that only the first verse requires *kavanah*. The rest of the first paragraph and the second and third paragraphs do not require *kavanah*. This brings us back to our original question: which of the three possible forms of *kavanah* are required for the first verse?

Rabbi Joseph B. Soloveitchik, in an essay on the subject of *kavanah*, analyzes the various options and concludes that Maimonides and R. Meir refer to concentration on the meaning of the words. As far as the other two categories of *kavanah* are concerned, viz., reading the words accurately and intending to fulfill the mitzvah, there is no reason to distinguish between the first verse and the rest of *Sh'mah*. The first verse, however, is unique in that it captures the essence of the mitzvah which is to proclaim one's belief in the Sovereignty and Unity of God. When a Jew recites the words "Hear O Israel ..." and concentrates on their meaning, he has fulfilled his obligation. If he did not concentrate on the message "Hear O Israel, the Lord is our God, the Lord is One," it is as though he has not recited *Sh'mah* at all, and the mitzvah remains unfulfilled until he recites *Sh'mah* again with *kavanah*. That is why Maimonides is insistent on this particular form of *kavanah* specifically for the first verse. As far as the other two forms of *kavanah* are concerned, they are not essential, as long as there was a proclamation of belief in God's Sovereignty and Unity.

Sh'mah is unlike most other mitzvot in this respect. When a Jew eats matzah on Passover eve or takes a *Lulav* and *Etrog* in hand on Sukkot, the action speaks for itself. Mental concentration on the meaning of the mitzvah is not necessary. *Sh'mah*, however, is totally meaningless, unless the worshipper has *kavanah*, removing from his mind all distractions and concentrating on the supreme testimony of Jewish faith.

In addition, explains R. Soloveitchik, because the essence of the mitzvah of *Sh'mah* is the *kavanah* of God's Sovereignty and Unity, no other *kavanah* is required. Once a person has recited the first verse of

Sh'mah while concentrating on the meaning of the words, he does not have to intend to fulfill the mitzvah. Furthermore, once the mitzvah has been fulfilled by reciting the first verse, no further *kavanah* is essential for the balance of *Sh'mah* (*Lectures in Memory of My Father, My Teacher* (Heb.), Rabbi J.B. Soloveitchik, Akiva Joseph Publ., 1983, pp. 24-33).

It should be stated that this technical analysis relates only to the essential requirement of the law. The debate as to whether mitzvot need *kavanah* or not applies to situations that are *fait accompli*, after the fact. Before the fact, however, there is universal agreement that mitzvot should be performed with a maximum of *kavanah*. The mitzvah establishes a connection between man and God. That connection should be approached with a sense of joyful obligation, with deep understanding, and with sincere devotion.

INTERRUPTIONS DURING PRAYER

When a person prays, he should devote all his attention and concentration to his prayers. He should make every effort to clear his mind of distracting thoughts, and he should certainly not interrupt his prayers with idle talk or conversation. The mishnah states, however, that there are situations in which a person may interrupt his prayers. The factors to be considered are: Is he between paragraphs or in the middle of a paragraph; is he addressing someone he fears or someone he respects; and, is he initiating the greeting or responding?

R. Meir makes no distinction between initiating and responding to a greeting. If approached by someone he fears, a person may greet and respond even in the middle of a paragraph. If approached by someone he respects, he may greet and respond only between the paragraphs.

R. Judah agrees with R. Meir insofar as greeting is concerned. He is more lenient, however, with regard to responding. In other words, there are situations in which it is forbidden to initiate a greeting, but if addressed, it is permitted to respond. Thus, it is permitted, even in the middle of a paragraph, to respond to the greeting of someone who is respected. It is certainly permitted to do so because of fear. Between the paragraphs, a person may respond to anyone's greeting.

The authorities differ as to the definitions of "fear" and "respect." Rashi explains "fear" to mean fear of death. Rosh and Rashba disagree with that definition, because when life is at stake, one may interrupt his prayers at any time, even if he is in the middle of the *Amidah*. They therefore interpret "fear" to mean reverence. This refers specifically to one's parent or teacher whom he is required to revere. All three authorities concur that "respect" is defined as referring to someone who should be respected, such as an elderly person, a Torah scholar, or a respected member of the community.

Maimonides takes a middle position with regard to "fear." He concurs with the objection that where there is fear for one's life, it is obvious that it is permitted to interrupt at any point of the prayers. The mishnah then is referring not to fear of death, but rather to fear of physical or financial harm. "Respect" refers to one's parent or teacher.

The halachah is decided in favor of R. Judah. "Respect" is defined as referring to someone who is to be respected (as held by Rashi, Rosh, and Rashba). "Fear" is defined as referring to a parent or a teacher (as held by Rosh and Rashba). In the case of fear of bodily or financial harm, or death, it is certainly permitted to greet (*Orach Chaim* 66:1).

R. Aharon Halevi of Barcelona (13th century) writes in his *Sefer Hachinuch* that as long as no one is offended, it is forbidden to interrupt even between the paragraphs (Mitzvah 419). *Magen Avraham* limits interruptions to a newcomer or stranger who may feel offended if he is not greeted. It is common practice nowadays not to interrupt at all during prayers in the synagogue.

The Spirit of the Law

DO MITZVOT REQUIRE *KAVANAH*?

The life of a Jew is filled with religious duties and responsibilities. There is no facet of life that is beyond the parameters of religious experience. From the moment he wakes up in the morning to the time he closes his eyes and falls asleep at night, the Jew's thoughts, words, and deeds are guided by religious principles and values. These principles and values are not remote, abstract theories. They are concrete, tangible mitzvot, commandments.

Every mitzvah is a link between God, the Commander, and man, the commanded. As a soldier in an army demonstrates his loyalty by faithfully obeying orders, the Jew expresses his loyalty to his Commander by faithfully observing the commandments. The performance of a mitzvah goes beyond the act itself. It is a statement, through deed, of the acceptance of God's divine sovereignty. Every mitzvah act is an acknowledgement of the Almighty as King of the universe and of the Jew as His humble, willing subject.

This is why *kavanah* plays such an important role in the fulfillment of a mitzvah. The mitzvah has meaning when it connects the Jew with God. That connection takes place when the mitzvah is performed with the awareness that it is a divine decree and its performance is a fulfillment of a religious obligation. Of what religious value is eating matzah on Passover night, if one is not cognizant of the fact that he is performing a mitzvah? What spiritual inspiration can be derived from donning *tefillin*, if the worshipper is not aware that he is fulfilling a mitzvah? Clearly, a *kavanah*-less mitzvah is no mitzvah at all.

There is one point of view that avers that mitzvot require *kavanah*. But, what of the other opinion that maintains mitzvot do not require *kavanah*? This does not imply that *kavanah* is not desirable or consequential. All are in agreement that *kavanah* is very important. But this second opinion believes that *kavanah* is not essential to the fulfillment of a mitzvah. The obligation can be fulfilled even when *kavanah* is lacking. What rationale is there to this point of view?

A KABBALISTIC ANSWER
One approach is that taken by the Kabbalah, which sees intrinsic value in a mitzvah, even when performed without *kavanah*. Every human act is a reflection of the divine emanation. The cosmic unity of creation is a reflection of the unity of the *Ein Sof*, the Infinite One. God and creation are inseparable. Therefore, every human act has a far-reaching effect even upon the highest spiritual realms. A pebble cast in a lake causes ripples to flow even to the most distant shore. Analogously, the performance of a mitzvah creates a ripple effect upon the entire spiritual universe.

R. Shneur Zalman of Lyady (1745-1813), the founder of Chabad (Lubavitch) Chasidism, addresses this question in his Kabbalistic work, *Tanya*. He writes that there are four levels of existence in the

CHAPTER 2: *Mishnah 1*   91

physical world: a) inanimate (*domem*), such as rocks, earth, dust, etc., b) vegetative (*tzome'ach*), such as plants, trees, grass, etc., c) animate (*chai*), living creatures, and d) man (*m'daber*). All four levels derive from the same divine Source. All are equally dependent upon divine Will for existence, and all are physical manifestations of God's infinite Spirit. They differ only insofar as they represent four stages of physical existence that are determined by the degree of contraction and expansion of the divine illumination. (All physical matter is made up of atoms. Atoms are the building blocks of the physical world. A rock, a blade of grass, and a human being are all made up of identical atoms. Yet, they differ widely. The Kabbalistic idea of physical existence is that the world is made up of spiritual atoms, all of which are part of the *Ein Sof*. The human being and the chair he sits on come from the same source.)

Kavanah is the soul that resides in the body of mitzvot. Even though a mitzvah performed with *kavanah* is infinitely superior to a mitzvah performed without *kavanah*, both derive from the same Will. "And although in both of them, in the commandment and in its *kavanah*, there is the same Will which is perfectly simple, without any change or multiplicity, God forbid, which is united with His blessed Essence and Being in perfect unity, nevertheless the illumination is not the same in respect to contraction and extension and it, too, is differentiated into four grades. For the 'body' of the commandments themselves constitute two grades, namely, the commandments involving real action and those which are performed verbally and mentally, such as the study of *Torah*, reciting *Sh'mah*, praying, saying Grace after Meals, and other benedictions. The *kavanah* of the commandments, i.e., the intention to cleave to His blessed Self, being like the soul to the body, is likewise subdivided into two grades, corresponding to the two categories of the soul which are present in corporeal bodies, namely in animal and in man respectively" (*Tanya*, Chapter 38).

The philosophy of Chabad which sees value even in mitzvot that are performed without *kavanah* is most manifest in the Lubavitch mitzvah "tanks" that travel the world. Manned by devoted followers of the Lubavitcher *Rebbe*, these "tanks" carry *tefillin*, Shabbat candles, books, and other religious articles to Jews in the most far-flung communities. It is not uncommon to find a Lubavitcher Chasid stationed at a busy thoroughfare asking passersby "Are you Jewish? Did you put on tefillin today?" He happily places *tefillin* on any Jew, even the most uncommitted, because the act of wearing *tefillin* has infinite worth, even when unaccompanied by *kavanah*.

A PSYCHOLOGICAL ANSWER

A second approach to comprehending the intrinsic value of a *kavanah*-less mitzvah is to recognize the influence external reality has upon the human soul. Modern psychology recognizes that motivation and behavior mutually affect each other. Motivation obviously stimulates behavior. Hunger drives a person to eat. The habit of eating may, in itself, however, become the motivation for eating, even when hunger does not exist. Each act of eating reinforces the pattern of behavior and strengthens the motivation. Is it any wonder that dieting is a national pastime in many affluent countries? Similarly, even a mitzvah performed without *kavanah* reinforces a pattern of behavior that strengthens the motivation to perform additional mitzvot. This concept is succinctly expressed in the Ethics of the Fathers (4:2): "Ben Azzai says: Run to do even a minor mitzvah and flee from transgression, because one mitzvah leads to another and one transgression leads to another. And the reward of a mitzvah is another mitzvah and the 'reward' of a transgression is another transgression."

The author of *Sefer Hachinuch* questions why there is a plethora of mitzvot related to the celebration of Passover. Would it not have been sufficient to have a single reminder of the Exodus? His response indicates a profound insight into human behavior: "Know that a person is affected by his actions. His heart and all his thoughts constantly reflect his activities, be they good or evil. Even if one were a totally evil person in his heart, and his thoughts were inclined towards evil all day long, if his spirit was stirred and he placed his efforts and actions diligently into Torah and mitzvot, even if not for heaven's sake, he would immediately be inclined towards good. And [performance] not for the mitzvah's sake will become for the mitzvah's sake. The strength of his actions will eliminate his evil inclination because *thoughts are affected by behavior*....

"Therefore, our Sages said, 'The Holy One, blessed be He, wanted to merit Israel, thus, he increased Torah and mitzvot for them.' In so doing, all of our thoughts and our activities will be absorbed by them. And this will be for our ultimate benefit because good deeds will cause us to be good and meritorious of eternal life. They, (the Sages) alluded to this when they said, 'Whoever has a *mezuzah* on his doorpost and wears *tzitzit* on his garment and *tefillin* on his head, is certain not to sin' (Menachot 43b). The reason is because these are constant mitzvot, and a person is affected by them constantly. (In Talmudic times *tefillin* were worn all day long.)

"Now that you understand this, it is not difficult for you to comprehend why there are so many mitzvot pertaining to the miracles of Egypt. For they are a great pillar in our Torah, and the more we are occupied with them the more we will be affected by them, as we have explained " (*Sefer Hachinuch*, Mitzvah 20).

Thus, if a person performs a mitzvah without *kavanah* it may be argued that his obligation is fulfilled because the very act of doing a mitzvah affects his personality and may ultimately lead to his performing other mitzvot. Many Jews have returned to Judaism because of a mitzvah that was performed without *kavanah*. For example, a person may visit a friend who is a Sabbath observer. In deference to his host, he, too, observes Shabbat. The experience may be so rewarding, that he considers becoming Shabbat observant himself. This point of view teaches us not to underestimate the value of performing a mitzvah even if performed not for the mitzvah's sake, because "not for the mitzvah's sake will become for the mitzvah's sake."

PRAYER AND RESPECT FOR PEOPLE
The mishnah discusses the opinions of R. Meir and R. Judah as to when a person is permitted to interrupt his prayers to greet or respond to the greeting of another. R. Judah takes a lenient point of view and allows a person to interrupt between the paragraphs by responding to anyone's greeting. The halachah is decided in favor of R. Judah.

There is a great moral lesson to be learned from R. Judah's words. Even when a Jew is praying, he should not be oblivious to another person's feelings. *Sefer Hachinuch* and *Magen Avraham* are quite explicit on this point (cited earlier, p. 89). A Jew wrapped in his *tallit* should not be wrapped up in himself. Even when he is reciting *Sh'mah* and affirming his faith in God, he may not embarrass or hurt a fellow human being who greets him.

Implicit in this law is a value system that attributes infinite worth to human beings. The feelings and sensitivities of a neighbor, friend, relative, or any other person may not be disregarded with the excuse of being occupied with a mitzvah. Preoccupation with God does not preclude preoccupation with others. Abraham serves as a wonderful role model for proper human conduct. Abraham was sitting in front of his tent one hot day recuperating from his painful circumcision operation. God suddenly appeared to visit the sick. No sooner does God appear, when Abraham interrupts the visit and runs off to welcome three desert wayfarers to his home (Gen.18:1-2; Rashi *ad. loc.*). Abraham was not concerned about hurting God's feelings. He understood that to show concern and respect for fellow human beings is to show honor to God. He knew that man is created in God's image. What greater honor can be paid to God than to give honor to a human being? It is in the spirit of this law that the Talmud says: "So great is the mitzvah of honoring one's fellow that it supersedes a negative commandment in the Torah" (Berachot 19b).

Judaism does not allow religious zeal to supplant humaneness. The value of the human being and the respect that is due every individual may not be sacrificed upon the altar of religious piety. All too often, learned, religious Jews who are seemingly successful in their relationship with God are dismal failures in their relationship with human beings. One wonders if there can be a true relationship with God if a person is insensitive to people. All too often, self-righteousness is mistaken for righteousness.

Those who hold themselves to be above fellow Jews who are less religious and less learned would do well to learn a lesson from R. Yanai. The Midrash relates that R. Yanai, a third-century sage of Eretz Yisrael, once met a well-dressed person and assumed that he was a Torah scholar. The stranger asked to be invited to a meal and R. Yanai happily agreed. During the meal, R. Yanai began to question the stranger. He soon discovered that his guest was not a Torah scholar, but an ignoramous, who was not even capable of leading the Grace after Meals. R. Yanai was so repulsed by his guest that he remarked: "Yanai broke bread with a dog." The stranger was enraged. He grabbed R.

Yanai by his coat and shouted: "You are witholding my inheritance from me!" R. Yanai was puzzled. "What do you mean," he asked. The stranger replied: "I was once walking past a schoolhouse and I heard the children reciting the verse 'The Torah was commanded to us by Moses; it is the inheritance of the congregation of Jacob' (Deut. 33:4). It does not say 'the inheritance of Yanai', it says 'the inheritance of the congregation of Jacob.' The Torah belongs to all Jews. Why do you deny me my inheritance by calling me a dog?" R. Yanai realized that he had made a terrible mistake. He had no right to insult his guest. He realized that this stranger, though not learned, did possess some Torah virtue. When he asked him what merit he possessed, the guest answered: "I have never gossipped nor spoken evil about another person, and whenever I see two people quarrelling, I always make peace between them" (*Lev. Rabbah* 9).

If R. Yanai had probed deeper into the character of his guest, he would have found a shining jewel, an individual whose humanity and sensitivity were exemplary. He did not possess Torah learning, but he felt proud to be part of the Jewish people, the "congregation of Jacob," and would not let anyone, even the great sage, deny him his inheritance.

There are many Jews today who are reminiscent of R. Yanai's guest. Their ignorance is no fault of their own. They were never afforded a proper Jewish education. At best, they attended an afternoon Hebrew School and studied for their Bar or Bat Mitzvah. With the built-in failures of the afternoon Hebrew School system, most graduates do not complete the equivalent of a first grade education. How can such a Jew be blamed for his lack of knowledge? Yet, this very same Jew who is incapable of translating a Hebrew verse in the Torah may have the finest human qualities in terms of his relationship with people, his giving of charity, his concern for the Jewish people and Eretz Yisrael. These qualities are not to be minimized. Perhaps, in the eyes of God, he is more beloved than the Jew who was privileged with a Yeshiva education and a religious home environment, but who does not live up to Torah standards. Only the True Judge knows who is more worthy.

It is told that the holy Baal Shem Tov was sitting at a Shabbat meal with his Chasidim when a poor, ignorant Jew entered the room. The

Baal Shem arose, greeted the man, and invited him to sit near him at the head of the table. The Chasidim were perplexed. Why did their *rebbe* place the ignoramous at a seat that is usually reserved for the most learned and pious? Later, the Baal Shem explained: "Someday, in the World to Come, I will want a 'seat' near the head of the table. When they ask me what merit do I possess to deserve such a high honor, I will tell them that here on earth I gave a seat of honor to a poor, ignorant Jew such as myself."

The Practical Law

1. It is essential to concentrate and pay attention to the meaning of the words of, at least, the first verse of *Sh'mah*. One who recites the first verse without such *kavanah* has not fulfilled his obligation. As for the rest of *Sh'mah*, one should try to have *kavanah*, although it is not essential (*Orach Chaim* 60:5).

2. One must have *kavanah* to fulfill his obligation to recite *Sh'mah* for all three paragraphs (*Mishnah B'rurah, ibid.*).

3. It is our custom nowadays not to interrupt the prayers by greeting others or responding to greetings. Even words of Torah may not be discussed during the prayers (*Mishnah B'rurah, ibid.* 66:1, no. 2). (See *The Practical Law*, next mishnah).

Mishnah 2

This is what is meant by "between the paragraphs": Between the first blessing[1] and the second,[2] (between) the second (blessing) and "hear,"[3] between "hear" and "and if you will carefully obey,"[4] between "and if you will carefully obey" and "and the Lord spoke,"[5] between "and the Lord spoke" and "true and certain."[6] R. Judah says: Between "and the Lord spoke" and "true and certain" it is forbidden to interrupt.

R. Joshua ben Korcha said: Why does "hear" precede "and if you will carefully obey"? In order to first accept upon oneself the yoke of the Kingdom of Heaven[7] and then

משנה ב

אֵלוּ הֵן בֵּין הַפְּרָקִים: בֵּין בְּרָכָה רִאשׁוֹנָה לִשְׁנִיָּה, בֵּין שְׁנִיָּה לְ"שְׁמַע", וּבֵין "שְׁמַע" לְ"וְהָיָה אִם שָׁמֹעַ", בֵּין "וְהָיָה אִם שָׁמֹעַ" לְ"וַיֹּאמֶר", בֵּין "וַיֹּאמֶר" לְ"אֱמֶת וְיַצִּיב". רַבִּי יְהוּדָה אוֹמֵר: בֵּין "וַיֹּאמֶר" לְ"אֱמֶת וְיַצִּיב" לֹא יַפְסִיק. אָמַר רַבִּי יְהוֹשֻׁעַ בֶּן קָרְחָה: לָמָּה קָדְמָה "שְׁמַע" לְ"וְהָיָה אִם שָׁמֹעַ"? אֶלָּא כְּדֵי שֶׁיְּקַבֵּל עָלָיו עֹל מַלְכוּת שָׁמַיִם תְּחִלָּה, וְאַחַר כָּךְ יְקַבֵּל עָלָיו עֹל מִצְוֹת. "וְהָיָה אִם שָׁמֹעַ" לְ"וַיֹּאמֶר"? שֶׁ"וְהָיָה אִם

---

1. FIRST BLESSING — *Yotzer ohr*.
2. SECOND — *Ahavah rabah*.
3. "HEAR" — *Sh'mah*.
4. "AND IF YOU WILL CAREFULLY OBEY" — *V'hayah im shamo'ah*.
5. "AND THE LORD SPOKE" — *Vayomer*.
6. "TRUE AND CERTAIN" — *Emet v'yatziv*.
7. "THE YOKE OF THE KINGDOM OF HEAVEN" — Acknowledging God's Sovereignty, which is the essence of the first verse of *Sh'mah*.

to accept upon oneself the yoke of Mitzvot.⁸ (Why does) "and if you will carefully obey" precede "and the Lord spoke"? Because "and if you will carefully obey" applies to (both) the day and the night, whereas "and the Lord spoke" applies only to the day.⁹

שְׁמַע" נוֹהֵג בַּיּוֹם וּבַלַּיְלָה, "וַיֹּאמֶר" אֵינוֹ נוֹהֵג אֶלָּא בַּיּוֹם:

---

8. "THE YOKE OF MITZVOT" — Acceptance of God's commandments, which is the subject of the second paragraph of *Sh'mah*.
9. ONLY TO THE DAY — The paragraph mainly speaks about the mitzvah of *tzitzit* which is required to be worn only during the daytime, as it says: "And you shall see it," meaning, it must be worn at a time when it can be seen, viz., daytime.

The Letter of the Law

The mishnah cites the blessings of the morning prayer. The definition of "paragraphs" applies, however, to the evening blessings, as well.

NOT INTERRUPTING BETWEEN "AND THE LORD SPOKE" AND "TRUE AND CERTAIN"

R. Judah says that the last words of the third paragraph of *Sh'mah* — "I am the Lord your God" — must be connected to the first word of the following blessing — "True." Even though the word "True" is not in the Torah, it must be linked to the third paragraph.

The authorities differ as to what R. Judah means by not interrupting. Rosh and R. Jonah interpret that there may be no interruption at all. Maimonides interprets that there may be no interruption as between the paragraphs, but, one may interrupt as in the middle of a paragraph, i.e., he may greet out of fear and respond out of respect.

R. Judah's ruling is based upon a verse in the Book of Jeremiah that contains the phrase, "But the Lord God is True" (10:10).

THE ORDER OF THE PARAGRAPHS

The Men of the Great Assembly selected the three paragraphs of *Sh'mah* for daily prayer and placed them in a sequence that does not correspond to the sequence in the Torah. The first paragraph of *Sh'mah* is in Deuteronomy, chapter 6, the second paragraph of *Sh'mah* is in Deuteronomy, chapter 11, but the third paragraph is in Numbers, chapter 15. Thus, the order in which the paragraphs are found in the Torah plays no role, as far as the order in the *Siddur* is concerned. R. Joshua ben Korcha offers a rational explanation for the order of the paragraphs. He says that there is an order of priorities. Before a Jew expresses his willingness to accept the commandments upon himself, he must first acknowledge that there is a Commander. The acceptance of God's Kingship is called *Kabbalat Ohl Malchut Shamayim*, the acceptance of the yoke of the Kingdom of Heaven. After proclaiming God as the supreme sovereign Ruler of the Universe, the next step follows, which is to accept His divine commandments. The second paragraph takes priority over the third, because the second paragraph refers to all mitzvot, those that must be performed by day, as well as those that must be performed at night. The third paragraph, however, speaks predominantly about the mitzvah of *tzitzit*, which a person is required to wear only by day. It therefore was placed last.

The Talmud offers a second explanation in the name of R. Simeon bar Yochai. The first paragraph contains three key elements in relation to mitzvot: learning ("and you shall speak of them"), teaching ("you shall teach them diligently to your children"), and observing ("you shall bind them... you shall inscribe them"). The second paragraph contains two elements: teaching ("you shall teach them to your children") and observing ("you shall bind them... you shall inscribe them"). The third paragraph only contains one element, viz., observing ("do all My commandments") (Berachot 14b).

The third paragraph of *Sh'mah*, however, is uniquely important. The Talmud gives an impressive list of fundamental principles that are contained in it — "Why was the paragraph of *tzitzit* included in *Sh'mah*? R. Judah ben Chaviva said: Because it contains five (according to another version, six) principles: 1) The mitzvah of *tzitzit*, 2) the Exodus, 3) the yoke of mitzvot, 4) admonitions against ideas of heresy, 5) immorality, and 6) idolatry" (Berachot 12b).

The Spirit of the Law

"THE LORD GOD IS TRUE *(EMET)*"

The inclusion of the word *"Emet"* in *Sh'mah* and its inseparability from "I am the Lord your God" is not merely due to a phrase used by the prophet. It is the context of the phrase that gives it special meaning and applicability to the third paragraph of *Sh'mah*. In chapter 10 of the book of Jeremiah, the prophet depicts the fallacy of idolatry. He proclaims: "Hear the word which the Lord spoke unto you, O House of Israel. So says the Lord: Do not learn from the ways of the nations, do not be dismayed at the signs of heaven; for the nations are dismayed by them. For the ways of the nations are empty; a tree is cut down from the forest, the work of the hands of the workman with the axe. They decorate it with silver and gold; they fasten it with nails and hammers that it should not move. They are like a hard post that cannot speak; they must be carried because they cannot walk. Do not be afraid of them for they have not the power to do evil or good.

"There is none like you, O Lord, You are great and Your Name is great with power. Who shall not fear You, King of the nations, for unto You it is fitting; there is none like You amongst all the wise men of the nations and in all their kingdoms. They are stupid and foolish all; their empty teaching is from wood. Beaten silver is imported from Tarshish, and gold from Ufa, the work of craftsmen and smiths; their garments are blue and purple, they are all the work of wise men. But the Lord God is True, He is the living God and King of the Universe" (10:1-10).

By linking the word *"Emet"* to the third paragraph of *Sh'mah*, we call to mind the words of Jeremiah, his ridicule of idolatry and his testimony of God's truthful existence. This message expresses the essence of *Sh'mah*. The negation of idolatry is alluded to in the third paragraph with the words: "Do not follow the desires of your heart and eyes which lead you astray." This verse is interpreted by the Talmud to be an admonition against immorality and idolatry (Berachot 12b). The negation of idolatry is also contained in the first verse: "the Lord is One," meaning, there is no other god. Thus, the addition of the word *"Emet"* brings *Sh'mah* to a full circle: "Hear O Israel, the Lord is our God, the Lord is One.... the Lord your God is True."

"TRUE" AT BEGINNING AND END

According to the Zohar, the 248 words of *Sh'mah* correspond to the 248 organs of the human body. Each word has a healing effect upon a particular part of the body. In reality, there are only 245 words in the *Sh'mah*. When, however, the reader repeats aloud the last three words, he brings the number to 248 (*Orach Chaim* 61:3). When a person prays alone, he should reach 248 words by preceding *Sh'mah* with the words *El Melech neh'eh'mahn*, "God is a faithful King" (*Ramah, ibid.*).

El Melech neh'eh'mahn has an additional importance. The initial letters, *aleph, mem, nun*, form the word "Amen". This is not mere coincidence. The Talmud states quite explicitly that the word "Amen", in fact, means *El Melech neh'eh'mahn*, "God is a faithful King" (Sanhedrin 111a). Amen has another connotation, as well. Amen means *Emet*, "true!" (*Orach Chaim* 124:6). Thus, *Sh'mah* is introduced with an affirmation that God is, indeed, the true and faithful King of the universe. *El Melech neh'eh'mahn* is a brief and appropriate prelude to *Sh'mah*. Again, we see the beginning and end of *Sh'mah* linked together by a single theme - truth.

Abudraham, a Spanish liturgical commentator (Seville, 14th century), notes that the letter *Ayin* in the word *Sh'mah* and the letter *Dalet* in the word *"Echad"* are written in the Torah scroll in an enlarged manner because these two letters form the word *"Eid,"* which means "witness." When a Jew recites *Sh'mah*, he bears witness to the absolute truth that "the Lord is our God, the Lord is One."

THE YOKE OF THE KINGDOM OF HEAVEN

The essence of Judaism is the recognition that there is One God. This fundamental principle is the foundation of the religion. The Torah, the mitzvot, the entire spectrum of life, are based upon this principle. The Ten Commandments begin with the words "I am the Lord your God." From this commandment, all the others emanate. Nachmanides, in his Torah commentary, writes: "This commandment, in the words of the Rabbis, is called the obligation 'to take upon oneself the yoke of the Kingdom of Heaven,' for these words [i.e., the eternal your God], which I have mentioned, indicate a King addressing His people. Thus the Rabbis have said in the Mechilta: 'Thou shalt have no other gods before Me'. Why is this said? Because it says, 'I am the Eternal thy God.' This can be illustrated by a parable: A king invaded a country, and his attendants said to him, 'Issue decrees to us.' He, however, refused, saying: 'No! When you have accepted my sovereignty, I will issue decrees to you, for if you do not accept my sovereignty, how will you carry out my decrees?' Similary, God said to Israel: 'I am the Eternal thy God, thou shalt have no other gods. I am He Whose sovereignty you have accepted in Egypt.' And when they said to Him: 'Yes,' [He continued]: 'Now, just as you have accepted My sovereignty, so you must also accept My decrees.' That is to say, 'Since you have accepted upon yourselves and have admitted that I am the Eternal, and that I am your God from the [time that you were yet in the] land of Egypt, then accept all My commandments'" (*Commentary on the Torah*, Chavel, Shilo Publishers, 1973, vol. 2, p. 286).

Maimonides opens his magnum opus, *Mishneh Torah*, with the words "The foundation of foundations and the pillar of all wisdom is to know that there is a First Being Who is the Creator of everything. Everything in heaven and earth, and everything in between, exists because of the truth of His existence. If you could imagine God's nonexistence, then nothing else could exist. And, if you could imagine all of existence not existing, He alone will exist. He will not cease to exist because they cease to exist, because everything needs Him, while He does not need them nor any one of them. Thus, His Truth (of existence) is not like any one of them. This is what the prophet said: 'The Lord God is True' (Jeremiah 10:10).... He is the Prime Mover... Knowing this is a positive commandment, as it says: 'I am the Lord your God' (Ex. 20:2)."

The commandment "I am the Lord your God" is so fundamental and basic, that the author of *Halachot G'dolot* does not consider it a commandment at all. In his listing of the 613 commandments, he does not include belief in God, because it is not simply one of the commandments, it is rather the foundation upon which all commandments rest.

But what does belief in God mean? Most people, when asked, state unequivocally, "I believe in God." No doubt, most people do, in fact, believe in God. But the real question is — "To what degree does your belief in God affect your daily life?" In Judaism, belief in God is not enough. A Jew must go a long way beyond belief. He must develop a relationship with God, a paradoxical relationship that is both immeasurably close and infinitely distant. He must try to develop profound feelings of love, awe, and reverence. He must be willing to submit himself and all that he possesses to the divine Will. He must control his desires and appetites because God said so. He must harness all of his intellectual, emotional, and physical resources and use them in the service of God. This is the meaning of "the acceptance of the yoke of the Kingdom of Heaven." As Rabbi Samson R. Hirsch defines it: "The subordination of all of our personality and of our entire world to the one and unique dominion of God" (*Commentary on the Siddur*, p. 114).

A yoke is placed upon an animal so that his master can guide and direct him in his work. It is also a harness that joins him with another animal so that the two can work in unison. Accepting the yoke of the Kingdom of Heaven means expressing a willingness to accept divine guidance and direction. It means showing a readiness to serve the Almighty. It also means that a Jew is not alone when he demonstrates faith. He joins his fellow Jews who are also prepared to serve God. Together, under one yoke, they do God's bidding and draw the divine Chariot upon the face of the earth.

Belief is not enough. What is required is the recognition that God is the Supreme King whose Will is to be obeyed. "Make His Will your will" teaches Rabban Gamliel (Ethics of the Fathers 2:4). Furthermore, there must be a recognition that all that one has and possesses — money, material wealth, health, family, and life itself — belongs to God. All that one owns and enjoys is given on loan. The loan may be long — or short-term, but eventually the Owner will recall that which is rightfully His. This is what God told the Children of Israel just a few days before the Great Revelation and the giving of the Ten Commandments, "For the entire world is Mine" (Ex. 19:5). And this is what King David expressed in the verse: "The earth and all its fullness belong to the Lord, the entire world and its inhabitants" (Ps. 24:1).

When a person truly believes in God's ownership of all that exists and all that one possesses, if and when the time comes to separate from something or someone that is cherished, that separation is made easier. Letting go is more difficult than holding on. But if letting go means returning to the rightful owner, the sense of loss is mitigated and bereavement is assuaged. The Midrash relates that one Shabbat afternoon, the great Tanna, R. Meir, was teaching Torah in his *beit midrash*. Apparently, a plague was ravaging the city and on that day his two sons died. His wife, Bruriah, a woman noted for her brilliance and scholarship, placed her dead children on a bed and covered them with a sheet. That evening when R. Meir came home, he inquired about his sons. Bruriah evaded telling her husband of the tragedy that had befallen them. She prepared wine for *havdalah* and brought R. Meir his meal. After he had eaten, she said: "Meir, I have a question to ask you. Some time ago, someone came and left two precious jewels for me to take care of. Today, he returned and asked for them back. Shall I give them back to him or not?" R. Meir was puzzled by the question. "My dear, if someone gave you something to watch, of course you have to return it," he said. Without saying a word, Bruriah took her husband's hand and led him to the bedroom. She lifted the sheet, and there lay the two children. R. Meir broke into tears. "My children, my children," he cried. Bruriah tried to comfort him. "My husband," she said, "Do not cry, the Owner came and took back His jewels. The Lord gave and the Lord has taken, blessed be the Name of the Lord" (*Midrash Proverbs* 31).

Adam and Eve were granted Paradise. They were free to enjoy all the delicacies and delights of the Garden of Eden, with the exception of one tree whose fruit was forbidden. There was nothing exceptional or unnatural about the tree. It was an ordinary plant whose fruit might have been figs, or grapes, or *etrogim* (citrons) or, perhaps, even wheat (*Gen. Rabbah* 15). The Torah does not specify what the Tree of Knowledge was. It is not important. What is important is that its fruit was forbidden. Why, in fact, did Adam and Eve sin? Why were they so tempted by a single tree when virtually every other tree and fruit was permitted to them? What was the nature of their sin?

Rabbi Joseph B. Soloveitchik explains that Adam and Eve failed to recognize God's rightful ownership of all of creation. They believed in God. They had no doubt as to God's existence. Rather, their sin lay in their failure to recognize "for the entire world is Mine." "... the prohibition was intended to teach Adam the concept of *adnut*, [ownership], that God is not only the world's Creator and Sustainer, but also its Owner. *Vayetzav Hashem Elohim*, ['the Lord God has commanded,'] was a restrictive command intended to teach man that all benefits and pleasures are gifts of God, who offers them selectively and conditionally. They are privileges that are granted, not prizes freely to be taken. Adam viewed the world as ownerless property, *hefker*. He accepted that God was the Creator and Sustainer; this was indisputable to him. But he was unwilling to concede that God had retained proprietary rights over His creation; he refused to recognize any "no trespassing" restrictions. Rather, Adam claimed for himself carte blanche rights to partake as he pleased.

"This, therefore, was his sin, the crime of *gezelah*, robbery; he took that which was not his. *Adnut* insists that life and all its benefits stem from God and are granted only to the extent that we accept His will. We must be ready to surrender, to restrict our appetites, to control our fantasies. If we take possession contrary to His will, we are usurpers and thieves." (*Reflections of the Rav*, Abraham R. Besdin, Dept. of Torah Education and Culture in the Diaspora of the World Zionist Organization [Jerusalem: 1979], p. 18).

KABBALAT OHL MALCHUT SHAMAYIM IN *SH'MAH*

The Prayer Book is replete with prayers that express the idea of *Kabbalat ohl malchut shamayim*. In fact, every blessing contains acceptance of the yoke of the Kingdom of Heaven with the words, "Lord our God, King of the Universe." No prayer or blessing, however, expresses this idea more succinctly or more profoundly than "Hear O Israel, the Lord is our God, the Lord is One." This is why the Talmud states that *kavanah* is essential only for the first verse (Berachot 13b).

Two divine Names are mentioned in *Sh'mah*, the Tetragrammaton (*Yud, hay, vuv, hay*) and *Elohim (Elohaynu*, our *Elohim*). Implicit in these two Names are the meaning of God's Essence and His relationship with the world. The Tetragrammaton is also known as the Ineffable Name because today it is never pronounced. This name connotes God's essence. It means Merciful God. It also means Eternal God because the four letters spell the words *hayah, hoveh*, and *yihiyeh*, past, present, and future. As we saw earlier in Maimonides' opening words to *Mishneh Torah*, the world's continuous existence depends upon God's existence. Thus, the Name also implies God the Sustainer.

It is sometimes referred to as the *Shem ha-Havayah*, which means the Name of Existence that causes existence.

Elohim is derived from the word *el*, which means might or power. This Name connotes divine Omnipotence. It is the Name that is employed in the first chapter of Genesis because it also connotes Creator. It is not a coincidence that the *gematriyah*, the numerical values, of the Name *Elohim* and the word *ha-tevah*, nature, are identical. Each of them totals 86. This does not imply the pantheistic notion that God and Nature are one and the same. Rather, it implies that God is within Nature. *Elohim* means the God who is immanent, within the world. *Havayah* means the God who is transcendent, outside the bounds of Nature. This dual aspect of God is expressed in the verse: "Holy, holy, holy is the Lord of Hosts (transcendent), the whole world is filled with His glory (immanent)" (Isaiah 6:3). And lest the worshipper confuse God's dual aspect with duality, the first verse of *Sh'mah* concludes "the Lord is One." It is the limitation of human intelligence that perceives a dual aspect. In Essence, God is One.

"The Lord is our God, the Lord is One" consists of two separate phrases which require an additional mention of God's Name. Why does not the verse simply read: "The Lord our God is One"? This is probably the question that prompted Rashi to explain the verse in the following manner:

"Hear O Israel, the Lord is *our* God" today, because other nations do not believe in the God of Israel. There will come a time, however, when "the Lord is One" for the entire family of nations, as it says: "For then I will turn the nations to be pure of speech that they may all call upon the Name of the Lord, to serve Him together" (Zephaniah 3:9); and it says: "On that day the Lord will be One and His Name One" (Zechariah 14:9). According to Rashi, *Kabbalat Ohl Malchut Shamayim* consists not only of our affirmation in our belief in God. It includes a second affirmation, that someday all people will unite in an enduring faith in God's Kingship and Unity.

THREE LEVELS OF FAITH
R. Joshua ben Korcha offers an explanation for the order of the three paragraphs of *Sh'mah*. The acceptance of the yoke of the Kingdom of

Heaven precedes the acceptance of the Yoke of mitzvot. And the acceptance of all mitzvot precedes the mitzvah of *tzitzit* which is observed only at daytime. R. Simeon bar Yochai offers a second explanation. The first paragraph speaks of learning, teaching, and observing; the second, teaching and observing; and the third, only of observing.

There is a third explanation. Each of the three paragraphs offers a basis for belief in God. The Sages saw a hierarchy of faith in the *Sh'mah* and placed the paragraphs in the order of their priority. The first paragraph speaks of faith based upon love of God, the second, faith based upon reward and punishment, and the third, faith based upon gratitude.

The most sublime relationship a human being can have with the Almighty is one of love. Maimonides speaks at length about the value of loving God: "Let not a man say that I shall perform the mitzvot of the Torah and engage in its wisdom so that I will receive all the blessings written in it, or so that I will merit life in the hereafter. And, I will refrain from sinning in order to be spared the curses that are written in the Torah, or, so that I will not be cut off from life in the hereafter. It is not fitting to serve the Lord in this manner, for whoever serves in this manner is serving from fear. This is not the level of prophets or wise men.... He who serves out of love engages in the Torah and the mitzvot and walks in the ways of wisdom, not for an ulterior motive and not from fear of evil and not to inherit good. But rather, he observes truth because it is truth, and goodness will follow by itself. This level is a very sublime one and not every wise person is privileged to reach it. It is the level of Abraham whom the Holy One, blessed be He, called His 'lover' because he served only from love. This is the level that the Holy One, blessed be He, commanded us through Moses, as it says, 'And you shall love the Lord your God!' When a person loves the Lord properly, he will automatically do the mitzvot out of love.

"What is meant by proper love? It is loving the Lord so greatly, so powerfully, that the soul is bound to its love for Him. It is to yearn constantly like one who is lovesick and cannot distract his mind from his beloved. He yearns for her constantly, while sitting or standing, while eating or drinking.... The entire Song of Songs is an allegory on this subject " (*Mishneh Torah*, Laws of Repentance 10:1-3).

It is clear that the first paragraph of *Sh'mah*, which emphasizes love for God, should precede the second paragraph, which speaks primarily of reward and punishment. A person should not perform the mitzvot with expectations of reward or because of fear of punishment. The mitzvot should be performed for their own sake. It is a privilege to be able to serve God through His commandments. Antigonus of Socho used to say: "Do not be like servants who serve their master for the sake of receiving a reward, but rather be like servants who serve their master without expecting reward" (Ethics of the Fathers 1:3).

It is told that the Jewish community of Vilna sent an emissary to purchase an *etrog* for their rabbi, the great R. Elijah, the Vilna Gaon. In the cold climate of Eastern Europe *etrogim* were difficult to obtain. So the emissary travelled from village to village and from town to town with a large sum of money in search of an *etrog*. He searched in vain. Nowhere could he find an *etrog* for his rabbi. The Sukkot festival was approaching, so in great disappointment he decided to return to Vilna. One night he entered an inn to find lodging. He told the innkeeper of his plight and his great disappointment. The innkeeper smiled broadly and proudly took a beautiful *etrog* out of a drawer. The emissary could hardly believe his eyes. He offered to buy the *etrog*, but the innkeeper refused. He offered a large sum of money, but the innkeeper still refused. Finally, in desperation, he said, "I am not looking to purchase an *etrog* for myself. I want to purchase an *etrog* for the Vilna Gaon." The innkeeper hesitated for a while and replied, "Alright, I am willing to sell you my *etrog*, but not for money. What I want in return is the Vilna Gaon's share in the World to Come. Only if you promise me that will I give you the *etrog*." The emissary agreed.

Upon returning to Vilna with the prized *etrog*, the emissary nervously told the Vilna Gaon of the bargain he had struck with the innkeeper. R. Elijah smiled and replied: "We do not know what reward we receive for mitzvot. But, let me assure you that I am happy to give away my portion in the World to Come for the opportunity to perform the mitzvah of *etrog*" (*Saray Ha'mayah*, vol. 2, pp.22-23).

Maimonides, in his lengthy introduction to the tenth chapter of Tractate Sanhedrin which deals with the World to Come, discusses the need for offering reward for the study of Torah and the performance of mitzvot. He gives the analogy of a child who does not see the value of education and does not want to learn. It is perfectly acceptable for the teacher to "bribe" his student with candies and sweets to motivate him to learn. When the child tires of these rewards, he may be offered gifts and money. And when the child matures and no longer wishes to accept these "bribes," he may be motivated by honor and the title "Rabbi." None of these is a valid reason for studying Torah. But until a person reaches the level of understanding that will enable him to perform the mitzvot for their own sake, let him perform them for an ulterior motive. Maimonides' pedagogic lesson is based upon the Rabbinic dictum: "Not for the mitzvah's sake will become for the mitzvah's sake" (Pesachim 50b). Observing the mitzvot because of reward and punishment is not a *desideratum*, but it is a means of reaching the higher level of observing mitzvot out of love (Commentary on the Mishnah).

The third level of faith is one that is based on the return of a favor. Sometimes a person may observe the requirements of his religion because he feels a deep debt of gratitude to God. Imagine a drowning person who is pulled from the water by a passerby. The person whose life was saved will undoubtedly feel eternally indebted to his rescuer. He will try to find some way of repaying his savior. No request made by the rescuer is too great or demanding. The third paragraph of *Sh'mah* speaks of this kind of faith: "It is for you to remember and do all of my commandments and be holy for your God (because) I am the Lord your God who brought you out of the Land of Egypt to be your God." *Sifre* comments on the verse: "I redeemed you from Egypt on condition that you accept My decrees." Here, the motivation for doing the commandments is neither love nor reward. Rather, it is a *quid pro quo* obligation based upon God's rescue of the Jewish people from bondage. A person who serves God in gratitude for what God has done for himself or his ancestors is also praiseworthy. This, too, is a valid acceptance of the yoke of the Kingdom of Heaven.

The order of the three paragraphs may, therefore, be seen as three levels of faith. The third is based upon events of the past. The second is based upon anticipation of the future. The first, and highest, level is based upon feelings of love that are felt in the present. All three levels express the various ways people express their faith in God and their acceptance of His absolute Sovereignty.

The Practical Law

1. It is our custom nowadays not to interrupt the prayers with greetings or responses, and certainly not with conversation. Even discussing Torah is forbidden after *Baruch she'amar (Mishnah B'rurah, Orach Chaim* 66:1).

2. Prayer responses, e.g., *Amen, Borchu, Modim, Kaddish, Kedushah*, at certain places in the prayer are permitted and at other places are prohibited. The following are some of the rules:

   a) Before *Baruch she'amar*, all prayer responses are permitted.

   b) *Adonai Elohachem emet* may not be interrupted.

   c) There may be no interruption between *Ga'ahl Yisrael* and the *Amidah*.

   d) There may be no interruption during the *Amidah*. One may join the congregation in *Kedushah* if he is at that place. After concluding the blessing *Shalom* and adding the words *Y'hiyu l'ratzon...*, it is permitted to interrupt as one would during the paragraphs of *Sh'mah*.

   e) From *Baruch she'amar* until *Borchu*, prayer responses are permitted. The response to *Kedushah* should be limited to the verses *Kadosh ..., Baruch...,* and *Yimloch....*

   f) Between the paragraphs, from *Borchu* until the *Amidah*, it is permitted to answer *Amen* to all blessings, *Amen, y'hay sh'may rabah*, and *Amen* after *da'amiran b'almah* in the *Kaddish*, the verses *Kadosh...* and *Baruch...* in the *Kedushah, Baruch Adonai...* after hearing *Borchu*, and the three words *Modim anachnu lach* in response to *Modim*.

   g) In the middle of the paragraphs, the rules are basically the same, with the exception of answering *Amen* to blessings. All *Amens* are prohibited except for the blessings *Ha'El Hakadosh* and *Shomayah tefillah (ibid.,* 66: 3, 5, 7, and *Mishnah B'rurah, ad.loc.).*

3. The correct order of the paragraphs is: *Sh'mah, V'hayah* and *Va'yomer (Mishneh Torah,* Laws of *Sh'mah* 1:2).

Mishnah 3 / משנה ג

He who recites *shm'ah* inaudibly has fulfilled his obligation. R. Yosi says: He has not fulfilled his obligation.

If he recited without pronouncing the letters distinctly[1] — R. Yosi says: He has fulfilled his obligation. R. Judah says: He has not fulfilled his obligation.

He who recites[2] in the wrong order has not fulfilled his obligation. If he recited and erred[3], he must return to the place where he erred.[4]

הַקּוֹרֵא אֶת שְׁמַע וְלֹא הִשְׁמִיעַ לְאָזְנוֹ, יָצָא. רַבִּי יוֹסֵי אוֹמֵר, לֹא יָצָא. קָרָא וְלֹא דִקְדֵּק בְּאוֹתִיּוֹתֶיהָ — רַבִּי יוֹסֵי אוֹמֵר: יָצָא, רַבִּי יְהוּדָה אוֹמֵר: לֹא יָצָא. הַקּוֹרֵא לְמַפְרֵעַ, לֹא יָצָא. קָרָא וְטָעָה, יַחֲזֹר לַמָּקוֹם שֶׁטָּעָה:

1. WITHOUT PRONOUNCING THE LETTERS DISTINCTLY — By slurring the words or letters, improper accentuation or running one word into another.
2. HE WHO RECITES — The verses.
3. ERRED — By skipping a word or a verse.
4. WHERE HE ERRED — To the beginning of the verse in which he had erred.

The Letter of the Law

"HEAR" O ISRAEL

The word *Shmah* has two meanings: "hear" and "understand." R. Yosi takes *Sh'mah* to mean "hear." A person reciting *Sh'mah* must hear the words he is reciting. The Sages, however, argue that *Sh'mah* means "understand." In other words, if one does not understand Hebrew, he may recite *Sh'mah* in the language he understands. What is important is not the audibility of *Sh'mah* but its comprehension. We find the word *Sh'mah* meaning "understand" in II Kings. The delegates of Hezekiah say to the Assyrian general Rab-shakeh: "Speak unto your servants Aramaic for we understand (*shomim*) it" (18:26). R. Yosi, however, takes the word *Sh'mah* to mean "hear" as it is found most frequently in the Bible.

According to most authorities, the Sages, who do not require audibility, do require verbalization. In other words, though it is not necessary to hear the words of *Sh'mah*, they must at least be pronounced. If a person were to recite *Sh'mah* mentally, without uttering the words, he will not have fulfilled his obligation. This is based on the principle: "thinking is not speaking." And even according to those authorities who permit a mental recitation of Grace after Meals and other blessings, *Sh'mah* must be verbalized because the Torah says "and you shall speak of them" (*Torah T'mimah*, Deut. 6:6).

RECITING IN THE WRONG ORDER

If a person recites the words or the verses in the wrong order he has not fulfilled his obligation. The Talmud bases this law upon the words "And these words shall be....," i.e., they must be recited in the order in which they appear in the Torah (Berachot 13a). It is obvious that if a person recited the words of *Sh'mah* backwards he has not fulfilled his obligation because the meaning would be totally confused and distorted. "And these words shall be ..." teaches us that even a reversal of the verses would disqualify the reading of *Sh'mah*. A reversal in the order of the paragraphs, however, does not invalidate *Sh'mah*. Each paragraph is an independent unit. Maimonides explains that since the order of the paragraphs was not established to coincide with the order in which they are found in the Torah, they do not have to follow the sequence of the *Siddur*. The sequence of paragraphs suggested by R. Joshua ben Korcha in mishnah 2 is preferred, but not essential (*Mishneh Torah*, Laws of Reciting *Sh'mah* 2:11).

We explained in the previous mishnah that each of the three paragraphs expresses a different level or degree of faith experience. However, they all share the common theme of the acceptance of the yoke of the Kingdom of Heaven. Thus, the order in which they are recited is not crucial to the fulfillment of the mitzvah of reciting *Sh'mah*.

The Spirit of the Law

VERBALIZATION AND AUDIBILITY

When a person recites *Sh'mah*, he externalizes his innermost feelings and thoughts of faith. The words of *Sh'mah* give expression to a sincere belief in God and an enthusiastic willingness to serve Him. The essential obligation, according to the Sages, is to verbalize that faith. Verbalization is a sufficient testimony of faith, even if inaudible. R. Yosi, on the other hand, insists that the words must be audible because testimony implies audibility. Furthermore, faith must not only be externalized, it must be internalized. A person must hear his own recitation of *Sh'mah* in order to reinforce his faith and belief in God. When a Jew recites *Sh'mah*, he becomes the audience to his own testimony.

The Practical Law

1. One should recite *Sh'mah* audibly. If, however, he recited inaudibly, he has fulfilled his obligation provided that he enunciated the words (*Orach Chaim* 62:3). If he merely read *Sh'mah* without enunciating, he has not fulfilled his obligation (*Mishneh B'rurah, ibid.*).
2. One should make every effort to read the words carefully and pronounce them clearly. If he did not do so, he has still fulfilled his obligation. If, however, he skipped over words or deleted letters, he has not fulfilled his obligation (*Orach Chaim* 62:1).
3. If one recited the words or verses in the wrong order, he has not fulfilled his obligation. If, however, he recited the paragraphs in the wrong order, he has fulfilled his obligation (*ibid.*, 64:1).
4. If one skipped a verse he must return to the verse that was skipped and continue from there. If he does not remember at what point he skipped, he must return to the beginning of the paragraph (*ibid.*, 64:2).
5. If one concluded one of the first two paragraphs and is not sure which, he must return to the beginning of the second paragraph (*ibid.*, 64:3).

Mishnah 4 / משנה ד

Workers may recite[1] on top of a tree or on top of a wall, which they are not permitted to do for *t'fillah*.[2]

הָאֻמָּנִין קוֹרִין בְּרֹאשׁ הָאִילָן אוֹ בְּרֹאשׁ הַנִּדְבָּךְ, מַה שֶּׁאֵינָן רַשָּׁאִין לַעֲשׂוֹת כֵּן בַּתְּפִלָּה:

1. MAY RECITE — *Sh'mah*.
2. *T'FILLAH* — The *Amidah*, or *Sh'moneh Esray*. The *Amidah* is prayer par excellence. That is why it is referred to as *T'fillah*.

The Letter of the Law

KAVANAH DURING SH'MAH AND THE AMIDAH

In order to fulfill the obligation to recite *Sh'mah*, one need only have *kavanah* for the first verse. The *Amidah*, on the other hand, requires *kavanah* for all nineteen blessings. Therefore, the halachah does not require workers to climb down from the tree, wall, or scaffolding on which they are working to recite *Sh'mah*. They can do this without climbing down. The *Amidah*, however, requires an extended period of concentration. Such concentration is difficult on top of a tree or a wall. They, therefore, are permitted to climb down to pray. Maimonides adds that the workers must recite not only the first verse with *kavanah*, but the first paragraph, as well. If they were only required to recite one verse, they may take *Sh'mah* too casually (*Mishneh Torah*, Laws of Reciting *Sh'mah*, 2:4).

The Spirit of the Law

STEALING TIME

Only the first verse of *Sh'mah* requires total concentration and devotion. The Sages did not obligate workers to climb off a tree or scaffolding to recite *Sh'mah* for the sake of the first verse, as this would cause an unnecessary monetary loss to the employer. The worker who is idle on his employer's time is guilty of theft. Thus, writes Maimonides: "Just as the employer is enjoined not to steal the salary of the poor worker and not to delay payment, so too, is the worker enjoined not to steal the work of his employer by wasting a little time here and a little time there and ending up spending the day deceitfully. Rather, he is obligated to be punctilious with his time. It is for this reason that they (the Sages) insisted that he not recite the fourth blessing of the Grace after Meals. He must also work to the best of his ability, for Jacob, the righteous one, said, 'I have worked for your father with all my strength'(Gen. 31:6). He was accordingly rewarded for this in this world, as it says: 'And the man (Jacob) prospered very much' "(*ibid.*, 30:43) (*Mishneh Torah,* Laws of Employees 13:7).

Just as an employee must be considerate of the time that belongs to his employer, the employer must be considerate of the religious needs of his employee. The employee may not take unfair advantage of his employer by using an excessive amount of time to pray. The employer, on the other hand, may not deny his employees their right to worship God. In this manner, Judaism sets a fair balance between the needs of both parties.

The Practical Law

1. If a person is engaged in work and wishes to recite *Sh'mah*, he may stop working in order to recite the first paragraph (*Orach Chaim* 63:7).
2. Workers or employers who are working in tree tops and on scaffolding may recite *Sh'mah* where they are and do not have to descend (*ibid.*, 63:8).
3. A porter may recite *Sh'mah* while carrying a load. He may not, however, recite while loading or unloading (*ibid.*, 63:9).

Mishnah 5

משנה ה

A bridegroom[1] is exempt from reciting *Sh'mah* from the first night[2] until Saturday night — if he had not performed the act.[3] It happened that Rabban Gamliel recited (*Sh'mah*) on his wedding night. His students said to him: "Did you not teach us, our Rabbi, that a bridegroom is exempt from reciting *Sh'mah* on the first night?" He said to them: "I will not heed you to absolve myself from the sovereignty of Heaven, even for one hour."[4]

חָתָן פָּטוּר מִקְּרִיאַת שְׁמַע בַּלַּיְלָה הָרִאשׁוֹן עַד מוֹצָאֵי שַׁבָּת, אִם לֹא עָשָׂה מַעֲשֶׂה. מַעֲשֶׂה בְרַבָּן גַּמְלִיאֵל שֶׁקָּרָא בַלַּיְלָה הָרִאשׁוֹן שֶׁנָּשָׂא. אָמְרוּ לוֹ תַלְמִידָיו: לֹא לִמַּדְתָּנוּ, רַבֵּנוּ, שֶׁחָתָן פָּטוּר מִקְּרִיאַת שְׁמַע בַּלַּיְלָה הָרִאשׁוֹן? אָמַר לָהֶם, אֵינִי שׁוֹמֵעַ לָכֶם לְבַטֵּל מִמֶּנִּי מַלְכוּת שָׁמַיִם אֲפִלּוּ שָׁעָה אֶחָת:

1. A BRIDEGROOM — Whose bride is a virgin.
2. THE FIRST NIGHT — His wedding night. In the time of the Mishnah, it was customary to marry on Wednesday night. Thus, the bridegroom is exempt from reciting *Sh'mah* four nights.
3. THE ACT — The consummation of marriage with sexual intercourse.
4. ONE HOUR — Even for a brief moment.

The Letter of the Law

There is a Talmudic principle, "One who is occupied with a mitzvah is exempt from performing other mitzvot." The bridegroom is preoccupied with the mitzvah of performing sexual intercourse with his bride; therefore, he is exempt from the mitzvah of reciting *Sh'mah*. This exemption extends only four days. If intercourse did not take place by Saturday night, it is assumed that the groom's preoccupation has lessened and he must recite *Sh'mah* the following morning. According to Maimonides, the exemption applies to *Sh'mah* in the morning, as well as to *Sh'mah* in the evening (*Mishneh Torah*, Laws of *Sh'mah* 4:1). R. Mano'ach, in the name of Rabad, says that during the day the groom is less preoccupied with his first intercourse and is, therefore, obligated to recite *Sh'mah* (cited in *Kesef Mishneh*, *ibid.*).

Another example of this principle is found in chapter 3, mishnayot 1 and 2. A mourner who is preoccupied with the burial is also exempt from *Sh'mah*. Still another example: If a person is travelling during the Sukkot festival, on his way to perform a mitzvah such as studying Torah or greeting his rabbi, he is exempt from eating in a *sukkah* (Sukkah 2:4).

The principle "One who is occupied with a mitzvah is exempt from performing other mitzvot" is derived from a verse in *Sh'mah*, "When you are sitting at home and when you are going on the way." This is not a literal translation of the Hebrew. "*B'shivt'chah b'vaytechah u'v'lech'techa vaderech*" literally reads: "In *your* sitting at home and in *your* going on the way." The Talmud derives from the emphasis on "your," that when you are occupied with *your* affairs you must interrupt them to recite *Sh'mah*. If, however, you are occupied with God's affairs, i.e., a mitzvah, you are exempt from reciting *Sh'mah* (Berachot 16a).

Rabban Gamliel recited *Sh'mah* on his wedding night even though he was exempt. He was capable of concentrating properly and having proper *kavanah* even though he was preoccupied with the mitzvah of his wedding night. Therefore, he took it upon himself to recite *Sh'mah* in order not to "absolve himself from the Sovereignty of heaven even for one moment." (See mishnah 8.)

The Spirit of the Law

MARRIAGE IN MISHNAIC TIMES

The Jewish wedding consists of two stages: the betrothal, *kiddushin*, and the nuptials, *chuppah*. *Kiddushin* is a legal act by which the husband "acquires" a wife. The first mishnah in Tractate Kiddushin states: "A woman is acquired in one of three ways: with money, with a contract, and with sexual intercourse." The first method, with money, means that if a man gives a woman money or an object of monetary value (today, a ring is used) in the presence of two valid witnesses and declares his intent to betroth her and she accepts the gift, she is legally betrothed. In the second method, a written document which contains the names of the couple and the declaration of betrothal is used. This too must be given in the presence of two valid witnesses. The third method consisted of a declaration of intent to betroth and the man and woman retiring to a private place with the intent to perform intercourse. Again, two witnesses are required to see them enter the private place, though they need not witness the act of intercourse itself. This third method was banned in the third century because of its immoral overtones.

A betrothed woman has the legal status of a married woman. The bond of marriage is formally sealed with the betrothal. Thus, even though the marriage has not, as yet, been consummated, the couple is legally married. The husband and wife, however, are not permitted to live together until the *chuppah*. If the wife were to have sexual relations with another man, it would constitute an act of adultery and she would be prohibited from ever living with her husband.

The *chuppah*, or nuptials (also called *nissuin*), is the second stage of the marriage ceremony. The term *chuppah* means wedding canopy. The wedding canopy is the prelude to the consummation of the marriage when the couple is permitted to live together as husband and wife. The *chuppah* ceremony consists of the seven wedding blessings and *yichud*, the bride and groom spending time alone together in a private room. Both *kiddushin* and *chuppah* are required for the finalization of a marriage.

During the Mishnaic period and until the twelfth century, it was customary to wait twelve months between the betrothal and the nuptials. The reason for the delay was to give the bride, who was usually quite young, an opportunity to prepare her trousseau, learn the culinary arts, and psychologically prepare herself for marriage. The bride continued to live in her parents' home and, no doubt, received all the necessary instruction that would enable her to properly fulfill her role as homemaker. The perils of medieval Europe, however, led to radical changes in a number of Jewish customs and traditions. With the onset of the Crusades and the rise in popular anti-Semitism, Jewish communities were under constant fear of attack and expulsion. Jews often had to flee for their lives to distant places. Under these circumstances, situations arose in which a betrothed couple was separated, leaving husband and wife never able to find each other again. Unable to obtain a *get*, a religious divorce, the wife remained an *agunah*, a woman who was legally forbidden to remarry. In order to prevent such tragedies, the rabbis enacted that the *kiddushin* and the *nissuin* take place in immediate succession. If forced to flee, the couple could leave together as husband and wife. This practice has continued in modern times. In the contemporary wedding ceremony, the groom gives the bride a ring (*kiddushin*), the *ketubah* is read, the seven blessings are recited under the wedding canopy (*chuppah*) and the couple retires to a private room. The reading of the *ketubah* signifies a separation between the two stages of the marriage ceremony.

WEDNESDAY WEDDINGS
The first mishnah in Tractate Ketubot reads as follows: "A virgin is wedded on Wednesday... because twice a week, on Mondays and Thursdays, the religious courts held session in the cities, and if the husband had a complaint about his wife's lack of virginity, he could appear at the religious court the following morning." (The reason why the wedding should not take place on Sunday is because no wedding preparations may be made on Shabbat.)

The mishnah is based on a law that prohibits a man from living with his wife if she committed adultery during the betrothal period. Rather than allow a single day to pass where there is doubt as to the wife's moral behavior before the nuptials, the matter is to be swiftly adjudicated the very next day. The court would then hear testimony and receive evidence. If the court was convinced that the wife committed adultery after her betrothal, the couple was required to divorce. On the other hand, if there was no evidence of adultery, the court was in a position to allay the husband's suspicion and doubts. The absence of blood stains would certainly not incriminate the wife because it is not uncommon for the hymen to be ruptured by causes other than intercourse.

The ancient practice of holding weddings on Wednesdays was designed not to destroy marriages but to preserve them. It was deemed important by the Sages for the husband to bring the matter to court almost immediately so that the crisis in the couple's relationship could be resolved. If even a few days were to elapse between the wedding night and the court appearance, the damage done to the marriage might be irreparable. A prompt clarification on the part of the court was essential for a harmonious relationship. If, in a rare instance, the court ascertained that the wife had, in fact, committed adultery, the marriage had to be dissolved.

PREOCCUPATION WITH A MITZVAH
"One who is occupied with a mitzvah is exempt from performing other mitzvot," says the Talmud. What does "occupied" mean? It would seem, on the surface, that being occupied means being actively involved in performing a mitzvah. We see from the mishnah that such is not the case. Even if a person is not actually performing a mitzvah, if his thoughts are absorbed by a mitzvah which he intends to fulfill, it is considered as though he were actually performing the mitzvah. Preoccupation with a mitzvah is a mitzvah in itself. Mental involvement and psychological preparation for the performance of a mitzvah have intrinsic religious value. Chasidism places a special emphasis upon spiritual preparations prior to the performance of mitzvot. Many Chasidim immerse in a *mikveh* (ritual bath) and recite special preparatory prayers in anticipation of a mitzvah. Chasidism recognizes that such preparations not only enhance the mitzvah, but also are mitzvot in themselves.

The Practical Law
Nowadays, most people do not concentrate sufficiently when they pray; therefore, a bridegroom must recite *Sh'mah* (*Orach Chaim* 70:3).

Mishnah 6

He[1] bathed[2] on the night his wife died. His students said to him: "Did you not teach us, our Rabbi, that a mourner is forbidden to bathe?"[3] He replied to them: "I am not like everybody else; I am sensitive."[4]

משנה ו

רָחַץ לַיְלָה הָרִאשׁוֹן שֶׁמֵּתָה אִשְׁתּוֹ. אָמְרוּ לוֹ תַּלְמִידָיו: לֹא לִמַּדְתָּנוּ, רַבֵּנוּ, שֶׁאָבֵל אָסוּר לִרְחֹץ? אָמַר לָהֶם: אֵינִי כִּשְׁאָר כָּל אָדָם, אִסְטְנִיס אֲנִי:

1. HE — Rabban Gamliel.
2. BATHED — In warm water.
3. TO BATHE — In warm water.
4. SENSITIVE — And must bathe for reasons of health.

The Letter of the Law

The seven day mourning period that begins with the day of burial is called *shiva*, which means "seven." During the *shiva*, the mourner is forbidden to enjoy the pleasure of studying Torah and certain physical pleasures such as marital relations, wearing new or freshly laundered garments, shaving, wearing leather shoes, using cosmetics, and bathing. Bathing is forbidden only when it involves personal pleasure and comfort. Therefore, it is not permitted to wash with warm water, or to bathe the entire body even with cool water. It is permissible, however, to wash one's hands and face, and separate parts of the body, with cool water. Such washing is a matter of hygiene and not pleasure. A person who is required to bathe in warm water for medical reasons is also permitted to do so. If a person will experience severe discomfort if he does not bathe, as in Rabban Gamliel's case, he also may bathe, even in warm water.

The Spirit of the Law

MISHNAIC STYLE

This mishnah and the next are unrelated to the laws of *Sh'mah*. Mishnaic style, however, allows for digressions. Since the previous mishnah related an incident in which Rabban Gamliel conducted himself in an exceptional manner, two similar incidents are also related.

THE MOURNING EXPERIENCE

Many of the laws that pertain to a mourner are reminiscent of Yom Kippur. On Yom Kippur, bathing, using cosmetics, wearing shoes, and engaging in marital relations are prohibited. These prohibitions apply to a mourner during *shiva*, as well. Rabbi Joseph B. Soloveitchik, on the occasion of the funeral of Rabbi M.Z. Twersky, the Talner *Rebbe,* in 1972, delivered a eulogy in which he explained the equation between Yom Kippur and mourning. These two events, he said, share in common the act of expiation of guilt. On Yom Kippur, the Jew fasts and prays for divine forgiveness and atonement. The sins of the past are recalled and the penitent worshipper pleads for God's merciful judgment. The mourner, too, feels a profound sense of guilt. When death snatches away a loved one, the mourner asks himself, "Why was I not more loving, more sensitive to him/her?" Memories of past wrongs and hurts haunt the mourner. He feels ridden with guilt because he could have been a better child, spouse, or parent.

Rabbi Soloveitchik quoted the passage in the Talmud that tells of the guilt felt by the students of Rav. When Rav died, his students followed his bier to the burial. Upon their return, they stopped at a riverside to eat their meal. When it was time to recite Grace after Meals, a question arose which they were not able to resolve. Whereupon, R. Addah bar Ahavah rose and rent his garment which had already been torn. He exclaimed: "Rav is dead and we have not even learned the laws of Grace" (Berachot 42b). Though they admired and revered their teacher in his lifetime, they were not aware of the full measure of his greatness and their dependence upon him until he died.

The mourner needs an opportunity to expiate and atone for whatever feelings of guilt he has vis-a-vis the deceased. That is why many of the rules of mourning are identical to those of Yom Kippur. By observing these laws, the mourner has an opportunity to go on with his life without a haunting sense of guilt. In mourning, he finds atonement for the human weakness of insensitivity.

The Practical Law

1. A mourner may not bathe his entire body, not even in cold water. He may, however, wash his hands and face in cold water, but not in warm water (*Yoreh Day'ah* 381:1).

2. A woman after childbirth who is a mourner is permitted to bathe. A person may shampoo his hair for medical reasons. A person who is extremely sensitive about cleanliness may bathe if his not bathing will cause him great discomfort (*ibid.*, 381:3).

Mishnah 7 / משנה ז

And when Tabi, his slave,[1] died, he[2] accepted condolences.[3] His students said to him: "Did you not teach us, our Rabbi, that we do not accept condolences for slaves?" He replied to them: "My slave Tabi is not like other slaves. He was a worthy man."[4]

וּכְשֶׁמֵּת טָבִי עַבְדּוֹ, קִבֵּל עָלָיו תַּנְחוּמִין. אָמְרוּ לוֹ תַלְמִידָיו: לֹא לִמַּדְתָּנוּ, רַבֵּנוּ, שֶׁאֵין מְקַבְּלִין תַּנְחוּמִין עַל הָעֲבָדִים? אָמַר לָהֶם: אֵין טָבִי עַבְדִּי כִּשְׁאָר כָּל הָעֲבָדִים, כָּשֵׁר הָיָה:

1. SLAVE — A Canaanite bondman.
2. HE — Rabban Gamliel.
3. CONDOLENCES — After the funeral.
4. A WORTHY MAN — Very religious; according to some commentators, a great scholar.

The Letter of the Law

It was the custom in Mishnaic times, as today, for those who attended a funeral to form a row after the burial and for the mourners to walk past the row of people. As the mourners passed, they were consoled with the words: "May the Omnipresent comfort you among the mourners of Zion and Jerusalem."

Condolences are extended in this manner only to mourners who have lost one of seven relatives: father, mother, sister, brother, son, daughter, or spouse. The laws of mourning do not apply to other relatives.

The Vilna Gaon explains that Rabban Gamliel's students asked two questions. Firstly, why did he accept condolences for a Canaanite bondman when he himself had taught them that condolences are not offered for a bondman? Secondly, even if Tabi was a freeman, how could Rabban Gamliel be considered a "mourner," in the halachic sense of the word, since Tabi was not one of the seven relatives? Rabban Gamliel's response answered both questions. Tabi was a worthy man. He observed the mitzvot fully. (According to some commentaries, he was a Torah scholar). He deserves to be mourned at his funeral as one would mourn for a near relative. Rabbi Akiva Eiger interprets the mishnah differently. He quotes the Jerusalem Talmud which states that a student and a faithful slave are like one's own children. Therefore, Tabi was to be mourned by Rabban Gamliel.

The Vilna Gaon's interpretation implies that not only was Rabban Gamliel required to mourn; indeed, everyone should have received condolences upon this loss. According, however, to Rabbi Akiva Eiger, only Rabban Gamliel was required to receive condolences.

The Spirit of the Law

TABI

Tabi was the slave of Rabban Gamliel II, who lived in the late first and early second centuries C.E. The Mishnah in Tractate Sukkah quotes Rabban Gamliel as saying to the Sages: "See what a scholar my slave Tabi is. He knows that slaves are exempt from the mitzvah of *sukkah*; therefore, he sleeps under the bed" (2:1). The Talmud states that he slept there in order to hear the words of the scholars. Tabi also wore *tefillin* even though slaves are not obligated to do so (Jerusalem Talmud, Eruvin 10:1). The Midrash relates that once Tabi was serving his master and a group of scholars. R. Elazar ben Azariah said: "Tabi should be seated and I should be standing" (*Midrash Proverbs* 9:2).

Tabi was once sent to the marketplace with instructions to purchase some good food. He returned with a tongue. Then he was sent to purchase some bad food, and again, he returned with a tongue. When asked why he bought tongue both times, he responded: "Good and evil derive from the tongue. When it is good, there is nothing better, and when it is bad, there is nothing worse" (*Lev. Rabbah* 33).

The Practical Law

If a person attends the funeral of his servant, the assembled do not form a row, nor do they offer the mourner condolences. It is, however, proper to say: "May the Omnipresent fill your loss." (*Yoreh Day'ah* 377:1).

CHAPTER 2: *Mishnah 8*

Mishnah 8 / משנה ח

A bridegroom may recite *Sh'mah* on his wedding night if he so wishes. Rabban Simeon ben Gamliel says: not everyone who wishes to assume the name[1] may do so.

חָתָן אִם רָצָה לִקְרוֹת קְרִיאַת שְׁמַע לַיְלָה הָרִאשׁוֹן, קוֹרֵא. רַבָּן שִׁמְעוֹן בֶּן גַּמְלִיאֵל אוֹמֵר: לֹא כָל הָרוֹצֶה לִטֹּל אֶת הַשֵּׁם יִטֹּל:

1. THE NAME — Of someone who is pious.

The Letter of the Law

This mishnah is a continuation of mishnah 5, in which Rabban Gamliel chose to recite Sh'mah on his wedding night, even though he was exempt. Rabban Gamliel was on a very high spiritual level. His mental concentration enabled him to put aside the normal anxieties of his wedding night and focus his attention on *Sh'mah*. But, said R. Simeon, his son, not everyone is on such a high level. Thus, reciting *Sh'mah* under such circumstances appears haughty and boastful. It is better to be humble and refrain from reciting *Sh'mah* than to compare oneself to Rabban Gamliel and recite. The *Tannah Kamah*, the first opinion in the mishnah, disagrees. One need not be on the level of a Rabban Gamliel to recite *Sh'mah* on his wedding night. As long as the bridegroom feels that he can concentrate properly, he should recite *Sh'mah*.

R. Yitzchak Alfasi and Maimonides adopt the view of the *Tannah Kamah*. They say that the average bridegroom is exempt from reciting *Sh'mah*. A person who feels, however, that he can concentrate properly may recite, if he so wishes. Tosafot and Rosh hold an opposing view. They agree in principle with R. Simeon ben Gamliel. It is their view, however, that: "Nowadays, we do not pray with adequate *kavanah*. Thus, a bridegroom who does not recite *Sh'mah* appears haughty. It is as though he were saying: 'I usually pray with *kavanah*, but, tonight I can't!' " It is their conclusion that nowadays a bridegroom must recite *Sh'mah* (*Tosafot*, Berachot 17b). (Based on *Tosafot Yom Tov*'s interpretation of the controversy; see his commentary, Pesachim 4:5.)

R. Akiva Eiger makes a very insightful point in his commentary on the mishnah. He says that the bridegroom's exemption applies only to the first night. When he recites *Sh'mah* on the other three nights he does not give the appearance of acting haughtily, because people will simply assume that intercourse took place on the first night, and now he is obligated to recite *Sh'mah* like everyone else.

WHEN TO GO BEYOND THE LETTER OF THE LAW

Not everyone who wishes to go beyond the letter of the law may do so. To perform a mitzvah when it is not appropriate to do so merely demonstrates false piety and self-righteousness. R. Simeon ben Gamliel prohibits a Jew from reciting *Sh'mah* if it may lead to pride and self-aggrandizement. We have seen earlier (Berachot 1:3) that R. Tarfon was severely rebuked by his colleagues for having adopted the stricter opinion of Beit Shammai by lying down to recite *Sh'mah*. He was censured because he went beyond the letter of the law. We find other examples, as well, of halachah restraining a person from doing what he is not required to do. If a person eats or sleeps in a *sukkah* when it is raining, not only does he not receive reward, he even is called a fool (*Orach Chaim* 639:2; *Hagahot Maimoniyot*, Laws of *Sukkah*, chap. 6). The Jerusalem Talmud makes a sweeping statement: "Whoever is exempt from a mitzvah and does it anyway is called a fool (Shabbat 1:1-2; 2:9).

The Vilna Gaon, in his Mishnah commentary, raises a very important and difficult question. The above examples seem to contradict many other Talmudic sources that praise the one who is *machmir*, who goes beyond the letter of the law. Here are some such examples:

1. A mishnah in Tractate Sukkah relates that on the festival of Sukkot, R. Yochanan ben Zakkai and Rabban Gamliel were given some food to eat. The food was merely a snack and not a meal. It was,

CHAPTER 2: *Mishnah 8* 129

thus, permissible for them to eat their food outside the *sukkah*. But they instructed their students: "Bring it into the *sukkah*." R. Zadok, on the other hand, ate his food outside the *sukkah* (Sukkah 2:5). Maimonides concludes: "It is permitted to drink water and eat fruits outside of the *sukkah*. The person, however, who is stringent upon himself and does not taste even water outside of a *sukkah* is deemed praiseworthy" (*Mishneh Torah*, Laws of *Sukkah* 6:6).

2. A person is required to recite Grace after Meals in the place where he ate. What if he forgot, left the place where he ate, and later remembered? Is he required to return to where he ate or not? This question is the subject of a debate between Beit Shammai and Beit Hillel. Beit Shammai says he must return, while Beit Hillel says he may bless in the place where he remembered (Berachot 8:7). The Talmud relates an incident in which a student forgot to bless and returned to the place where he had eaten. He conducted himself in accordance with the view of Beit Shammai, even though the halachah is in accordance with Beit Hillel. For his effort, says the Talmud, he was rewarded with finding a bag of gold (Berachot 53b). Unlike R. Tarfon, who was criticized for adopting Beit Shammai's viewpoint, the student was rewarded by heaven for his efforts.

The question is — when is it an act of piety to go beyond the letter of the law, and when is it foolishness?

The Vilna Gaon concludes that if there is an element of mitzvah in going beyond the letter of the law, doing so is praiseworthy. If, however, going beyond the letter of the law has no basis whatsoever, if there is no mitzvah element in the act, then it is sheer foolishness (*Sh'not Eliyahu*, Berachot 1:3).

Our mishnah's controversy between the Sages who permit a bridegroom to recite *Sh'mah* on his wedding night, on the one hand, and R. Simeon ben Gamliel who prohibits, on the other, focuses on this very question. Is the *Sh'mah* of a bridegroom on his wedding night a mitzvah? According to the Sages, it is a mitzvah and a bridegroom may accept upon himself to recite *Sh'mah* voluntarily. R. Simeon ben Gamliel, however, says that if there is not proper *kavanah*, not only is there no mitzvah, but, to do so is simply a sign of haughtiness.

Rabban Gamliel did recite *Sh'mah* on his wedding night even though he was exempt. But Rabban Gamliel is an exception. R. Simeon ben Gamliel admits that someone who is deeply pious and learned may recite *Sh'mah*, as did his father.

R. Tarfon was censured because there is no mitzvah whatsoever in lying down to recite the evening *Sh'mah*. This is precisely the point of Beit Hillel, that *Sh'mah* may be recited in any position. In the case of eating or sleeping in the *sukkah* while it is raining, the mitzvah is to live in a *sukkah* as though it were home. People do not normally live in a house that is not protected from the rain. Here, too, there is no mitzvah of *sukkah* while it is raining.

When a person goes beyond the letter of the law and he, in fact, performs a mitzvah, he is deemed praiseworthy. Though R. Yochanan ben Zakkai and Rabban Gamliel were not required to eat their fruit and drink their water in a *sukkah*, by doing so, they fulfilled a mitzvah. Similarly, though Beit Hillel does not require a person who forgot to bless in the place where he ate to return, they admit that to do so is a mitzvah. That is why the student was rewarded with finding a bag of gold.

We see from this halachic discussion that before a person takes upon himself to do more than what is religiously required of him, he should ascertain whether or not he is fulfilling a mitzvah. This often requires a thorough study of the mitzvah at hand, or asking a Torah scholar. Knowing when to be *machmir* can make the difference between educated piety and ignorant foolishness.

The Spirit of the Law

ON PIETY AND POMPOSITY

There is a very fine line between piety and pomposity. Judaism can be a source of sublime spiritual expression and it can be a source of religious excess and pietism. The framework of halachah provides clear-cut guidelines that prevent extremism and abuse of Torah teaching. Life without an halachic framework is usually spiritually vacuous. People need a structure and a system in which they can express themselves spiritually. Halachah is such a system. Sometimes, however, moral judgment can be misguided as a result of religious feelings. Religion can be carried too far. Grievous errors can be committed in the name of religion. Even with the best of intentions, religious principles can be abused and misconstrued. As Samuel Johnson put it: "Hell is paved with good intentions."

KING SAUL
King Saul certainly had noble intentions when he spared the life of Agag, king of the Amalekites. He took pity on the enemy king who suffered the annihilation of his people. But Saul had defied the prophet Samuel who commanded that no one be spared. Saul's defiance cost him his throne. The prophet rebuked Saul: "Because you have rejected the word of the Lord, He has rejected you from being king" (I Sam. 15:23). In going beyond God's command, Saul brought tragedy upon himself and near tragedy upon the entire Jewish people. Generations later, a descendant of King Agag came close to annihilating the Jewish nation. His name was Haman (Megillah 13a). The Talmudic judgment of Saul's misplaced piety is expressed in the wise words of King Solomon: "Do not be overly righteous" (Eccl. 7:16) (Yomah 22b).

Saul was punished because he violated a clear mandate given to him by the prophet. But not all mandates are clear. When laws are applied to real life situations, they are not always easy to interpret. Sometimes, even literal readings of the law may be too extreme. It takes enormous scholarship to be able to apply a law correctly to each given situation. Rabbi Chaim Soloveitchik was known to be very lenient with regard to matters pertaining to health. When colleagues criticized him for his leniencies he would respond: "I am not lenient with regard to Shabbat and Yom Kippur. I am simply *machmir* (strict) in the law of saving a life."

A WEDDING ON SHABBAT
R. Moses Isserles (1525 or 1530-1572) was one of the great halachic authorities in Jewish history. His mastery of Jewish law, his knowledge of philosophy and science, and his methodical approach earned him the title of "the Maimonides of Polish Jewry" by his contemporaries. He is known to students of halachah by the acronym of his name, "the Ramah." For more than twenty years he served as the rabbi of Cracow, one of Poland's largest and most prestigious Jewish communities.

The Ramah was a prolific writer. Most of his works were on the subject of halachah. He also wrote on philosophy and Kabbalah. His most famous and important work is *Darkay Moshe*, notes and supplements to R. Joseph Karo's *Beit Yosef. Darkay Moshe* later served as the basis for the Ramah's glosses on the *Shulchan Aruch*, the Code of Jewish Law. R. Joseph Karo's *Shulchan Aruch* is a masterful compendium of Jewish Law. The name *Shulchan Aruch*, the Set Table, is quite apropos because its massive body of Jewish law is neatly arranged and well organized. R. Joseph Karo, a Sephardi, based his halachic rulings mainly upon the views of R. Isaac Alfasi and Maimonides, who themselves were Sephardim. Ashkenazic Jewry had need of a comparable work that followed Ashkenazic tradition. R. Moses Isserles filled that need. Not lacking a sense of humor, he wrote supplements and additions to "The Set Table" which he called *Hamapah*, "The Tablecloth." By spreading his "tablecloth" over R. Karo's "table," Jews of Central and Eastern Europe could also feast on the delicacies of Jewish law.

As a world renowned authority, the Ramah's opinion was solicited by the leading rabbis of his time. Many of his responsa were later collected and published. They clearly demonstrate an encyclopedic knowledge of halachic sources, clarity of exposition, and bold forthrightness. He did not hesitate to offer opinions that differed from those of his colleagues. One responsum deals with a matter that pertained to the Ramah personally. He had made a legal decision in his own community that inspired a deluge of criticism and debate. This particular responsum begins with the words: "I heard behind me a great noise" (Ezek. 3:12).

The incident that prompted the criticism and debate, and the Ramah's responsum, related to a wedding ceremony that he had performed on Friday night. It is forbidden for marriages to take place on Shabbat. This is a rabbinic decree designed to prevent a possible violation of Shabbat by the writing of the *ketubah*, the marriage document, which usually takes place before the ceremony. A second reason for the prohibition of weddings taking place on Shabbat is that all forms of legal acquisitions are forbidden on Shabbat. Nevertheless, the Ramah performed a wedding ceremony on Friday night.

The story was as follows: A match had been arranged for a young man and woman who lived in Cracow. A significant sum of money had been promised to the groom as the bride's dowry. Shortly before the wedding, the bride's father died. The mother of the bride had died earlier. The orphan-bride went to live with the family of her uncle.

The wedding date was set for Friday afternoon. Just before the ceremony was to take place, the groom was informed that the dowry promised him was no longer forthcoming. His response was: "No dowry, no wedding!" The members of the bride's family begged and pleaded with him to change his mind, but he refused. The young bride sat with a veil over her face and wept. Without a dowry, her chances of finding another bridegroom were slim. The bridegroom was unmoved by her plight. Her family persisted in trying to persuade him, but to no avail. While the haggling and negotiations were going on, the sun began to set. Friday ended and Shabbat began. Finally, after an hour and a half, the bridegroom conceded. Without a moment's delay, R. Moses Isserles set up the wedding canopy. He would not risk the possibility of the bridegroom reneging. The blessings were made, the ring was placed on the finger, the wine was drunk, and the wedding was completed. The bride and groom left to establish a family, the relatives of both sides smilingly departed, and the Ramah went to his synagogue to pray.

In his lengthy responsum, the Ramah carefully analyzes the legal sources. He cites interpretations of earlier opinions that lean toward leniency. Rabbeinu Tam, Rashi's grandson, had written: "In case of emergency it is permitted to marry on Shabbat." The Ramah concludes with a bold statement: "There is no greater emergency than this case. The young orphan would have been shamed and embarrassed for the rest of her life. 'So great is the mitzvah of honoring one's fellow human being, that it takes precedence over a negative commandment in the Torah' (Berachot 19b). Here we are only dealing with a rabbinic law" (Dr. Asher Ziev, *Responsa of the Ramah*, [N.Y.: Feldheim, 1970], Responsum 125).

KASHRUT

Kashrut is an area of halachah in which many *chumrot*, stringencies, have been adopted by observant Jews. Many of these stringencies are well-founded and commendable. It is an act of piety to ensure against eating food that is not kosher. Historically, Jews have gone through great lengths and even danger to avoid eating nonkosher foods. It should be recalled that the Maccabean revolt was sparked by the martyrdom of old Eleazar and the seven sons of Hannah who refused to eat pork (IV Maccabees). *Kashrut* is a bedrock of the Jewish home. Jews have expressed their intuitive understanding of the importance of the *kashrut* laws by observing them with care and meticulousness.

Unfortunately, zealousness in the laws of kashrut has sometimes led to serious abuses in the laws that pertain to ethics and morality. Rather than being a source of *kedushah*, holiness, and service of the Lord, *kashrut*, in many instances, has become a paradigm of sin between man and his fellow. *Kashrut* supervision is a necessary component in ensuring halachic standards. But when *kashrut* supervision becomes "big business" replete with cutthroat competition, dishonesty, slanderous rumor-mongering and economic coercion, it becomes a desecration of God's Name and a mark of shame for the Jewish people. When Jews who observe *kashrut* are forced to pay exorbitant prices for kosher meat, it is no longer a matter of piety, it is a matter of public thievery. When a storekeeper, a butcher, or a caterer's reputation is scurrilously defamed for less than noble motives, it is tantamount to bloodshed. Many of these activities take place under a cloak of piety and in the name of religion. The *chumrah* becomes a thin veil for corruption, deceit, and mistrust. Spiritual values are distorted and holiness becomes abomination.

When we study the teachings and practices of truly pious rabbis, we find great empathy and compassion for fellow human beings. These spiritual leaders did not lose sight of the needs of others. They did everything in their power to help people, even if it meant finding leniencies in the laws of *kashrut*. One such saint was R. Abraham Abusch.

R. Abraham Abusch (1700-1769) was the pious and humble rabbi of Frankfurt. His kindness and charity are legendary. A great Talmudic scholar and community leader, he served as president of the Council of Four Lands, the central institution of Jewish self-government in Poland and Lithuania. R. Abraham Abusch was known to be lenient in matters of *kashrut*. Questions of ritual slaughter and the *kashrut* of animals after slaughter were frequently brought to him. Often, he declared meat kosher that many of his colleagues would declare *treife*. When asked about his lenient stance on these matters he would explain: "If a rabbi makes a mistake and declares the nonkosher to be kosher, he has sinned against God, and Yom Kippur will atone for his sin. But if he makes a mistake and declares the kosher to be nonkosher, he has caused a monetary loss to his fellow Jew. This is a sin between man and his fellow for which even Yom Kippur will not atone."

Once, a local ritual slaughterer approached R. Abusch and his colleagues with a question concerning a blemish on the lung of an animal. R. Abusch stood alone in declaring the lung kosher. The other rabbis protested: "How can you say it is kosher when the Ramah and all other authorities say it is *treife*?" R. Abusch replied: "When the day comes after my death and I will have to face the Final Judgment, I would rather face the Ramah than the butcher. What will I answer the heavenly court when the poor butcher claims that I caused him a financial loss by declaring his meat *treife*? But if the Ramah and the other authorities confront me, I am sure that I will be able to convince them of the validity of my argument" (*Saray Ha'may'ah*, vol.I, p. 195).

Another great sage and pious rabbi was Rabbi Yechiel Michal Epstein (1829-1908) of Novogrudok, Belorussia, where he served as rabbi for thirty-four years until his death. Rabbi Epstein is most noted for his work *Aruch Hashulchan*. As Maimonides saw the need to codify the halachah in his time, and R. Yosef Karo in his, Rabbi Epstein felt there was a new need to update the Code of Jewish Law based on the rulings and decisions that had been made since the time of R. Yosef Karo. Following the arrangement of the *Shulchan Aruch*, Rabbi Epstein included the earlier opinions that formed the basis of the halachah and rendered his own decisions, many of which differed from prevailing views. There is a general tendency in his work to rule leniently in many controversial matters.

His disciple, Rabbi Yehuda Leib Maimon, the author of *Saray Ha'may'ah*, who was ordained by Rabbi Epstein, received the following advice from his teacher: "If a matter pertaining to a prohibition comes before you, you must always remember that it is presumed permitted. Only after you have studied all the *Rishonim* (early scholars) and you cannot find any possibility of permissibility, you are obliged to rule that it is forbidden. To my great sorrow, I know many rabbis who are Torah scholars, but their piety precedes their wisdom. They judge a question from the perspective of presumed *treife* and forbidden, and thereby unnecessarily cause monetary loss to a Jew. This is a sin worse than a sin between man and God."

Rabbi Maimon recalls an incident when one Passover eve Rabbi Epstein came home from the synagogue and the family prepared to begin the *Seder*. Suddenly, a woman knocked on the door with a question of *kashrut*. The obvious answer was *treife*. But such an answer would have rendered not only her food, but her utensils nonkosher, as well. Rabbi Epstein saw that the woman was poor and most likely had no other utensils to use on Passover. He told her to wait as he proceeded to his study. He began to thumb through books looking for a lenient opinion. Time passed and his family grew impatient. After about two hours, his grandson entered and said: "Grandpa, you are detracting from the festival joy. If you can't find a leniency, it is *treife*." The rabbi replied: "My dear grandson, I understand that you want to celebrate the holiday eve, but if I render a decision of nonkosher, this poor woman won't have a celebration for the entire holiday." Finally, after more searching, he found a source that ruled kosher. He triumphantly entered the dining room and told the woman: "Everything is kosher." The woman left happily and Rabbi Epstein sat down with his family to celebrate the *Seder* (*ibid.*, vol. 6, pp. 112, 114).

JACOB'S LADDER
"And he dreamed, and behold, a ladder was set upon the earth, and its top reached to heaven. And behold, the angels of God were ascending and descending on it. And behold, the Lord stood above it..." (Gen. 28:12-13).

There is a great spiritual ladder that connects heaven and earth. Every human being stands at some point on the ladder. No one is at the very bottom, and only God is at the very top. Like the angels in Jacob's dream, people either go up or go down. Few stay on the same rung for very long. The human being's mission in life is to strive to go upward, to try each day to grow a little closer to God. Spiritual descent is a tragic failure in life's mission. Spiritual ascent is the fulfillment of man's most noble goal. Life's never-ending challenge is to climb step by step, rung by rung, in the direction of God and godliness.

As people grow religiously, they often observe more mitzvot and are more stringent in the mitzvot they already perform. This is a healthy sign of religious growth. Sometimes there are outward manifestations of that religious growth. Such externals are meaningful only if they meet two criteria: 1)They should be placed in a correct order of priorities, and 2)they should truly reflect inner spirituality. It makes no religious sense for a person to wear his *tzitzit* outside his clothing if he does not don *tefillin*. It makes no sense for a person to wear a *gartel*, the cloth belt worn by Chasidim when praying, if he does not pray with *kavanah*. Furthermore, externalization should not be a substitute for internalized religious feeling. Externals should reflect internal religiosity.

Religious growth may be evolutionary or revolutionary. Some people grow closer to God and Torah through a slow and deliberate process. Step by step, they learn more, do more, and feel more. The process may continue for many years, sometimes a lifetime. There are others who return to Judaism in one precipitous, radical sweep. Making a one hundred and eighty degree turnabout, they abandon their secular lifestyle and immerse themselves in religious observance and Torah study. The past is uprooted and all energies are focused upon establishing a new future. This kind of return often entails an upheaval in patterns of daily life, familial relationships, and social contacts. One value system is shattered and another takes its place. Such a return to Judaism is sometimes manifest in outer dress, as well. Outward appearances become a very important identification with religion.

Both approaches to return have merit. The person who slowly evolves, as well as the person who quickly changes into a religious personality, manifest religious growth. Both climb the ladder. The one, however, who makes a precipitous leap is in greater danger of falling. A sudden upheaval in lifestyle and relationships can snatch away the pillars of stability and security. There has not been sufficient time to become firmly rooted in a religious way of life. The pressures that are brought to bear by relatives and friends who have not had time to comprehend and accept the change further weaken the underpinnings. Also, there has not been an adequate opportunity to study the myriad of laws, prohibitions, rules, and regulations. "An ignoramous cannot be pious" (Ethics of the Fathers 2:6). It takes an enormous investment in time and effort before a person is sufficiently knowledgeable to be fully observant. As a result of cataclysmic change, the *baal teshuvah*, the returnee to religion, confronts internal frustrations and external pressures. These may cause a total collapse of a hastily-built framework.

The slow growth method has distinct advantages. The individual affords himself time to study and understand what he is doing and why. Family and friends have more time to adapt to the changes they see in their loved one. It is easier for them to be more accepting of those changes. The *baal teshuvah* himself has the opportunity to adapt to a more religious life with fewer tensions and apprehensions. He climbs each rung of the ladder slowly and carefully, reducing the risk of falling off. With each new step, he can pause and enjoy the new spiritual height which he has attained.

WHEN TO BE *MACHMIR*

When should a person be *machmir*? When should he do more than what the law requires? The answer depends on the individual. If being *machmir* is a manifestation of inner piety, it is praiseworthy. But if it is a manifestation of pomposity, it is a sign of foolishness. If a person is motivated by a sincere desire to climb the religious ladder and feel closer to God, the *chumrah* is in order. But if he is being *machmir* to impress others or himself with his piety, the *chumrah* is self-defeating.

The Talmud relates that Mar Ukvah used to praise his father's piety. His father would wait twenty-four hours before eating cheese after meat while Mar Ukvah only used to wait until the next meal. "I am like vinegar compared to wine in this matter," he said (Chulin 105a). One could ask, if Mar Ukvah was so impressed with his father's piety, why did he not also wait twenty-four hours before eating cheese after meat? Apparently, Mar Ukvah felt that he was not on a high enough spiritual level to adopt such a strict practice. For him, waiting twenty-four hours would have been a less than honest display of piety. His heightened integrity was sensitive to the difference between piety and pomposity.

THE IMPORTANCE OF STUDY

Study is the key to piety. Observance of mitzvot should be rooted in knowledge and understanding. Most daily rituals are based on sound reason and logic. The halachic structure was not haphazardly thrown together. The Sages of old, over a period of many centuries, developed an halachic system that provides the Jew with a maximum opportunity for religious self-expression. They were the architects of an intricate and beautiful spiritual edifice. The grandeur and majesty of that edifice can only be appreciated and understood by someone who has studied their designs very carefully. This is why the study of Talmud is so very important. The Talmud provides the sources, the logic, and the historic background of halachah. Rather than perform mitzvot in ignorance, a Jew should strive to delve into their meaning and their purpose. Without knowledge, halachah is incomprehensible. Without understanding, even the most well-intentioned Jew is bound to make mistakes.

A group of teenagers once attended a weekend Torah seminar. Though they had very little religious background, they were interested in learning about Judaism. On Friday evening, before the meal, the students lined up to ritually wash their hands before eating. One young lady approached another and asked to borrow her ring. When asked why she needed a ring, she replied: ":Well, I see all the girls removing their rings before washing and I do not have a ring to remove." One memorable lesson that young lady learned at the seminar is that the ring is removed so that the water should wash every part of the hands.

When a person does not understand the background and the basis for halachah he is likely to attribute importance to things that are not important. He may be *machmir* where no *chumrah* is called for. The innocent young lady who asked for a ring found herself in a similar situation to that of a Chasid who lived about two hundred years ago. The Chasid noted that his *Rebbe*, the famous R. Naphtali Zvi Ropshitzer (1760-1827), one of the leading Chasidic rabbis of Galicia, would cut his fingernails after immersing in the *mikveh*. The Chasid asked: "*Rebbe*, please tell me why you cut your nails after immersing in the *mikveh* when everyone else cuts his nails before immersing?" The *Rebbe*, whose sense of humor is legendary, replied, "This is a great secret which can be revealed only to someone who is on a very high spiritual level." The Chasid asked: "What can I do, *Rebbe*, to be worthy of learning the secret?" Said R. Naphtali: "Whoever wishes to know the secret of the fingernails must first repent for every sin he has committed. Then he must fast a total of seventy days and immerse in the *mikveh* seventy times. Only then will he be worthy of knowing the secret."

The eager Chasid did as the *Rebbe* prescribed. He spent many days and nights cleansing himself of all sins and wrongdoings. He fasted and immersed the required number of times. Finally, he returned to R. Naphtali and said: "*Rebbe*, I have done all that you have commanded. Now, please reveal the secret of the fingernails to me."

R. Naphtali said: "Lean forward and I will whisper the secret in your ear." The trembling Chasid bent his ear to catch his *Rebbe*'s every word. "It is the nature of fingernails," whispered the *Rebbe*, "to soften in warm water. It is easier to cut them after immersion" (*Saray Ha'may'ah*, vol. 4, pp. 97-98).

THE 36

There is a Chasidic belief that the world continues to exist because of the merit of thirty-six righteous men in every generation. The *lamedvavnikim*, as they are called, are hidden saints. Nobody is aware of who they are. Their piety and saintliness are disguised. Outwardly, they appear to be ordinary folk, engaged in ordinary occupations. Secretly, however, they are God's favorites. The *Messiah* is counted as one of the 36. The origin of this belief derives from a statement in the Talmud: "Abaye said: There are no less than 36 righteous men in the world in every generation who receive the Divine Presence" (Sanhedrin 97b, Sukkah 45b). The belief in the 36 has been the source of many Chasidic folktales and legends.

Are the *lamedvavnikim* hidden because they are righteous or are they righteous because they are hidden? Perhaps the answer is both. Jewish tradition has always venerated the righteous person whose piety is private and not on display. All too often, people flaunt their piety by trying to be more *frum*, more religious, than the next person. It is as though they are engaged in a competition of religiosity. Each tries to out-*frum* the other by being more stringent. Such conduct is not piety, it is pomposity. The prophet admonishes these pompous individuals: "Walk humbly with your God" (Micah 6:8).

R. Yosef Baer Soloveitchik (1820-1892), the great grandfather of my teacher who bears his name, was very intolerant of people who were religiously stringent in order to demonstrate their piety. He was equally intolerant of those who acted piously out of ignorance rather than knowledge. Once, R. Yosef Baer noticed such an individual pouring an excessive amount of water on his hands for the ritual washing. He caustically commented: "There goes his piety down the drain" (*Saray Ha'may'ah*, vol. 5, p. 206).

NOT AT OTHERS' EXPENSE
Piety is laudable, but not at the expense of other people. Sometimes a person may become so engrossed in fulfilling his religious duties that he is oblivious to the needs of others around him. Those who often suffer the most are loved ones and family members. Responsibility for the financial and emotional needs of one's wife and children does not cease because of involvement with mitzvot and Torah study. A telling lesson may be derived from a Talmudic anecdote. A certain R. Rechumi used to travel every year to Mechoza to study Torah with Rava and would return home on the eve of Yom Kippur. One year he was so engrossed in his studies that he neglected to return home. His wife waited and waited, hoping that he would enter at any moment. The hour grew late and she realized that her husband was not coming home for Yom Kippur. A single tear trickled down her cheek. At that very moment, the roof on which her husband was sitting collapsed and he fell and died (Ketubot 62b).

One of the saintliest souls who lived in the nineteenth century was R. Yisrael Lipkin, better known as R. Yisrael Salanter (1810-1883). His ethical conduct and his sensitivity to his fellow human beings are legendary. He founded the Musar Movement which stressed refinement of character and sincere caring for people. Though R. Yisrael wrote very little, his conduct became a living textbook. He understood and practiced, better than most, the true meaning of piety. He used to say: "A person should be more concerned with his spiritual needs than his physical needs. This is true, however, only with regard to one's self. With regard to others, we should be more concerned about their physical needs than their spiritual needs."

R. Yisrael Salanter was once a house guest of a wealthy Jew in Kovno named R. Yaakov Karpas. R. Yaakov noticed that when R.

Yisrael would ritually wash his hands before eating, he would measure the water and spill only a minimal amount. When questioned why he was so frugal in his use of water, he replied: "I see that the maid has to bring water from the well that is quite a distance from the house. She can hardly carry the bucket of water on her shoulder. One should not be pious at the expense of someone else's shoulder."

R. Yisrael used to personally supervise the baking of *matzot* for Passover. From the time the wheat was harvested to the time the dough was placed in the oven, he himself watched to make sure the *matzot* were free of leaven. One year, R. Yisrael was ill and was not able to supervise the baking of *matzot*. He asked several of his students to supervise for him. Not having done this before, they asked him: "*Rebbe*, what should we be most careful of during the preparation of the *matzot*?" He replied: "Be sure that you do not scold or embarrass the woman who kneads the dough. She is a poor widow."

One year, the second day of Rosh Hashanah fell on Friday. The *gabba'im* who were in charge of the prayer services approached R. Yisrael and asked: "*Rebbe*, we do not want to prolong the services today, because people need time to prepare for Shabbat. What *piyutim*, liturgical poems, may be deleted from the prayers?" R. Yisrael replied: "All of them, including *U'netaneh tokef*. But do not leave out the *piyutim* in the three long blessings of the *Mussaf* — *Malchiyot*, *Zichronot* and *Shofarot*." "Why are these any different from the others?" asked the *gabbaim*. "While these are said by the congregation, the cantor will have a chance to rest and regain his strength," he said.

In many congregations it was customary for only one mourner to recite *Kaddish*. When more than one person was required to say *Kaddish*, priority was given to the one observing *yahrtzeit*, the anniversary of the death of a parent. Once, on the *yahrtzeit* of his father, R. Yisrael relinquished his right and told a Jew who had come to say *Kaddish* on the *yahrtzeit* of his daughter to recite the prayer. Several people questioned R. Yisrael's action. "Was he not dishonoring his late father by not reciting *Kaddish*?" they asked each other. R. Yisrael overheard the whispers. He turned around and said: "I know the importance of saying *Kaddish*. But relieving a little of the pain of a man who lost his daughter is worth more than a hundred *Kaddeshim*."

R. Yisrael Salanter took it upon himself to collect funds for the poor. He viewed charity collection as a supremely important mitzvah. There was a particularly destitute family in Kovno that R. Yisrael wanted to help. So he approached a number of wealthy Jews and asked them for their contributions. One Jew who was particularly "pious" refused to give. "Why won't you help this family?" R. Yisrael asked. "They are not so religious," answered the wealthy Jew. "Now I understand the wise words of our Sages," said R. Yisrael. " 'Jews are holy. There are those who want to give but do not have, and there are those who do not want to give' (Chulin 7b). Now, I can understand that someone who wants to give but does not have should be called 'holy.' But why should someone who does have and does not want to give be called 'holy'? Our Sages, however, wished to teach us a great lesson. There are some people who can afford to give charity but don't want to. So they look for excuses not to give. Suddenly they become 'holy' and 'pious' and begin to find fault with the poor who need their help. These are the 'holy ones' who have but do not want to give" (*Saray Ha'may'ah*, vol. 2, pp. 272-278).

The Practical Law

1. Nowadays, most people do not concentrate sufficiently when they pray; therefore, a bridegroom must recite *Sh'mah* (*Orach Chaim* 70:3).

Chapter Three

Introduction

The previous chapter concluded with the law of the bridegroom who is exempt from reciting *Sh'mah* as a result of his preoccupation with performing a mitzvah. Chapter 3 discusses additional classes of individuals who are exempt from reciting *Sh'mah*. The mourner prior to the burial of his dead and participants in the funeral procession are occupied with the mitzvah of burial. Women, bondsmen, and minors are also exempt. A person who experienced a seminal emission may not recite *Sh'mah* verbally, but he must mentally contemplate prayer. *Sh'mah* may not be recited in the presence of nudity, foul odors, or excrement.

The reasons for these exemptions vary in each of the above cases. Burial is a mitzvah to which the rule "He who is occupied with a mitzvah is exempt from performing other mitzvot" applies. Women, bondsmen, and minors are exempt due to their particular legal status. The exemption of one who experienced a seminal emission derives from a rabbinic decree that was eventually abolished. The association of prayer with *kedushah*, holiness, necessitates praying in a place whose sanctity is not voided as a result of nudity or uncleanliness.

Mishnah 1

He whose dead[1] is lying before him[2] is exempt from reciting *Sh'mah*, from *Tefillah*,[3] and from donning *Tefillin*.[4] Those who carry the bier[5] and those who exchange with them, and those who exchange with them[6] — whether they are in front of the bier or behind the bier — those that are needed for the bier[7] are exempt and those that are not needed[8] for the bier are obligated.[9] These and those[10] are exempt from *Tefillah*.[11]

מִי שֶׁמֵּתוֹ מֻטָּל לְפָנָיו, פָּטוּר מִקְּרִיאַת שְׁמַע וּמִן הַתְּפִלָּה וּמִן הַתְּפִלִּין. נוֹשְׂאֵי הַמִּטָּה וְחִלּוּפֵיהֶן וְחִלּוּפֵי חִלּוּפֵיהֶן, אֶת שֶׁלִּפְנֵי הַמִּטָּה וְאֶת שֶׁלְּאַחַר הַמִּטָּה, אֶת שֶׁלַּמִּטָּה צֹרֶךְ בָּהֶן — פְּטוּרִין, וְאֶת שֶׁאֵין לַמִּטָּה צֹרֶךְ בָּהֶן — חַיָּבִין. אֵלוּ וָאֵלוּ פְּטוּרִין מִן הַתְּפִלָּה:

1. WHOSE DEAD — Any one of the seven relatives for whom it is required to mourn, i.e., mother, father, sister, brother, son, daughter, or spouse.
2. LYING BEFORE HIM — Prior to burial.
3. *TEFILLAH* — The *Amidah (Sh'moneh Esray)* prayer.
4. TEFILLIN — Phylacteries.
5. BIER — Or, coffin.
6. WHO EXCHANGE WITH THEM — It was customary to relieve the pallbearers so that others can participate in the mitzvah of burial.
7. THOSE THAT ARE NEEDED FOR THE BIER — Those who are going to be pallbearers.
8. THOSE THAT ARE NOT NEEDED — Either because they will not have a turn carrying the bier or they have already had their turn.
9. OBLIGATED — To recite *Sh'mah* and don *tefillin*. Though they are walking, they are able to pause and fulfill their obligation by reciting the first verse of *Sh'mah*.
10. THESE AND THOSE — The pallbearers and those who are in the cortege.
11. *TEFILLAH* — Unlike *Sh'mah*, whose obligation is from the Torah, *tefillah* is a rabbinic obligation and the Rabbis exempted *tefillah* in this circumstance (Rashi, Tosafot, Berachot 17b). Another explanation is that the emotional grief experienced by the participants in the funeral cortege precludes sufficient concentration for *tefillah* (Maimonides).

The Letter of the Law

THE *ONEN*

A mourner (one who lost one of seven close relatives, i.e., mother, father, sister, brother, son, daughter, or spouse), from the time of death until the burial, is called an *onen*. Though the mishnah enumerates only three mitzvot from which the *onen* is exempt, in point of fact, he is exempt from all positive mitzvot. Thus, during the period of *aninut*, the *onen* does not don *tefillin*, pray, or recite Grace after Meals or blessings. The only blessing the *onen* is required to bless is *Baruch dayan ha'emet*, "Blessed is the True Judge." Various reasons are given for this halachah:

1) The *onen* is mentally preoccupied with the mitzvah of burying his dead. As was stated earlier with regard to the bridegroom (2:5), "He who is occupied with a mitzvah is exempt from performing other mitzvot" (Rashi, Berachot 17b).

2) If the *onen* interrupts his feelings of grief and bereavement in order to perform a mitzvah, he is dishonoring the deceased. He must honor the deceased by focusing his attention on his grief and by not being distracted, even to perform a mitzvah (Semachot, chap. 10; Jerusalem Talmud, Berachot 3:1).

3) "There is none other to carry his burden." In other words, the *onen* is occupied with the burial arrangements and is, therefore, relieved of other religious obligations (Jerusalem Talmud, *ibid.*). The implication of this statement is that in a situation where the funeral arrangements are being taken care of by others, e.g., a *chevrah kadishah* or a funeral parlor, the *onen* is obligated to perform mitzvot.

4) The *onen* is in a state of confusion and is incapable of performing mitzvot in a proper manner (*Deut. Rabbah*, chap. 9).

5) "So that you will remember the day of your departure from the Land of Egypt all the days of your life" (Deut. 16:3) — when you are occupied with life, not when you are occupied with death (Jerusalem Talmud, quoted by *Tosafot*, Berachot 17b).

WHAT IS THE MEANING OF "EXEMPT?"

When the mishnah says that the *onen* is exempt from *Shm'ah*, *tefillah*, and *tefillin*, does it mean that he is not obligated to perform mitzvot, but may voluntarily do so, or, does it mean that he is precluded from performing mitzvot, even voluntarily? It was stated earlier (2:8) that a bridegroom who is preoccupied with a mitzvah may recite *Sh'mah*, even though he is not obligated to do so. If the reason for the *onen*'s exemption were solely preoccupation with a mitzvah, as in the case of the bridegroom, he, too, would be permitted to recite *Sh'mah* if he so desired. Because, however, there are other factors that play a role in the *onen*'s exemption, viz., "honoring the dead" and "there is no other to carry his burden," he is precluded from mitzvot, and may not perform them, not even voluntarily. If the *onen* were to distract himself with prayers and other mitzvot, he would be dishonoring his deceased relative. Not all authorities agree, however, with this analysis. Rashi's opinion is that the *onen* may pray if he chooses to do so (Berachot 17b). Maimonides states: "Whoever is exempt from *Sh'mah* may be stringent and recite *Sh'mah* if he so desires, provided he is able to concentrate" (*Mishnah Torah*, Laws of *Sh'mah* 4:7). The implication is that the *onen*, too, may recite *Sh'mah*. Most authorities, however, are of the opinion that the *onen* may not recite *Sh'mah*, nor perform other mitzvot (*Tosafot*, Rosh).

THE PALLBEARERS
It is a mitzvah to bury the dead. Attending a funeral and participating in the burial is an expression of honor and respect for the deceased. Thus, those who carry the coffin and those who simply join in the funeral procession are exempt from *tefillah*. Insofar as *Sh'mah* is concerned, however, the mishnah distinguishes between those who are directly involved in carrying the coffin and those who are walking in the procession. The pallbearers and those who are going to be pallbearers are exempt from *Sh'mah*. Those who do not carry the coffin and have not as yet recited *Sh'mah* must pause to recite the first verse because they are not directly involved with the burial.

The Spirit of the Law

THE MENTAL STATE OF THE *ONEN*
Death creates a religious crisis in the mind of the mourner. When torn by the painful grief of losing a loved one, the foundations of the mourner's faith are shaken. He experiences great difficulty in

reconciling his belief in a God who is good with the harsh reality of bereavement. It is not unusual for the mourner to question God's goodness and omnipotence. Often he expresses outright anger: "God, how could you have done this to me? Why did You steal away my parent (spouse, sibling, child)? Where is Your love? Where is Your justice?" When such anger and doubt are directed towards the Almighty, the entire Torah is called into question, as well. When faith is so very difficult, obeying commandments is even more difficult.

The human being is a creature who wishes to understand all, but understands so very little. The human being is the only creature on earth who suffers existentially from an awareness of his own mortality. "Man is like a breath, his days are like a passing shadow," (Ps. 144:4) exclaims the Psalmist. Man's limited intellectual capacity, his ignorance of the complexities and intricacies of the workings of the cosmos, his exclusion from the spiritual dimension which is barred to him like the entrance to the Garden of Eden, and his hopeless inability to comprehend his Creator, cause him to live in the shadow of doubt and fear, frustration and anger.

All these latent feelings rise to the surface in the face of death. The confrontation with the Angel of Death is a confrontation with one's own mortality and helplessness. When "his dead is lying before him" the mourner, as an *onen*, evinces a silent scream of despair. Job was an exception. His story is told in the Bible because "despite all this (that befell him), Job did not sin and did not cast reproach on God" (Job 1:22).

The halachah does not deny the mourner his grief and suffering. It does not impose itself upon the *onen* who feels helpless and shattered. The mitzvot recede to the background and allow the *onen* to vent his anger and frustration. Patiently and lovingly, God allows the *onen* to feel and express his fears and confusion. Until the burial, he is relieved of all of his religious obligations.

AFTER THE BURIAL
After the burial, doubt and despair must come to an end. After the coffin has been lowered and covered with earth, the mourner must attempt to put aside his gnawing thoughts and painful feelings. He must try to achieve a degree of acceptance that will make normal living

possible again. It is at this point in time that the mourner is called upon to make an heroic effort to reaffirm his faith in the Almighty and return to the observance of mitzvot.

AHVELUT
Interment marks the transition from the state of *aninut* to the state of *ahvelut*. Once the burial is concluded, the mourner emotionally moves from despair to hope, from doubt to faith. He expresses a beautiful testimony of faith that is contained in the *Tziduk hadin* prayer, "Justifying the judgment": "The works of the Creator are perfect, for all His ways are justice. A faithful God without fault, righteous and upright is He...." He then recites the *Kaddish* as an admission of his inability to fathom the ways of the Almighty and his public acceptance of the divine decree. As an *onen*, the mourner was exempt from mitzvot. As an *ahvel*, all religious obligations return.

THE *KADDISH* PRAYER
The *Kaddish* prayer is an important element in the burial ritual. The officiating rabbi often goes to great lengths to ensure that a *minyan* (a quorum of ten) is present at the burial so that the mourner will be able to recite the *Kaddish*. The mourner himself will make every effort to attend services daily throughout his period of mourning so that he will be able to recite *Kaddish*. Oddly enough, this ancient Aramaic prayer originated, not as a mourner's prayer, but rather as a prayer to be recited at the conclusion of Torah study. Yet, the Jewish people has universally adopted the custom of reciting *Kaddish* upon the occasion of burial and mourning, even though it contains no allusion to death. Why then was the *Kaddish* inseparably linked with the mourning experience?

As explained earlier, bereavement often shakes the foundations of faith, even in the believer. The dark cloud of grief obscures the radiance of the Almighty. This is true for the mourner, and to a lesser degree, for all who witness the grisly presence of death. Life is a manifestation of the Divine Presence. Death is a manifestation of *Deus absconditus*, the hidden God. A very special task is assigned to the mourner at the gravesite. It becomes his role to sanctify the Name of God. His task is to publicly declare that God, who is obscured by death, is, in fact, manifest. The declaration: *Yitgadal v'yitkadash shmay rabah*, "May the great Name be magnified and hallowed," strengthens the faith of all who are present and reaffirms the faith of the mourner himself.

God's Name is the human perception of the divine essence. No human being can comprehend God's true essence. "No man can see Me and live' (Ex. 33:20). At best, we can know the Almighty only through His works and His Torah. "And you shall see my Back, but, my Face shall not be seen" (*ibid.*, 33:23). Human knowledge of the divine is limited to His footprints left in the sands of time. The *Kaddish* addresses itself to the Name of the Almighty. It is a prayer for greater awareness and recognition of the Divine Presence in our midst. The *Kaddish* fulfills the words of the prophet: "Thus will I be magnified and sanctified, and I will make myself known in the eyes of many nations; that they shall know that I am the Lord" (Ezekiel 38:23). Thus, the mourner recites: "Magnified and hallowed be His great Name in the world which He has created according to His will. May He establish His kingdom during your life and during your days, and during the life of all the house of Israel, speedily and soon, and say, Amen!" The listeners respond: "Amen! May His great Name be blessed forever and to all eternity."

THE *KADDISH* AND *SH'MAH*

Sh'mah, like the *Kaddish*, is a prayer that sanctifies the Name of God. It, too, is an affirmation of God's presence and the greatness of His Name. As mentioned earlier (pg. 106) Rashi interprets the clauses "The Lord is our God" and "The Lord is One" as referring to two separate eras in the history of mankind. In the present, "The Lord is *our* God." "The Lord is One" is a prophecy for the future. There will come a time, in the days of the Messiah, when all nations of the world will join the Jewish people in their belief in the One God. This is the prophetic vision of Zechariah: "The Lord shall be One and His Name One." No longer will human beings see the world as being anchored to the confusion and void from which it was created. No longer will we see a world filled with conflicts and paradoxes. Life and death, good and evil, will not be viewed as independent forces governing the affairs of humanity. All mankind will perceive the unity of creation and the Creator. Thus, *Sh'mah* is not only a testimony to the belief in One God, it is a testimony to the Jew's faith in the spiritual redemption of all mankind.

A clear link between *Kaddish* and *Sh'mah* is also contained in the words that immediately follow the first verse: "Blessed be the Name of His glorious majesty forever and ever." Here, as in the *Kaddish*, God's Name is blessed. In fact, the Aramaic translation of "Blessed be the Name..." is almost identical with the congregational response in the *Kaddish*: "Yehay sh'may rabah..." (Jerusalem Targum, Gen. 49:1, Deut. 6:4).

The Practical Law

1. The *onen* is exempt from *Sh'mah*, *tefillah*, *tefillin*, blessings, and Grace after Meals. He may not be included in the quorum of a *minyan* (*Gesher Ha'chaim*, vol. 1, chap. 18).

2. The *onen* may not perform mitzvot, even if he wishes to do so voluntarily (*Orach Chaim* 71:1, *Yoreh De'ah* 341:1).

3. All who are involved in carrying the coffin are exempt from reciting *Sh'mah*. The others in the cortege are obligated to recite *Sh'mah* (*Orach Chaim* 72:1). They must recite the first verse while standing still and must concentrate on the words. The rest of *Sh'mah* may be recited while walking (*Mishnah B'rurah*, *ibid.*).

4. All participants in the funeral procession are exempt from *tefillah* (*Orach Chaim* 106:1).

CHAPTER 3: *Mishnah 2*   155

Mishnah 2   משנה ב

After the burial, when they have returned[1] — if they can begin and complete[2] before reaching the line — they begin. If not, they do not begin.[3] Those who stand in the line — the inner ones[4] are exempt[5] and the outer ones[6] are obligated.

קָבְרוּ אֶת הַמֵּת וְחָזְרוּ — אִם יְכוֹלִין לְהַתְחִיל וְלִגְמֹר עַד שֶׁלֹּא יַגִּיעוּ לַשּׁוּרָה, יַתְחִילוּ; וְאִם לָאו, לֹא יַתְחִילוּ. הָעוֹמְדִים בַּשּׁוּרָה — הַפְּנִימִים פְּטוּרִים, וְהַחִיצוֹנִים חַיָּבִין:

---

1. RETURNED — From the gravesite to the place where the line is formed. Those attending the funeral form a line. As the mourners walk past the line, they are consoled with the words: "May the Omnipresent comfort you among the mourners of Zion and Jerusalem."
2. COMPLETE — If there is time to complete the first paragraph of *Sh'mah* (R. Ovadiah Bertinoro). According to another opinion, even the first verse (*Tiferet Yisrael*).
3. NOT BEGIN — Rather, they should first comfort the mourners and address them with words of consolation.
4. INNER ONES — I.e., those who can see the mourners and address them with words of consolation.
5. EXEMPT — From reciting *Sh'mah*.
6. OUTER ONES — I.e., those who are unable to see the mourners.

The Letter of the Law

RECITING *SH'MAH* OR COMFORTING THE MOURNER?

One who is occupied with the mitzvah of comforting a mourner is exempt from performing other mitzvot, including reciting *Sh'mah*. The mishnah is not specific as to whether there is time to recite *Sh'mah* afterwards or not. Does the mishnah mean that comforting the mourner takes priority over *Sh'mah*, even if the time for reciting *Sh'mah* will elapse; or is the mishnah referring to a case in which there is time to recite *Sh'mah* afterwards, and only then does comforting the mourner come first? In other words, if the choice is between comforting the mourner or reciting *Sh'mah*, which of the two mitzvot takes precedence?

There are two arguments in favor of giving precedence to *Sh'mah*. Firstly, *Sh'mah* is a mitzvah commanded by the Torah, whereas comforting the mourner is only a rabbinic law. Secondly, while a person is waiting on the line, he is not yet occupied with the mitzvah of comforting the mourner. Thus, he must fulfill the mitzvah of *Sh'mah*, even if it means missing the opportunity to comfort the mourner as he passes. Maimonides supports this opinion: "If the people are able to begin and complete even the first verse before they arrive at the line, they must begin (to recite *Sh'mah*). If not, they may not begin, but they must comfort the mourners, and after they have left, they must recite *Sh'mah*" (*Mishneh Torah*, Laws of *Sh'mah* 4:6). The implication is that comforting mourners takes precedence only if there is time to recite *Sh'mah* afterwards.

There is a contrary opinion, however, that argues with both premises. *Shitah M'kubetzet* holds the view that comforting the mourner is a Torah law, no less than *Sh'mah*. Furthermore, the mitzvah of comforting the mourner begins immediately, even while standing in line before the mourners arrive. Thus, according to this opinion, comforting the mourner takes precedence over *Sh'mah*, even if the mitzvah of *Sh'mah* will be forfeited (quoted in *Tosafot Anshay Shem*). According to this opinion, the mishnah means that comforting the mourner takes precedence over *Sh'mah*, whether there is time to recite *Sh'mah* afterwards or not.

The Spirit of the Law

"LOVE YOUR NEIGHBOR"

Maimonides writes: "It is a rabbinic positive commandment to visit the sick, to comfort mourners, to escort the dead, to dower the bride, to escort guests, to engage in all the burial requirements, to carry the coffin, to walk before it, to eulogize, to dig the grave and to bury the dead, to bring joy to the bride and groom and to provide them with all their needs. These are acts of kindness that a person performs physically and for which there is no limit. Even though all these mitzvot are of rabbinic origin, they are subsumed under the mitzvah 'Love your neighbor as yourself.' Whatever you wish others to do for you, do them for your brother in Torah and mitzvot" (*Mishneh Torah*, Laws of Mourning 14:1).

Maimonides teaches us an important principle. All acts of kindness and concern are a fulfillment of the mitzvah "Love your neighbor as yourself." Furthermore, we see that this mitzvah does not apply only to the living. "Love your neighbor" applies even to the dead. Tending to burial arrangements and attending a funeral are no less important than visiting the sick or rejoicing at a wedding.

BURYING THE DEAD

When Jacob lay on his deathbed, he called for his son Joseph and asked him to take an oath that he will bury his father in Eretz Yisrael. "Do unto me kindness and truth, please do not bury me in Egypt" (Gen. 47:29). "Kindness and truth" succinctly expresses the essence of the mitzvah of burying the dead, as Rashi comments: "Kindness done for the dead is a true kindness because there is no expectation of reward" (*ad loc.*). When a favor is done for a friend or neighbor, even with altruistic motives, there is always the possibility of the favor being returned. But when kindness and respect are shown for the dead, there is no possibility of reciprocation. It is a deed that is performed without any expectation of recompense, or even a "thank you." It is a "true kindness."

The Talmud derives the mitzvah to bury the dead from the verse "... you shall surely bury him on that day..." (Deut. 21:23) (Sanhedrin 46b). The Torah teaches that even the criminal who received a death sentence by the hands of the court must be afforded the dignity of a burial. The human being is created in the image of God. Within the human body resides a spark of divinity, a soul. It is that spark of divinity that distinguishes the human being from all of God's creations. Man's capacity to discern between right and wrong, to feel pangs of conscience, to be motivated towards goodness, to strive for spirituality, are all manifestations of his unique divine endowment.

Man's capacity to display animal behavior — aggression, lust, gluttony, territorial domain, etc. — is derived from his physical essence.

The human body which houses the divine spark originates from dust. "And the Lord God formed man of the dust of the ground and breathed into his nostrils the breath of life" (Gen. 2:7). The "dust" ingredient is man's biological aspect. The "breath of life" is his spiritual essence. The composite of the two combine to form a creature whose destiny is to live with a constant tension between biological and spiritual drives. Each individual must determine which of the two shall predominate. Each human being carries the awesome responsibility of shaping his own spiritual destiny.

The struggle ends with death, which marks the separation of body from soul. "The dust returns to the earth as it was, and the spirit returns to God who gave it" (Eccl. 12:7). The body which housed the soul during its brief sojourn on earth must be treated with dignity and respect. There are many laws which govern the treatment of the dead. The body must be bathed. It must not be left unattended. Embalming is prohibited. Autopsies are forbidden except under special circumstances. The entire community is called upon to pay last respects by attending the funeral. The Talmud says: "He who sees the dead and does not escort him reflects the verse: 'One who mocks the poor insults his Maker' (Proverbs 17:5)" (Berachot 18a). Failure to pay respect to the dead, who in his lifetime was "the image of God," is deemed an insult to God. On the other hand, paying respect to the dead is deemed a demonstration of respect for the Creator Himself.

COMFORTING THE MOURNER
Bereavement is one of the most painful human experiences. After the initial trauma of losing a loved one, the mourner suffers the anguish of helplessness and loneliness. He feels isolated and abandoned. He feels cut off from the society around him that proceeds as though nothing has happened, nothing has changed. It is during this very difficult seven day *shivah* period that the halachah calls upon friends and neighbors to ease the mourner's pain and suffering.

It is God Himself who demonstrated the importance of consoling the bereaved. As the Torah says: "And it was after the death of Abraham that God blessed his son Isaac" (Gen. 25:11). God's personal visitation was a consolation and a blessing to Isaac. The importance of comforting the mourner was taught to us by Moses, too. The Torah relates that Aaron suffered the tragic loss of his two sons, Nadab and Abihu, on the day the Sanctuary was dedicated (Lev. 10:1-2). We can only imagine the severity of Aaron's grief at that time. Moses approached his brother and consolingly said to him: "This is what the Lord has spoken, saying, 'By them that are near to me, I will be sanctified, and before all the nation I will be honored' " (ibid., v.3). Moses was saying, in effect, that God had dealt harshly with Nadab and Abihu because they were so great and holy. Their sin might have been overlooked if they had been on a lower spiritual level. But God is most exacting with those who are close to Him. Aaron heard Moses' words and was consoled: "And Aaron was silent" (ibid.).

The best way to console a mourner is by physically being in his presence and showing care and concern. Words are usually inadequate and sometimes counterproductive. Job's friends sat with him in silent sympathy for seven days. In the presence of caring neighbors and friends, the mourner's sense of isolation is mitigated. Just being with him offers comfort, as the Psalmist says: "I shall be with him in time of trouble" (Ps. 91:15). The only formal statement that is customarily said to the mourner is the formula: "May the Omnipresent comfort you among the mourners of Zion and Jerusalem." God is referred to as the Omnipresent, in order to indicate that God is present in the house of mourning, too.

Maimonides sums up the importance of comforting the mourner with the following words: "It seems to me that comforting mourners takes precedence over visiting the sick, because comforting mourners is an act of kindness to both the living and the dead" (*Mishneh Torah*, Laws of Mourning 14:7).

G'MILUT CHASSADIM

Burying the dead and offering condolences to the mourner are counted amongst the ways of fulfilling the mitzvah of *G'milut chassadim*, "acts of kindness." The Talmud states: " 'You shall walk after the Lord, your God' (Deut. 13:5). Is it possible for a person to walk after the Divine

Presence? Is it not already written: 'For the Lord your God is a consuming fire' (Deut. 4:24)? Rather, one should walk after (emulate) the attributes of the Holy One, blessed be He. Just as He clothes the naked, as it is written: 'And the Lord God made garments for Adam and his wife and He dressed them' (Gen. 3:21), so shall you clothe the naked. Just as the Holy One, blessed be He, visits the sick, as it is written: 'And the Lord appeared to him in the terebinths of Mamre' (Gen. 18:1), so shall you visit the sick. Just as the Holy One, blessed be He, comforted the mourners, as it is written: 'And it was after the death of Abraham that God blessed his son Isaac' (Gen. 25:11), so shall you comfort the mourners. Just as the Holy One, blessed be He, buried the dead, as it is written: 'And He buried him in the valley' (Deut. 34:6), so shall you bury the dead" (Sotah 14a).

G'milut chassadim is one of the cornerstones of the Jewish way of life. It is a mitzvah that governs our relationship with spouse, friends, relatives, neighbors, and even total strangers. It is a mitzvah that can be performed in an infinite variety of ways; with a kind word, friendly advice, a financial loan, a gift to the poor, doing a favor, cheering one who is depressed, praying for the ill, etc. *G'milut chassadim* is counted among the three pillars upon which the world stands (Ethics of the Fathers 1:2). It is a mitzvah which a person "eats the fruits thereof in this world and the principle remains in the world to come" (*Siddur*). So fundamental is this mitzvah, that "he who does not believe in *G'milut chassadim* does not believe in the existence of the Almighty" (*Kohelet Rabbah* 7).

These are but a few of the numerous quotes pertaining to *G'milut chassadim* that are found in the Talmud and Midrash. Clearly, our Sages understood that Judaism is far more than a tedious rulebook of do's and don'ts. Behind the letter of the law is a spirit which helps build and mold human character. The law covers every facet of life so that the Jew constantly and consistently has a standard by which he can measure his behavior. Spiritual development is inseparable from human development. Religiosity is both the catalyst for ethical conduct, and the result of ethical conduct. The integrated religious personality is unified in its relationship with God and its relationship with fellow human beings. Ritual and righteousness fuel each other. Ritual inspires spiritual refinement; spiritual refinement inspires sensitivity and caring for others; sensitivity and caring for others inspire a greater receptivity for spiritual elevation.

Torah may be subdivided into numerous categories. There is the Written Law and the Oral Law; there are laws governing our relationship with God, and laws governing our relationship with our fellow. There are rational mitzvot, symbolic mitzvot, and mitzvot which are statutes for which there are no rational explanations. There are positive commandments and negative commandments. There are mitzvot which are constant, and others that are related to specific time periods. These numerous categories and divisions of Torah often obscure the totality of the forest because of the individual trees. The ideal, however, is to be able to perceive not a forest, but rather a single tree made up of various parts. The Torah Tree of Life has roots and trunk, branches and leaves. It is a tree that bears the sweetest of fruits for all who are privileged to dwell in its shade. The Jew who perceives Torah in its totality achieves a level of holiness that is otherwise unobtainable. Isn't it interesting that Webster's Unabridged Dictionary enters the word "holism" after the word "holiness"?

The Practical Law

1. After the burial, when the people are walking to the place where the line will be formed to comfort the mourners, if there is time to recite, even the first verse, before reaching the line, they must recite. If not, they may not begin (*Orach Chaim* 72:4).

2. This law applies only when there is time to recite *Sh'mah* afterwards. If the time for reciting *Sh'mah* will elapse, they must recite *Sh'mah* first (*Ramah, ibid.*).

Mishnah 3 / משנה ג

Women, servants,[1] and minors[2] are exempt from reciting *Sh'mah* and from *Tefillin*. But they are obligated for prayer, *mezuzah*, and Grace after Meals.

נָשִׁים וַעֲבָדִים וּקְטַנִּים פְּטוּרִין מִקְּרִיאַת שְׁמַע וּמִן הַתְּפִלִּין; וְחַיָּבִין בַּתְּפִלָּה וּבַמְּזוּזָה וּבְבִרְכַּת הַמָּזוֹן:

1. SERVANTS — Canaanite bondsmen who have been circumcised and have immersed in a *mikveh*. Their legal status, insofar as mitzvot is concerned, is similar to that of a woman. They are obligated to observe all negative commandments and are exempt from certain positive commandments with a fixed time period.
2. MINORS — Before the age of Bar Mitzvah, i.e., thirteen years and a day.

The Letter of the Law

WOMEN AND MITZVOT

The issue of women and halachah has been at the forefront of debate and controversy for the past several decades. The role and status of women have changed radically in modern times. These changes have precipitated serious criticism of woman's role in Judaism. Efforts have been made in certain circles to "correct" the situation by altering Jewish tradition to make it compatible with current trends. Unfortunately, much of the debate and criticism fail to deal with the issues with scholarly understanding and intellectual honesty. A full treatment of the subject of women and halachah is beyond the scope of this work. For a detailed analysis of the subject, the reader is referred to: *Jewish Woman in Jewish Law* by Moshe Meiselman, Ktav/Yeshiva University Press, 1978; *Contemporary Halachic Problems*, vol.1, by J. David Bleich, Ktav/Yeshiva University Press, 1977, pp. 78-83; "The

Status of Women in Halakhic Judaism," by Saul Berman, *Tradition*, vol.14, no. 2 (Fall, 1973).

Those who are exempt from reciting *Sh'mah*, as listed in the first two mishnayot of this chapter (the *onen*, those involved in the burial, and those who are occupied with comforting the mourner), are exempt because of the particular circumstances in which they find themselves. Women, bondsmen, and minors, on the other hand, are exempt because of their unique legal status. Women and Canaanite bondsmen share the same legal obligations. They are obligated in all negative commandments and are exempt from a number of time-oriented positive commandments. *Sh'mah* must be recited "when you lie down and when you arise." *Tefillin* must be worn by day, but not at night, nor on Shabbat and festivals. Thus, they are exempt from these mitzvot.

The *mezuzah* must be affixed to the doorpost at all times. It is a positive commandment without a fixed time. Thus, women and bondsmen are obligated. Grace after Meals is, also, a positive commandment without a fixed time. Whenever a person has eaten an amount of bread that constitutes a meal, he/she is obligated to recite Grace after Meals. There is, however, a debate amongst halachic authorities as to whether a woman's obligation to recite Grace after Meals is of Torah or rabbinic origin. The Talmud leaves the question unresolved (Berachot 20b). Grace after Meals is clearly a positive commandment without a fixed time. The text of the second blessing, however, contains references to mitzvot from which women are exempt, i.e., inheritance of the Land of Israel, circumcision, and Torah study. These mitzvot would not have been included if woman's obligation were of Torah origin. Thus, their obligation may be only of rabbinic origin.

There are legal ramifications as to whether a woman's obligation to recite Grace after Meals is of Torah or rabbinic origin. If her obligation is of a rabbinic nature, a woman may not recite Grace after Meals on behalf of a man, whose obligation is Biblical. In addition, there is a principle that states that if a person is in doubt as to whether he recited a rabbinic blessing, he may not recite the blessing. If, however, the doubt concerns a Biblical blessing, he must recite the blessing. Thus, if a woman ate a meal and was satisfied, and she does not remember if she recited Grace after Meals or not — if her obligation is Biblical, she must recite Grace after Meals. If her obligation is rabbinic, she may not recite Grace after Meals.

TIME-ORIENTED MITZVOT

The mishnah cites just two examples of time-oriented mitzvot from which women are exempt, *Sh'mah* and *tefillin*. The two relate to prayer and are the subject matter of Tractate Berachot. A general rule, however, is stated in Tractate Kiddushin 1:7: "All positive commandments with a fixed time — men are obligated and women are exempt. And all positive commandments without a fixed time — both men and women are obligated. And all negative commandments, with or without a fixed time — both men and women are obligated."

What appears as a categorical statement about women's obligations is, in fact, not categorical at all. There are many exceptions to the rule. The mishnah in Kiddushin is simply offering a general guideline that pertains to some mitzvot. There are, however, many time-oriented positive commandments in which women are obligated, as there are many non-time-oriented mitzvot from which women are exempt. Of the 248 positive Biblical commandments, women are exempt from: *sukkah, lulav, shofar*, counting the *Omer* (which, according to most authorities, is a rabbinic commandment nowadays), *tefillin, tzitzit, Sh'mah* (and in Temple times: the pilgrimage on the festivals and the festival offering). Biblical time-oriented positive mitzvot which women are obligated to perform are: matzah, *Kiddush*, rejoicing on festivals (and in Temple times: *maror* (bitter herbs), the Paschal lamb, and the national assembly after the Sabbatical year). Maimonides emphatically makes this point in his Mishnah Commentary: "As you know, we have a rule, 'we do not learn from rules.' The word 'all' means 'most.' The entire scope of positive commandments in which women are obligated and not obligated has no rule. They have been transmitted orally and are tradition. As you know, eating matzah on Passover, rejoicing on festivals, assembling every seven years, prayer, reading the *megillah*, Chanukah lights, Shabbat lights, *Kiddush*, all of these are positive commandments which have a fixed time period, yet, men and women share the same obligation. Furthermore, bearing children, studying Torah, redeeming the firstborn, and waging war with Amalek — these are all positive commandments which do not have a fixed time, yet, women are not obligated to fulfill them. These are all based on tradition, as we have explained."

WOMEN AND PRAYER
The Mishnah states that women are obligated for prayer. It does not specify, however, if women must pray three times a day (as men are obligated to do), or once a day. There are differing opinions on the subject. According to Maimonides, every Jew is obligated to pray once a day: "It is a positive commandment to pray every day as it is written: 'And you shall serve the Lord your God' (Ex. 23:25). Tradition teaches that 'service' means prayer, as it is written: 'And to serve Him with all your heart' (Deut. 11:13). The Sages said: 'What is service of the heart? — Prayer.' The number of prayers is not from the Torah, neither is the formulation nor the specific times. Therefore, women and bondsmen are obligated to pray because it is a positive commandment with no fixed time" (*Mishneh Torah*, Laws of Prayer 1:1-2). Maimonides is of the opinion that, from the Biblical standpoint, men and women share an equal obligation to pray once a day. Biblically, there is no fixed time or formulation for prayer. Rabbinic law introduced the obligation to pray morning and afternoon, *Shacharit* and *Minchah*. The evening prayer, *Arvit*, was originally optional, but later was voluntarily adopted as an obligatory prayer.

Maimonides makes no clear reference to a rabbinic obligation for women to pray three times a day. In his Mishnah Commentary (Kiddushin 1:7), however, he does include prayer in a list of time-oriented positive commandments in which women are obligated. This would imply that, rabbinically, women are obligated to pray three times daily.

Several authorities conclude that, according to Maimonides, there is no obligation whatsoever for women to pray three times a day. A brief prayer once a day, in any language, is sufficient. These authorities suggest that the practice of many pious women who do not pray three times daily is justified by Maimonides' opinion (*Magen Avraham, Orach Chaim*, 106:2, *Aruch Hashulchan, Orach Chaim*, 106:7).

Rashi and Tosafot disagree with Maimonides. In their opinion, there is no Biblical mitzvah to pray. Maimonides' source, that equates "service" with prayer, is not to be construed as a literal commandment to pray. Rather, the origin of the obligation to pray is rabbinic. When the Rabbis established the rule to pray three times daily, they did not distinguish between men and women. Rashi and Tosafot differ, however, in one point. According to Tosafot, though prayer is a rabbinic time-oriented mitzvah, the importance of entreating God's mercy is so important that it overrides the time-oriented aspect. According to Rashi, the time-oriented exemption does not apply to rabbinic laws. Some authorities distinguish between *Shacharit* and *Minchah*, on the one hand, and *Arvit*, on the other. *Arvit*, which was originally optional, was adopted as an obligation only by men. Thus, women are not required to pray *Arvit*.

WOMEN AND *MINYAN*

A *minyan* is defined as a quorum of ten individuals for whom public prayer is obligatory. Whoever does not possess an obligation to pray publicly cannot discharge the obligation of public prayer. Thus, women, who are not obligated to pray publicly, may not be included in a *minyan*. It is erroneous to view woman's exclusion from the *minyan* as an indication of inferior status, because in certain instances, men also may not be included in a *minyan*. For example, the *onen* (the mourner from the time of death until the burial), who is exempt from prayer, is also ineligible to be counted for a *minyan*. Furthermore, in those instances in which women share the same obligation as men, they, in fact, may be counted in the *minyan*. Thus, according to Rabbeinu Nissim, women, who share the same obligation to read the *megillah* as men, may be counted in a *minyan* for this purpose. In addition, the mitzvah of *Kiddush Hashem*, "the sanctification of God's Name," martyrdom, requires ten Jews, not necessarily males. Here, too, women may be counted as part of a *minyan* in the fulfillment of this mitzvah (*Gilyonay Hashas*, Sanhedrin 74b). There is a minority opinion that holds that a woman may be counted in a *minyan* for the purpose of reciting the *zimun* blessing of Grace after Meals (*R. Simcha*, quoted in *Mordechai*, Berachot 45b).

WOMEN AND THE CONDUCTING OF PRAYER SERVICES

There is an halachic principle that one who is not obligated to perform a mitzvah may not fulfill another's obligation. It is for this reason that a woman may not conduct the services. Women are exempt from public prayer; therefore, they may not lead the services. Again, the same is true for an *onen*. In those mitzvot, however, in which women share the same obligation as men, they may fulfill the man's obligation. For example, men and women share the same obligation to recite *Kiddush* on Friday night. It is, therefore, permissible for a woman to recite *Kiddush* for a man. Similarly, a woman may light Chanukah lights for a man.

THE SINGLE WOMAN

Some argue that the woman's exemption from time-oriented mitzvot should not apply to women who do not have family responsibilities. There are many single women, divorcees, and widows, and even married women with children, who have ample time to participate in communal life and pray with a congregation three times daily. Why shouldn't they share the same obligation as men? Here too, the answer lies in understanding the legal structure. Halachah operates with archetypal categories. Once exceptions to the rule are permitted, there is no rule. The law, therefore, focuses on the ideal situation which sees woman in the context of family. It should again be stressed that in those situations in which a woman can participate in communal religious life she is encouraged to do so.

"WHO HAS MADE ME ACCORDING TO HIS WILL"

There are two blessings that are recited in the morning prayers that seem highly objectionable and offensive to women. A man recites the blessing: "Blessed...who has not made me a woman" and a woman blesses: "Blessed...who has made me according to His will." The three blessings: "Who has not made me a heathen," "Who has not made me a slave" and "Who has not made me a woman" are problematic from a textual standpoint. The standard version of these blessings is in the negative: "Who has not made me, etc." Many authorities and early editions of the *Siddur*, however, present the blessings in the positive: "Who has made me a Jew," "Who has made me a free person," and "Who has made me a man." This version is found in the Mantua edition (1558), the Tehengan edition (1560), and the Prague edition

(1566). The Gaon of Vilna, indeed, adopted the view that these blessings should be recited in the positive form. The blessing "Who has not made me a woman" is in no way intended to denigrate women. Rather, it is man's expression of gratitude for having been granted more mitzvot than woman. Mitzvot are viewed as a privilege for which he is grateful.

The woman's blessing "Who has made me according to His will" is problematic insofar as its origin is concerned. Unlike the other blessings, there is no reference to it in the Talmud. For this reason R. Yaakov Emden suggests that it should be recited without mentioning God's Name. R. Yechiel Michal Epstein is of the opinion that women should not recite the blessing at all (*Aruch Hashulchan* 46:11). Most *Siddurim* today do include the blessing. Though easily misconstrued, the blessing was never intended to be disparaging of women. R. Samson Raphael Hirsch's comment on the three blessings recited by men and the blessing recited by women captures the spirit in which they are intended: "This is not a prayer of thanks that God did not make us heathens, slaves or women. Rather, it calls upon us to contemplate the task which God has imposed upon us by making us free Jewish men, and to pledge ourselves to do justice to this mission. These three aspects of our own status impose upon us duties much more comprehensive than those required of the rest of mankind. And if our women have a smaller number of mitzvot to fulfill than men, they know that the tasks which they must discharge as free Jewish women are no less in accordance with the will and desire of God than are those of their brothers" (Hirsch *Siddur*, p. 13).

BONDSMEN
The Canaanite bondsman is exempt from time-oriented mitzvot for reasons totally different from that of the woman. Time is a key element in halachah . Many mitzvot wholly depend upon the time factor for their observance. Shabbat, festivals, fast days, prayer, the eating of sacrifices, etc., are directly linked to time. A time differential of one brief moment can make the difference between the observance or the desecration of Shabbat. One minute can determine if a person has fulfilled his obligation to recite *Sh'mah* or not. To observe halachah properly, a Jew must have an accurate wristwatch and a keen sense of time-awareness.

Rabbi Joseph B. Soloveitchik explains that a bondsman is exempt from time-oriented mitzvot because he lacks time consciousness. "Time-awareness is the singular faculty of the free man, who can use or abuse it. To a slave, it is a curse or a matter of indifference. It is not an instrument which he can harness to his purposes. The free man wants time to move slowly because, presumably, it is being employed for his purposes. The slave may want to accelerate time, because it will terminate his oppressive burdens. Not being able to control time, the slave grows insensitive to it; inexactitude and unawareness characterize his schedule...

"In the concentration camps, night and day became indistinct and blurred. What was not done one day could be done the next; opportunities lost or anticipated generated no great excitement. Time was loosely and meaninglessly structured. This is the condition of the slave. Any mitzvah, therefore, which is defined within a time context does not devolve upon a slave. These mitzvot are meaningful only in their being related to what preceded their performance and to what will follow thereafter. They are time-structured. Their significance is derived from their association with a particular segment of time" (*Reflections of the Rav*, Abraham Besdin, pp. 201-202).

MINORS

Mitzvah obligations of women and bondsmen are determined by the nature of the particular mitzvah. They are exempt from *Sh'mah* and *tefillin*, which are time-oriented mitzvot. They are obligated, however, for prayer, *mezuzah*, and Grace after Meals because these are not time-oriented mitzvot. (As explained earlier, according to Tosafot, prayer is a rabbinic time-oriented mitzvah. The importance of imploring God's mercies is so important, however, that it overrides the time-oriented mitzvah exemption. Rashi argues that the time-orientation exemption does not apply to rabbinic laws.) But, as far as minors are concerned, why is there a distinction made between mitzvot? Minors should be either obligated or not obligated to perform mitzvot. Furthermore, it is an established principle that until the age of Bar Mitzvah, i.e., thirteen years and a day old, a boy has no legal obligations, as it says: "Thirteen is the age of mitzvot" (Ethics of the Fathers 5:21). A girl is not legally obligated to perform mitzvot until the age of twelve. "A twelve-year-old girl and a thirteen-year-old boy who have at least two pubic hairs are considered as adults as far as all mitzvot are concerned" (*Shulchan Aruch, Orech Chaim* 616:2). (Girls mature intellectually sooner than boys. This is derived from the verse which speaks of the creation of Eve, "And He built the rib" [Gen. 2:22] The Hebrew word *vayiven*, "built" is related to *binah*, "understanding" [*Tosafot Harosh*, Nidah 45b]). If so, why does the Mishnah obligate minors in the mitzvot of prayer, *mezuzah*, and Grace after Meals?

In point of fact, minors have no legal obligations. The mishnah addresses itself to the parent who is obligated to educate his/her child to live a Torah life. Parents, says the mishnah, are responsible to teach their child to don *tefillin*, to affix a *mezuzah*, and to recite Grace after Meals, as soon as the child is old enough to grasp the meaning of these mitzvot. *Sh'mah* and *tefillin*, however, are exceptions. Even if the child is old enough to comprehend the meaning of these *mitzvot,* the parent is not obligated to teach him. (These mitzvot apply to males. Women are exempt from *Sh'mah* and *tefillin*, as stated earlier.) The reason why the parent does not have an obligation to teach his child *Sh'mah* is because the parent is not always with his child at the time when *Sh'mah* must be recited. The reason why the parent does not have an obligation to instruct his son to don *tefillin* is because children, even when old enough to know how to don them, very often do not treat them with sufficient respect. This is the explanation of the mishnah according to Rashi (Berachot 20a).

Rabbeinu Tam, Rashi's grandson, views the mishnah differently. His interpretation radically changes the *prima facie* reading of the mishnah. In his view, the mishnah addresses itself solely to minors at a pre-educable age. A minor who is old enough to comprehend a mitzvah must be taught how to perform the mitzvah. As the mishnah speaks of a child at a pre-educable age, it is clear that the parent is not obligated to teach his child the mitzvot of *Sh'mah* and *tefillin*. But, how does Rabbeinu Tam interpret the latter part of the mishnah? It is inconceivable that the parent of a child who is too young to comprehend the meaning of prayer, *mezuzah*, and Grace after Meals should be obligated to teach him. Rabbeinu Tam offers a daring approach to the mishnah here. The word "minors" simply does not apply. The mishnah speaks only of "women and bondsmen" as being obligated in prayer, *mezuzah*, and Grace after Meals. The word "minors" was inserted only because the Mishnah in other places generally groups together "women, bondsmen, and minors" as a single category. From the standpoint of actual law, the word "minors" could be deleted (*Tosafot, ibid.*)

The debate between Rashi and Rabbeinu Tam, each with his respective interpretation of the mishnah, is highly significant insofar as a parent's duty to train his children in reciting *Sh'mah* and donning *tefillin* is concerned. According to Rashi, a child need not be instructed to recite *Sh'mah* until he is available and accessible for daily instruction, morning and evening. As to *tefillin*, a child should not begin donning them until he is capable of treating them with proper respect. But according to Rabbeinu Tam, *Sh'mah* and *tefillin* are not different from all other mitzvot. As soon as the child is of educable age, his parent must train him to don *tefillin* and accord them due respect. And as soon as a child is old enough to comprehend the meaning of *Sh'mah*, he should be instructed in its recitation.

The Spirit of the Law

SOCIETIES DIFFER

Each society operates within its own value system and legal structure. Societies differ greatly in their mores, their juridical systems, and their ideals. One could hardly expect modern Western culture to be in total conformity with the Jewish religion, which is based upon a God-given Law and a rabbinic tradition that span some 3,500 years. There are certain fundamental issues that highlight the differences between the two cultures. These stark contrasts are dramatically reflected in their respective legal and value systems.

Modern Western society is rights-oriented. The preamble to the French Revolution was the Declaration of the Rights of Man and of the Citizen. In the dawn era of the United States, ten amendments to the Constitution, known as the Bill of Rights, were adopted. In more recent times, the struggle for women's rights has been accompanied by struggles for human rights, civil rights, minority rights, children's rights, etc. These important issues place special emphasis upon the rights of the individual and the group. Judaism, on the other hand, is duty-oriented. It is a religion based on Torah laws and mitzvot. Judaism consists of a very elaborate and intricate edifice that stands on a strong foundation of ethical-religious-legal responsibilities. Rights do play a major role within the Jewish framework, but these derive from duties and responsibilities (e.g., the rights of an employee derive from the obligations of an employer vis-a-vis the employee).

Modern Western society highly values the freedom of the individual. The individual's privacy is cherished. The tendency of the law is to avoid peering into keyholes of closed doors, unless serious criminal offences are suspected. The individual is free to conduct himself in the manner of his choice, unless his behavior is deemed harmful to others. Judaism has a different perspective. The conduct of the individual is highly regulated in all ethical, moral, and religious matters. His behavior is subject to the scrutiny of the law both in public and in private. In addition, Judaism's primary concern is the physical and spiritual welfare of society and the family unit. Society's needs supercede individual freedoms. For example, whereas in Western society giving charity to the poor is a matter of individual choice, in Torah society it is a religious obligation.

Modern Western society cherishes the concept of equality. The banner of the French Revolution read "Liberty, Equality, and Fraternity". America's Declaration of Independence proclaims: "We hold these truths to be self-evident; that all men are created equal." On the spiritual level, Judaism shares the concept of equal worth of all human beings. All people are created in God's image, regardless of race, color, or creed. On a functional level, however, Judaism does not favor equality. Halachic Judaism establishes a complex structure in which there is a clear division of labor. These divisions were more apparent and operative during Biblical and post-Biblical times. In the Temple, the *Kohain Gadol*, the High Priest, had a special function. Special tasks were assigned to the *Kohanim* and Levites. Israelites were prohibited from infringing on the special roles of their *Kohain* and Levite brethren. Halachic Judaism also established unique and distinct roles for men and women. The ideal Torah society sees each individual as a member of a group whose task is to serve the ideals of the community.

Much of the criticism directed at the role of women in halachah is based upon a Western value system. A true understanding of the issues can be acquired only if seen within the context of the Jewish legal framework and value system. Judaism does not purport to be reconcilable with Western ideals. Thus, the first step in achieving an understanding of the role of women in Judaism is to recognize the fundamental differences and unbridgeable gaps that separate Judaism from modern Western culture.

THE STATUS OF WOMEN
Woman is not a second-class citizen in Judaism. Critics and detractors of halachah point to the fact that women may not be included in a *minyan*, they may not conduct services or be called for an *aliyah* to the Torah, and are segregated from men during prayer. The woman's blessing "Who has made me according to His will" is often cited to support their argument. These claims of woman's inferior status in Judaism are spurious for two reasons: 1) they derive from the value system and legal structure of Western culture, and 2) they do not recognize the value system and legal structure of halachic Judaism.

Torah's starting point in its attitude towards woman is beautifully expressed in the story of Creation in Genesis. "And God created man in His image, in the image of God He created him, male and female He created them" (Gen. 1:27). Man and woman are created in God's image. Both are endowed with spiritual and intellectual qualities that make them God-like. The use of the singular "He created him" followed by the plural "He created them" indicates the inherent unity of man and his female counterpart.

"And the Lord God said: It is not good for man to be alone, I shall make for him a helpmate" (*ibid.*, 2:18). This verse is often misconstrued and misinterpreted as an indication of woman's lowly station in her relationship to man. The original Hebrew is far more telling than the English translation: "I shall make for him an *ezer k'negdoh*, a helpmate opposite him." Woman is not simply a helper. She is an independent personality. Her personality is not submerged in his. Man and woman share a complementary relationship. Neither is whole without the other. This is precisely why God chose to form Eve from Adam's rib. Man is incomplete without woman.

Rabbi Joseph B. Soloveitchik explains the "helpmate" concept in this manner: "A wife is needed not solely for cooperation or partnership, to lighten the burden, or for procreation, sex or love. More profoundly, it is a union of two lonely souls whose existence would be incomplete, who are individually overpowered by anxiety for reasons not logically apparent, who are ridden with self-doubt in their individual role, work or ambition. For such, marriage is an ontological fulfillment, not just utilitarian. The word *"ezer"* suggests something more pragmatically useful than the fact that 'she cooks well.' ... Adam needs human companionship. In marriage, husband and wife share common dreams (*ezer*) but she is also an opponent (*k'negdoh*), someone different, feminine, mysterious, incomprehensible. Perhaps, she's an aid (*ezer*) and fascinates him precisely because she is different, seemingly unfathomable. Men and women should not be identical copies. This is the strength of marriage; the concept of unisex is unreal and inherently self-defeating. In Genesis I, the man and woman were the same, except for *zachar v'nekevah*, 'male and female,' a physiological differentation; both are called *adam* ... Here in Genesis II, she is an *ishah*, woman, and not an *ish*, man, suggesting an ontological individuality; she is not merely a shadow of man. Through each other they find salvation and redemption" (Quoted from Rabbi Abraham Besdin's reconstruction of Rabbi Soloveitchik's lecture on Adam and Eve).

TIME-ORIENTED MITZVOT

It is a mistake to view woman's exemption from time-oriented mitzvot as discriminatory. If anything, women are exempt from these mitzvot because they do not need them. The symbolic significance of *tzitzit* and *tefillin*, for example, are vital religious reminders which men require more than women. R. Samson Raphael Hirsch, in his Torah commentary writes: "... the Torah did not impose these mitzvot on women because it did not consider them necessary to be demanded from women. All time-oriented mitzvot are meant, by symbolic procedures, to bring certain facts, principles, ideas and resolutions, afresh to our minds from time to time to spur us on afresh and to fortify us to realize them to keep them. God's Torah takes it for granted that our women have greater fervour and more faithful enthusiasm for their God-serving calling, and that this calling runs less danger in their case than in that of men from the temptations which occur in the course of business and professional life. Accordingly it does not find it necessary to give women these repeated spurring reminders to remain true to their calling, and warnings against weakness in their business lives. Thus, at the very origin of the Jewish People, God's foresight did not find it necessary to ensure their bond with Him by giving women some permanent symbol in place of *Mila* (circumcision) for men. So, also, at the Lawgiving on Sinai, God reckoned first of all (Ex. XIX, 3) on the faith and devotion of the women. So also, the Jewish Nation has established the fact — and all our generations have inherited it — that in all the sins into which our nation has sunk, it has been the faithfulness of our women to their convictions and sense of duty which has preserved and nurtured the seed of revival and return" (Hirsch *Pentateuch*, Lev., vol 2, p. 712).

DIFFERENT ROLES
From the standpoint of spiritual worth, man and woman are equal. The halachah, however, assigned different roles and responsibilites to man and woman. The wisdom of Torah and the Sages deemed a division of labor as being most beneficial to the family unit and to society as a whole. Woman is assigned the responsibility of home and family. Abudraham, in his compilation of laws and customs of prayer, explains that women are exempt from time-oriented mitzvot as these may conflict with domestic duties. She is not called upon to neglect the family to perform a time-oriented mitzvah. Her role as wife-mother-homemaker is of supreme importance when viewed in the context of Judaism's lofty regard for family and home. Man, on the other hand, is assigned a public role. His major responsibility is to contribute to the spiritual welfare of the community. He is called upon to pray with a *minyan* and to listen to the public Torah reading. He is obligated to interrupt his work schedule to perform time-oriented mitzvot.

The community role of man and the home role of woman are not exclusive. Neither is precluded from participating in the other's domain. Men not only may, but should, assist their wives in domestic responsibilities. The Talmud relates how the greatest of rabbis would assist their wives in the preparation of Shabbat. "Love thy neighbor as thyself" does not exclude one's own wife. Quite the contrary, a husband should be more considerate of his wife's needs and feelings than those of a stranger. As the Talmud says: "He who loves his wife as himself and honors her more than himself will enjoy peace" (Yevamot 62b). Women, too, are not excluded from communal activities. Though not obligated, a woman may and should pray with a congregation and participate in communal endeavors. What is important, however, is that she be mindful of her primary responsibilities. Communal participation should not be at the expense of family responsibilities.

SLAVERY

The institution of slavery is recognized by Biblical and Rabbinic law. At a time when slavery was universally practiced, it was not forbidden for Jews to own slaves. What set the Jewish people apart was the manner in which their slaves were treated. A religion that sees "the image of God" in every human being could not accept even the slave being reduced to a mere chattel. The spirit of Jewish law as it pertains to slaves is beautifully summed up by Maimonides at the conclusion of his Laws of Slaves:

"It is permitted to make a Canaanite slave work hard. Though this is permitted by law, however, it is a trait of piety and the way of wisdom that a person be compassionate and fair and not place a heavy yoke on his slave and not torment him. Rather, he should give him of all food to eat and of all drinks to drink. The Sages of old used to give their slaves from whatever food they were eating. They would feed their animals and slaves before they sat down to eat. Behold, Scripture says: 'As the eyes of slaves to the hand of their masters, as the eyes of a maidservant to the hand of her mistress' (Ps. 123:2). So, too, he should not embarrass him by lifting his hand or by using words. Scripture gave slaves for service, not for humiliation. He should not shout at him or be overly angry with him, but rather speak to him gently and listen to his complaints. So it is stated explicitly by Job, who prided himself in his good ways: 'If I did despise the cause of my slave and my maidservant when they contended with me.... Did not He who made me in the belly make him? Did He not make us in one womb?' (Job 31:13, 15).

"Cruelty and arrogance are only to be found amongst star worshippers and idol worshippers. But as for the seed of Abraham, our

Father, namely, the people of Israel, upon whom the Holy One, blessed be He, has bestowed the goodness of Torah and whom He commanded just statutes and laws, they are compassionate to all. So, too, with regard to the qualities of the Holy One, blessed be He, whom we are commanded to imitate, it is said: 'And His mercy is upon all His works' (Ps. 145:9). Whoever is himself compassionate will be treated compassionately, as it is said: 'And He will give you compassion and have compassion for you and increase you' (Deut. 13:18)" (*Mishneh Torah*, Laws of Slaves 9:8).

EDUCATION
Abraham, The First Educator
Education is one of Judaism's primary goals. From its earliest history, studying and teaching the young have been hallmarks of the Jewish way of life. The home was a veritable educational institution. The Torah records that God chose Abraham to be the founder of the Jewish nation because of his unique capacity to instill the way of God in his children and in his household: "Shall I hide from Abraham that which I plan to do; seeing that Abraham shall surely become a great and mighty nation, and all the nations of the world shall be blessed in him? For I know him, that he will command his children and his household after him, and they shall keep the way of the Lord, to do righteousness and justice" (Gen. 18:17-19). The father of the Jewish people became a parent-teacher role model for all future generations. His example provided light and spirit to his descendants. It is the strength of education that makes the Jewish people an eternal nation.

Chinuch
The "way of the Lord" is to be found in the Torah. The study of the divine Law opens the path to a life dedicated to holiness and service of God. "And you shall be unto Me a kingdom of priests and a holy nation" (Ex. 19:6) was the singular goal of the divine Revelation at Mount Sinai. That goal is to be achieved by Israel's resolute commitment to study Torah and observe the commandments. The Hebrew word for education, *chinuch*, also means dedication or consecration. The Jewish people is both dedicated and consecrated by its devotion to Torah study.

Universal Education

The Jewish perception of universal education views Torah study as a lifetime commitment for every Jew. Education was never viewed as an occupation only for the young. "Provide yourself with a teacher" (*Ethics of the Fathers* 1:6,16) applies to young and old alike. The universality of Jewish education is expressed succinctly by Maimonides: "Every Jew is obligated to study Torah; poor or rich, healthy or afflicted with pain, young or feeble with age, even a poverty-stricken beggar and even a man with wife and children — they are all obligated to set a time for Torah study by day and by night, as it is written: 'And you shall meditate therein day and night' (Joshua 1:8)" (*Mishneh Torah*, Laws of Torah Study 1:8). Torah study and proper ethical conduct are viewed by the Talmud as the most meaningful ways of expressing love for God: " 'And you shall love the Lord your God'- let the Name of Heaven be loved because of you; read Scripture, study Mishnah, cater to Torah scholars, deal honestly in business, and speak gently to people" (Yomah 86a). A lifelong pursuit of Torah knowledge helps the Jew to constantly refine and perfect his integrity and character.

Goals of Education

Jewish education has two primary goals: 1) serving God through knowledge and observance of the mitzvot, and 2) appreciating God's role in Israel's unique history. Law and history are the framework of the Jewish experience. The Jewish way of life is experienced in the study and observance of mitzvot. Jewish nationhood is experienced in an understanding and appreciation of Jewish history and destiny.

The Passover *Seder* is a most remarkable educational experience. The *Seder* brings together these two aspects of education, law and history. *Seder* means "order." On Passover eve the family joins in a prescribed ritual of prayers, songs, story-telling, and eating of symbolic foods. Each member of the family holds a *Haggadah* and shares in the Passover experience. Special emphasis is placed upon involving the children in the *Seder* ritual. A vegetable is dipped in salt water, a matzah is broken, the *Afikoman* is "stolen"; these and other customs are observed in order to arouse the curiosity of the children, who are the focus of the *Seder*. The youngest child asks the Four

Questions. The Four Sons are included in the text of the *Haggadah*. The entire *Seder* is an experiential learning experience. The Jew who eats matzah and *maror* on Passover night and relates the story of the Exodus, is spiritually linked to his ancestors who ate the same foods on the night before their departure from Egypt. On Passover night we relive the Exodus experience. "Every person should view himself as having personally left Egypt," reads the *Haggadah*. Eating the prescribed foods and experientially relating the story of the Exodus puts each Jew in touch with his Law and history.

Educating Children
Though education is the occupation of every Jew, special emphasis is placed upon teaching the young. Not only on Passover when we are enjoined by the Torah: "And you shall tell your child on that day saying: Because of this has the Lord done for me when I went out of Egypt" (Ex. 13:8), but all through the year the parent is instructed to teach his children, as it says: "And you shall teach them to your children, speaking of them when you sit at home and when you go on the way, and when you lie down and when you rise up" (Deut. 11:19). The wise King Solomon said: "Educate a child according to his way, so that even when he grows old he will not turn away from it" (Proverbs 22:6). The Torah addresses the young and reminds them of the importance of knowing their past: "Remember the days of old, understand the years of generations; ask your father and he will tell you, your elders and they will say unto you" (Deut.32:7). Parents have a duty to pass on to the next generation the experiences of the past so that the young may learn from them. The transmission of the past is the best guarantor for the future. The Psalmist writes: "O God, with our ears we have heard, our fathers have told us, the works you performed in their days and in times of old" (Ps. 44:2); "I will open my mouth with a parable, I will utter riddles concerning ancient times. What we have heard and know, our fathers have told us. We will not withold them from their children even to the latter generation, telling the praises of the Lord, His might and wonders which He has done. For He established a testimony in Jacob and placed a Torah in Israel, which He commanded our fathers to make them known to their children. So that the latter generation shall know, they will bear children, they will

arise and tell their children; that they shall place their hope in God and not forget the works of God, but keep His commandments" (Ps. 78:2-7).

Education is the key to Jewish survival. For four thousand years, each generation was taught the accumulated knowledge and wisdom of previous generations. Where the young were taught their Jewish heritage, new links were added to the unbroken chain. Where the Jewish child did not receive a proper education, the chain ended. Abraham kindled the spark of education in his children and children's children for eternity. He is a living example of the parent whose responsibility is to "command his children and his household after him." The torch of Torah knowledge was ignited by Abraham and passed down from generation to generation for two hundred generations. The crises of modern assimilation and intermarriage are greatly due to the rapid decline in religious education that began with the Enlightenment in the nineteenth century.

For the majority of Jews today in the Western world, secular education has replaced Torah education. Many Jewish parents make great sacrifices to enable their children to achieve professional degrees and titles. They are motivated by a desire to see their children financially secure and socially respected. Perhaps this is the bitter fruit of nineteen centuries of poverty and degradation. The cost of secular "overkill" is religious vacuity. Rather than attempt to strike a harmonious balance between this-worldliness and other-worldliness, many well-intentioned parents condemn their children to a fate of religious illiteracy and spiritual poverty. The tragedy is compounded by the fact that many Jewish communities offer fine yeshivot and day schools where a dual education is available. But, most Jewish families do not avail themselves of a combined education, and, the results speak for themselves.

The pioneering spirit of the modern day school system was Rabbi Samson Raphael Hirsch (1808-1888, Hamburg). Rabbi Hirsch grew up in a German Jewry whose religious light had been eclipsed by the Reform movement and the Enlightenment. Traditional Judaism was regarded as archaic and anachronistic. Modernity was the Baal of German Jewry. Liberalism and humanism were deities. The minority of Jews who desperately clung to the religion of their parents were mocked and ridiculed. Aspects of Judaism that stressed ritual observance, the singularity of the Jewish people, the centrality of the Hebrew language, and Eretz Yisrael as a homeland, were singularly dismissed as primitive and old-fashioned. It was against this tide that Rabbi Hirsch courageously fought. He was able to see, long before many of his colleagues, that the future of Jewry lay in an educational system that was capable of synthesizing Torah values and ideas with worldly knowledge. Rabbi Hirsch saw Torah as eternal Truth. The movements and "isms" of his age were temporal waves that were sweeping over Western civilization. Judaism had nothing to fear in combining Torah truths with general knowledge. On the contrary, general knowledge offered much in the way of enhancing and appreciating the depth of Torah's divine wisdom. In order to propound his views to the new generation, he established a Jewish school system that was based upon his creed, *Torah im Derech Eretz*, "The study of Torah together with general culture."

Rabbi Samson Raphael Hirsch wrote a number of brilliant essays on the subject of Jewish education. What is most striking is that his words, written over a century ago, ring as clearly and as relevantly today as they did then. He, like rabbis of today, was faced with the dilemma of parents who were satisfied with the most minimal education for their sons' Bar Mitzvah. His forceful admonition to parents is conveyed in the following words:

"Consider, moreover, what you can achieve with the few 'religious lessons' which you let your children have as an extra to their other schooling, or perhaps only in 'preparation' for their Bar Mitzvah. At best, they may absorb something, a quintessence of the Divine word, simplified and adapted to their childish minds. But suppose now they have been Bar Mitzvah — or, as you would prefer to call it, 'confirmed' — and have successfully passed their public examination without their memories playing tricks with them so that answer B is trotted out in reply to question A; suppose the 'Articles of Faith' have been recited with childish feeling, uncles and cousins have expressed their congratulations, the religion copy-books have been gratefully put aside and the teacher of 'religion' has been suitably thanked — can you, Jewish father, stand before your God and say 'Blessed be He Who hath released me from responsibility for this boy'? Can you face your Father in heaven and say that you have discharged your duty as a father on earth, that you have made your child proof against all the struggles and temptations that await him? Can you claim that the responsibility is not yours if your child should in later years treat religion and morality with scorn; if he should be found wanting in his struggle with his desires and appetites, with error and delusion; if in his manhood he should deny the faith he learnt in his childhood lessons of religion? Can you assert that you are free from responsibility because you offered him all the means of knowledge and enlightenment, of sanctity and salvation for every Jew, which God has placed in your hands? That you cannot, Jewish father! That you cannot, because you considered 'religious instruction' as necessary only in the years of childhood, whereas Jewish religious instruction should in fact last as long as life itself, and both the young and the old should attend the school of God and of His prophets and Sages. You, however, did not open the mind of your child to understand the voice of his God, the language of his prophets, or the teachings of the Sages and his people.

"That you cannot do, because, though you gave your child all kinds of books and copy-books, the 'Book of books' remained a closed book to him. The purpose of this 'Book' is not to provide pretty sayings, nice adages for children, but to address words of fire to the growing youth, words of wisdom to the man, and words of Divine comfort to the aged, and to complete the education for living toward which your religious instruction made hardly a beginning.

"That you cannot do, because, though you gave your child all kinds of teachers, including the religious teachers, these trained your child to remain perpetually a spiritual minor, and accustomed him to use his teachers of religion as middlemen between himself and the Divine word throughout his life, to look up to them as his 'priests' and 'clergymen' who alone are privileged to approach the Divine word as the Holiest of Holies and to purvey some of it to the people — if indeed they come to hear it! They failed to lead your child to the source, to teach him at all times himself to drink of the eternal spring of life. They did not teach him to study for himself the words of God, of Moses, David and Isaiah, of Hillel and Shammai, Abbaye and Rava, Yehuda Halevi, and Caro; they did not make the Torah a Well of Miriam which would accompany your child through the wilderness of life even without their assistance; they kept the priestly sanctity to themselves and did not educate your child to be a son of the holy nation, of the kingdom of priests."

Rabbi Hirsch was well aware of the powerful motivation of Jewish parents to provide their children with a secular education. He was sensitive to the indictment of the education that produced a "ghetto" mentality. But he offered an alternative -

"But is it impossible. Our children have to study so much and such diverse subjects. We no longer live in the narrow confines of the ghetto. We move freely and our children will move more freely still; life now makes far greater demands on the educated man, in whose education and upbringing there is no room for 'Hebrew' instructions as it was given of old. Should our children be inferior to their contemporaries in knowledge and education? Should they not be equals in the languages and sciences? Should they perhaps retain the narrow outlook of the old ghetto? Should they forego the intellectual advantages of modern times?

"No, they should not!

"If, of course, they had to do so—if we had no other alternative but either to let our children remain ignorant of all knowledge which converts a Jew by birth into a Jew spiritually, or to let them do without much of the benefit of the new learning—we should not hesitate for a minute, in the face of the opposition of many of our contemporaries, to declare that we as Jews had to forgo intellectual advantages which could be acquired only at the expense of the Jewish spirit of our children. Our forefathers had to sacrifice much more for their Judaism. For us, too, it would be Judaism first, and then secular education. When we carried our little sons in our arms on the day of their Abrahamic dedication (circumcision) we vowed to God to bring them up as Jews. Our friends pronounced the customary blessings and good wishes, they prayed that the child should grow up to acquire first Torah and only then matrimony and good deeds. All their education, all their training for life's business has value, value and significance before God, only if their intellectual education rests on the broad basis of the Divine teachings and if their life is rooted in the Divine soil of Judaism. Indeed, just because our children move more freely, and will move more freely still, in the world at large, just because our children will be in closer and often more conflicting contact than their fathers with the education, views, principles and attitudes of non-Jewish minds, their need is the greater for a good Jewish education, so that they may learn consciously to know and value their Judaism; so that they may know the light and the truth which shines from it; so that they may taste of the glories which the chosen spirits of the age-long Jewish past have bequeathed to them. They must not be allowed to think that only elsewhere will they find the light and life for which their hearts and minds are yearning, while the holiness they see at home is dark and dismal. ... Our children need not forgo any of the advantages of a genuinely humanistic education, any of the fruits of knowledge and learning, in order to acquire the truths and the wisdom and the life-treasures of Judaism. Pursued hand in hand, there is room for both; each enhancing the value of the other and producing the glorious fruit of a distinctive Jewish culture which, at the same time 'is pleasant in the eyes of God and man' " (*Judaism Eternal*, Dayan I. Grunfeld, The Soncino Press, 1956, pp. 167-170).

The primary responsibility of educating the young rests with the parents. For many centuries, education was the domain of the home. "And you shall teach them to your children to speak of them" (Deut. 11:19) was practiced in a literal fashion. At the end of the Second Temple period, however, in the first century C.E., an elaborate school system was established that guaranteed universal religious education. The person responsible for this major development was a high priest named R. Joshua ben Gamla. "R. Judah said in the name of Rav: 'Truly, remember that man for good, and his name is R. Joshua ben Gamla. If it were not for him, Torah would have been forgotten from Israel. Originally, if a child had a father, his father taught him. Whoever did not have a father did not learn. So an enactment was passed that teachers be appointed in Jerusalem. But (the problem persisted because) whoever had a father was brought to Jerusalem, and whoever did not have a father did not study. Then they enacted that teachers be appointed in every district and students begin their education at age sixteen or seventeen. (This did not work because) those whose teachers got angry at them would rebel and leave. (This persisted) until Joshua ben Gamla enacted that teachers be appointed in every province and in every town, and that children begin their schooling at the age of six or seven' " (Bava Batra 21a).

The groundwork laid by R. Joshua ben Gamla remains intact to this very day. In almost every sizeable Jewish community there is at least one day school. Though we may bemoan the small percentage of Jewish children who actually attend these schools, the fact that they exist is a major accomplishment. The Torah U'Mesorah movement is to be greatly credited for the proliferation of day schools in the United States and Canada. One of the serious obstacles to increased enrollment is the heavy burden of tuition parents must pay to support their child's school. The burden of tuition for families with more than one child in school is often onerous. Is it any wonder that day school tuition has been termed "Jewish birth control"? It is vital for Jewish communities to share the burden by encouraging broader support for local day schools, and thereby relieving the parents of some of the financial pressure. Parents whose children no longer attend day school, and even parents whose children are in public school, will ultimately benefit from a stronger, more committed Jewish community.

Chafetz Chaim's Advice to Parents
Rabbi Israel Meir Ha-Kohen (1838-1933) was one of the most saintly figures in modern times. From the small village of Radun in Grodno, Poland, his reputation of piety spread throughout the world. Rabbi Israel Meir is universally known as the *Chafetz Chaim* (one who desires life), after the name of his first book. The title is based on the verse in Psalms: "Who is the man who desires life, who loves days that he may see good? Guard your tongue from evil and your lips from speaking guile. Depart from evil and do good, seek peace and pursue it" (Ps. 34: 13-15). These words of counsel guided the *Chafetz Chaim's* every word and deed. His famous book *Chafetz Chaim* is devoted entirely to the evils of gossip, slander and talebearing. Even today, the *Chafetz Chaim* is a living symbol of the sanctity of the spoken word.

My teacher, the late Rabbi Avigdor Cyperstein, of blessed memory, related that when the *Chafetz Chaim* was in his early sixties he became very ill. The doctors told him that his illness was terminal and he had but a short time to live. Upon hearing the medical report, the *Chafetz Chaim* retired to his room and began to pray. His devoted students who were standing in the adjoining room overheard his words intermingled with sobs: "Lord of the universe, all my life I have preached and taught the importance of guarding one's tongue from evil. I have taught that he who avoids slander and gossip will be granted a long life, as in the words of the Psalms: 'Who is the man who desires life ....' If you take me now, people will say that Scripture is not true, even the *Chafetz Chaim* was not granted a long life. Please give me a few more years that I may be a living testimony to the blessing granted to a person who avoids spreading evil of others."

The Chafetz Chaim lived for more than another thirty years, dying at the age of 95.

The most widely studied commentary on the *Orach Chaim* section of the *Shulchan Aruch* is the *Chafetz Chaim's* six-volume commentary known as the *Mishnah B'rurah*. The *Mishnah B'rurah* is an indispensable work on practical, everyday halachah. In his commentary, the *Chafetz Chaim* wrote the following words of advice and halachic guidelines for parents:

"If a person hears his young son or daughter speaking gossip, he should scold them and tell them to stop, and so with quarreling, lying, and cursing. In our multitude of sins, some people fail in this matter. They also allow their children to speak gossip, talebear, and curse to the extent that they become so used to it that when they grow up and someone tells them that it is greatly forbidden, it is difficult for them to break this habit of many years. They consider it perfectly permissible.

"Know that the guidelines for educating a child in performing positive commandments depends upon his intelligence and knowledge of each individual matter. For example, a child who understands the concept of Shabbat must be trained to hear Kiddush and Havdalah. A child who knows how to wear *tzitzit* is obligated to wear them. This is true for Biblical, as well as rabbinic positive commandments.

"As far as negative commandments are concerned, be they of Biblical or rabbinic origin, education begins as soon as the child is able to understand that such and such is forbidden to do or eat. But if a child has no understanding at all, his father is not obligated to forceably prevent him from eating forbidden foods or desecrating Shabbat, even if forbidden by the Torah, since he does not comprehend why he is being punished" (*Mishnah B'rurah, Orach Chaim* 343 no. 3).

The Practical Law

WOMEN AND PRAYER

1. The following prayers are the minimum that a woman is required to recite daily:

a) The blessing *ahl n'tilat yadayim* (for the washing of the hands).

b) The blessing *asher yahtzar* (after going to the bathroom).

c) The blessings on the Torah.

d) The morning blessings.

e) The first verse of *Sh'mah*.

f) One verse that recalls the Exodus from Egypt (the last verse of *Sh'mah*).

g) As to the *Amidah*, there are differing opinions. One opinion says that any petition of the Almighty is sufficient. Others require the *Amidah* of *Shacharit* and *Minchah* to be recited. Still others require the *Amidah* of *Arvit*, as well.

This is the minimum. It is, however, praiseworthy to pray additional prayers (*Am K'lahvee*, R. Shlomo Aviner, pp. 32-33).

The *Mishnah B'rurah* adds that women must also recite the blessing *emet v'yatziv* in order to link redemption with the *Amidah*. It is a subject of debate as to whether women are obligated to recite Mussaf or not (*Orach Chaim* 106:1, *Mishnah B'rurah* 4). In addition, *P'sukay d'zimrah* is required to be said, according to R. Akiva Eiger (*Orach Chaim* 70:1, *Mishnah B'rurah* 2).

2. Women are obligated to recite Grace after Meals. It is uncertain as to whether their obligation is of rabbinic or Biblical origin. Therefore, they may not fulfill the obligation for a man who has eaten to satiation and whose obligation is of Biblical origin (*Orach Chaim* 186:1).

If a woman forgot if she recited Grace or not, some authorities require her to recite Grace, while others say she should not (*ibid., Mishnah B'rurah* 3).

MINORS

1. Minors prior to educable age need not be instructed to recite *Sh'mah*. Educable-aged children must be instructed to recite *Sh'mah* twice daily (*Orach Chaim* 70:2).

2. Children aged 6-7 years old are considered of educable age (*Mishnah B'rurah, ibid.*, 6).

3. A minor may not wear *tefillin*. He must begin wearing *tefillin* when he is Bar Mitzvah (13 years and a day old) (*Ramah, Orach Chaim* 37:3).
4. It is now customary for a minor to begin wearing *tefillin* two or three months before his Bar Mitzvah (*ibid., Mishnah B'rurah* 12).
5. A minor of educable age must be taught to pray the *Amidah* three times daily (*Orach Chaim* 106:1).
6. A minor of educable age must be instructed to recite Grace after Meals (*ibid.*, 186:2).

CHAPTER 3: *Mishnah 4*   189

Mishnah 4   משנה ד

A *ba'al keri*[1] meditates in his mind.[2] He does not recite[3] the blessings before it[4] and after it.[4] He blesses after eating,[5] but not before.[6] R. Judah says: He blesses before them[7] and after them.[7]

בַּעַל קֶרִי מְהַרְהֵר בְּלִבּוֹ וְאֵינוֹ מְבָרֵךְ לֹא לְפָנֶיהָ וְלֹא לְאַחֲרֶיהָ. וְעַל הַמָּזוֹן מְבָרֵךְ לְאַחֲרָיו וְאֵינוֹ מְבָרֵךְ לְפָנָיו. רַבִּי יְהוּדָה אוֹמֵר: מְבָרֵךְ לִפְנֵיהֶם וּלְאַחֲרֵיהֶם:

1. *BA'AL KERI* — A person who had a seminal emission due to sexual intercourse or any other reason.
2. MEDITATES IN HIS MIND — He does not verbalize the words of *Sh'mah*, but rather contemplates them in his mind.
3. DOES NOT RECITE — Nor contemplate.
4. IT — *Sh'mah*.
5. AFTER EATING — The Grace after Meals is to be contemplated but not recited.
6. NOT BEFORE — The blessing before the meal, even through contemplation.
7. THEM — *Sh'mah* and Grace after Meals. The blessings before and after *Sh'mah* and the blessings of Grace after Meals are to be recited. *Sh'mah* itself must certainly be recited.

The Letter of the Law

HISTORICAL BACKGROUND

This mishnah is based upon one of the many edicts passed by Ezra the Scribe. Ezra played a major role in the spiritual rehabilitation of the Jewish community in Eretz Yisrael after the return of the Babylonian exile in the fifth century B.C.E. The Jewish community was small in number, beset by hostile neighbors, economically impoverished and militarily weak. While his counterpart, Nehemiah, worked on the physical reconstruction of Jerusalem's walls, Ezra built a Torah foundation for his people. He bravely waged a successful war against rampant intermarriage. His weapon was the enlightenment of Torah knowledge. So successful a teacher was he, that later generations ascribed to him the attribute of Moses, "If Moses had not preceded him, Ezra would have received the Torah" (*Toseftah*, Sanhedrin 4:7). He brought Torah to the masses by instituting public Torah readings on Shabbat afternoons and on Mondays and Thursdays. A widespread educational system was established with the opening of numerous schools.

Amongst his many enactments, Ezra decreed that Torah study be forbidden after sexual intercourse, or after any seminal emission, until immersion in a *mikveh*. This decree had nothing to do with the laws of purity and impurity. Torah is not subject to impurity, as stated by R. Judah ben Betayrah, "The words of Torah cannot become impure." The Talmud relates that a student who had experienced a seminal emission was stuttering on words of Torah in the presence of R. Judah ben Betayrah. The rabbi lovingly coaxed the student with the following words: "My son, open your mouth and your words will shine. The words of Torah cannot become impure, as it is written, 'Is not my Word like fire, says the Lord?' (Jeremiah 23:29). Just as fire cannot become impure, so too, the words of Torah cannot become impure" (Berachot 22a). Why then the need for ritual immersion after a seminal emission? Apparently Ezra wished to discourage his students' sexual activities so that their libidinal energies would be channeled into intensive Torah study. In the words of the Talmud: "So that scholars should not be with their wives like roosters" (*ibid*.). Like so many decrees, however, that were too demanding and ultimately fell by the wayside, this decree, too, was eventually nullified. The strict adherence to this decree resulted in two unacceptable results. Some students, in their devotion to Torah study, neglected their wives and failed to fulfill the mitzvah to "be fruitful and multiply." Others chose to remain unimmersed and, as a result, were banned from Torah study. These negative results, combined with the fact that this law was never fully accepted by the Jewish people as a whole, brought a repeal of Ezra's prohibition.

TWO INTERPRETATIONS OF THE MISHNAH
The *Tannah Kamah* (first opinion) distinguishes between *Sh'mah* and

Grace after Meals which are Biblical commandments, and the blessings of *Sh'mah* and the blessing before the meal, which are rabbinic commandments. According to the *Tannah Kamah*, Ezra's decree included prayer, as well as Torah study. Prayers prescribed by the Torah, however, must be mentally contemplated. Only reciting them verbally is forbidden. Rabbinic prayers are not required to be mentally contemplated.

R. Judah disagrees with the basic premise of the *Tannah Kamah*. In his opinion, Ezra's decree did not extend to prayer, but was limited strictly to Torah study. Therefore, all prayers, Biblical and rabbinic, must be recited.

Rabbi Akiva Eiger raises an interesting point concerning the *Tannah Kamah*'s opinion. Grace after Meals contains three blessings of Biblical origin, and a fourth blessing which is of rabbinic origin. Should not the fourth blessing be omitted from contemplation, as well? He concludes that since the mishnah did not distinguish between the first three and the fourth blessing, it too must be recited. Apparently, the Rabbis decreed that whenever Grace after Meals is recited, the fourth blessing must be included. The fourth blessing is an integral part of Grace after Meals, even though it is of rabbinic origin.

The Jerusalem Talmud interprets the mishnah differently. There is no dispute between the *Tannah Kamah* and R. Judah concerning prayers of Biblical origin. These must be recited in the usual manner. They disagree, however, with regard to blessings of rabbinic origin. According to the *Tannah Kamah*, these may only be contemplated. According to R. Judah, rabbinic prayers, as well, were not included in Ezra's decree and must be recited in the usual manner. According to this interpretation, there is no reference to *Sh'mah* in the mishnah, which refers only to its blessings (*Sh'note Eliyahu*).

The Spirit of the Law
SEVERE DECREES
Rabbinic decrees are designed to safeguard and strengthen the observance of Torah laws. (See 1:1, "Spirit of the Law," no. 4). The Sages of every generation are empowered by the Torah to use their good judgment in shoring up those areas of observance that are being neglected by the people. In Temple times, they saw fit to patch the cracks in the

observance of the purity laws. Many decrees were also issued to strengthen moral behavior. In certain points in history, emphasis was placed upon ethical conduct. In this manner, the rabbinic guardians of the Torah have been directly responsible for the perpetuation of Torah observance for the past three and a half millenia.

Rabbinic authority enjoys a good deal of power. This power, however, is not absolute. The Jewish checks and balances system prevents rabbinic authority from becoming too harsh and oppresive. Rabbinic authority is bound by an important rule: "No decree may be decreed unless most people can observe it" (Bava Batrah 60b). Maimonides writes in his *Mishneh Torah*: "Any court that wishes to issue a decree or enact an enactment or establish a custom must first consider whether or not the majority of the community is able to observe it. No decree may be decreed unless the majority of the community can observe it" (Laws of Rebellious Ones 2:5).

The Talmud derives this limitation of rabbinic power from a Scriptural source. The prophet Malachi admonishes his people for not observing the rabbinic decree of bringing tithes to the Temple storehouse: "You are cursed with a curse for you have robbed Me, this entire nation. Bring all the tithes to the storehouse so that there will be food in My house..." (Malachi 3:9-10). This verse is interpreted to mean: The entire nation had accepted the decree, upon threat of curse, to bring their tithes to the Temple. From this we derive the principle that a rabbinic decree must be accepted by the "entire nation" in order to be in force (Bava Batrah 60b).

We find several examples in the Talmud where rabbinic decrees were invalidated because most people were not able to observe them:

1) The Biblical Daniel decreed that oil belonging to Gentiles may not be used. His prohibition never became widespread and was nullified, because it was a decree which most people could not observe (Avodah Zarah 36a).

2) After the destruction of the Second Temple, many Pharisees expressed mourning by not eating meat and not drinking wine. R. Joshua asked them why they no longer partake of meat and wine. Their answer: "Shall we eat meat that was sacrificed on the Altar? Shall we drink wine that was poured on the Altar?" R. Joshua responded: "If so, you should not eat bread because the *Mincha* offering consisted of

bread." They said: "Then we shall not eat bread." R. Joshua continued: "You should also give up eating fruits because we no longer bring the *bikkurim* (first fruits)." They said: "Correct, we will not eat the seven species of fruits which were brought as *bikkurim*, but we will eat other fruits." "Then you must also stop drinking water because we no longer have the water libations," said R. Joshua. This time they had no answer. They were silent. Logic dictated that if they were to be consistent, they must give up the basic necessities of life in order to mourn for the Temple. But how were they to survive without bread and water? R. Joshua concluded: "My children, come and I will tell you what to do. It is not conceivable that we shall not mourn for the Temple. On the other hand, we may not mourn excessively, because no decree may be enacted unless most people can observe it. The Sages therefore said: When a person whitewashes his house he should leave a small section untouched in order to remember the Temple" (Bava Batrah 60b).

3) It is forbidden to raise small cattle in the cultivated parts of Eretz Yisrael because they eat the crops. Large cattle would have been included in the prohibition, as well. It was, however, possible to import small cattle from outside Eretz Yisrael, but not large cattle. Prohibiting the raising of large cattle would have been a decree that most people could not observe. Thus, the prohibition was limited to small cattle (Bava Kamah 79b).

4) A person who violated the Sabbatical year by plowing his field may not sow that field after the Sabbatical year. If he went ahead and sowed his field anyway, the produce is not forbidden, because it would be a decree that most people would not be able to observe (Jerusalem Talmud, Sh'vee'it 4:2).

The Practical Law

1. One who had a seminal emission is permitted to study Torah, recite *Sh'mah*, and pray. Such is the widespread practice (*Orach Chaim* 88:1).
2. There are pious people who still observe Ezra's enactment and immerse in a *mikveh* after a seminal emmision (*ibid., Mishnah B'rurah* No. 4).

Mishnah 5

משנה ה

If one, while standing and praying Tefillah,[1] reminded himself that he is a *ba'al keri*, he should not stop but should abbreviate.[2] If one[3] descended to ritually immerse himself[4] — if there is time to ascend and cover himself and recite[5] before sunrise[6] — let him cover himself and recite. If not, let him cover himself with the water[7] and recite. But, he may not cover himself with polluted water,[8] nor with steeping water[9] until he has spilled water into it.[10] How far must he distance himself

הָיָה עוֹמֵד בַּתְּפִלָּה, וְנִזְכַּר שֶׁהוּא בַעַל קֶרִי — לֹא יַפְסִיק, אֶלָּא יְקַצֵּר. יָרַד לִטְבּוֹל — אִם יָכוֹל לַעֲלוֹת וּלְהִתְכַּסּוֹת וְלִקְרוֹת עַד שֶׁלֹּא תָנֵץ הַחַמָּה, יַעֲלֶה וְיִתְכַּסֶּה וְיִקְרָא; וְאִם לָאו — יִתְכַּסֶּה בַּמַּיִם וְיִקְרָא. אֲבָל לֹא יִתְכַּסֶּה, לֹא בַמַּיִם הָרָעִים וְלֹא בְּמֵי הַמִּשְׁרָה, עַד שֶׁיַּטִּיל לְתוֹכָן מָיִם.

1. TEFILLAH — The *Amidah*, or *Sh'moneh Esray*.
2. ABBREVIATE — The blessings by reciting only the beginning and end of each blessing, omitting the middle part.
3. ONE — A *ba'al keri*.
4. IMMERSE HIMSELF — In a *mikveh*.
5. RECITE — *Sh'mah*.
6. BEFORE SUNRISE — As is the practice of the *vatikin*, those who recite *Sh'mah* before sunrise.
7. THE WATER — Up to his neck, provided that the water is not clear and his nakedness cannot be seen. If the water is clear, he is not covered.
8. POLLUTED WATER — Bad smelling.
9. STEEPING WATER — Water used for soaking flax which is malodorous.
10. SPILLED WATER INTO IT — The Talmud amends the text to read: "He may not recite near urine until he has spilled water into it." It must be diluted with at least a *r'vee'it* (between three and four ounces) of water.

CHAPTER 3: *Mishnah 5*

from it[11] and from feces? Four cubits.[12]

וְכַמָּה יַרְחִיק מֵהֶם וּמִן הַצּוֹאָה? אַרְבַּע אַמּוֹת:

11. FROM IT — From bad-smelling water. Some interpret, from urine which has not been diluted.

12. FOUR CUBITS — About six or seven feet. A distance of four cubits suffices if the feces is not in view. If it is in view in front of him, even beyond four cubits, he may not recite *Sh'mah* or pray.

The Letter of the Law

THE *BA'AL KERI* AND PRAYER
(See previous mishnah).

The laws in this mishnah are based upon the following verse: "Your camps shall be holy, that He see no sort of nakedness and turn Himself away from you" (Deut. 23:15). Though the context of the verse deals with pure and holy conduct in a military situation, the laws apply to general situations, as well. This is alluded to, says Rabbi Samson Raphael Hirsch, by the use of the plural "camps," which implies an army camp and any other place where Jews may settle.

The sanctity of Torah study and prayer requires that these activities be performed in a holy and clean environment. Where there is filth or nakedness there can be no holiness. Many laws of holiness are derived from this verse: "It is permitted to think of words of Torah everywhere except in a bathouse and a bathroom, as it is written: 'Your camps shall be holy' " (Shabbat 150a). " 'Your camps shall be holy,' from here they derived that a person should not recite *Sh'mah* next to dirty laundry, nor should he enter a bathouse or a tannery with holy books or *tefillin* in his hand, nor should he enter the Temple Mount carrying his staff, wearing shoes, or with dust on his feet" (*Sifre*). "It is forbidden to recite *Sh'mah* (even) in the presence of excrement that is passing by because the Torah says: 'Your camps shall be holy' " (Berachot 25a). "A pious Jew once asked Elijah: 'May a person who is naked recite *Sh'mah*?' He replied: 'That He see no sort of nakedness — naked speech' (*ervat davar* is interpreted as *ervat dibur*, 'naked speech')" (Jerusalem Talmud, Terumot 1:4).

"Your camps shall be holy" should be seen in the context of the passage in which it is found: "When you go forth to encamp against your enemies, you shall guard yourself against anything that is evil. If there be among you any man who is not pure through that which chances him at night, he shall go out of the camp, he shall not come into the midst of the camp. It shall be when evening comes, he shall bathe himself in water, and when the sun sets he may enter into the midst of the camp. You shall have a spade with your equipment so that when you sit down outside you shall dig with it and turn back and cover your excrement. For the Lord your God walks in the midst of your camps to save you and to give up your enemies before you; your camps shall be holy, that He see no sort of nakedness and turn Himself away from you" (Deut. 23:10-15).

"For the Lord your God walks in the midst of your camps" is interpreted by Rashbam and other commentators to refer to the Holy Ark which accompanied the Jewish army to war. The Holy Ark was a visible reminder of God's presence in time of combat. The soldier was to be constantly aware of the fact that victory will come "Not with might nor with strength, but with My spirit, says the Lord of Hosts" (Zechariah 4:6). The laws of holiness and purity, which keep away all that is unholy and unclean, make the Jewish army camp a suitable dwelling place for the Divine Presence. The Divine Presence resides not only in the army camp, but in every place in which a Jew prays or studies Torah. Thus, there may be no foulness, excrement, or nakedness in the place of prayer or Torah study.

The Spirit of the Law

"YOUR CAMPS SHALL BE HOLY"
One of Judaism's most lofty concepts is the sanctification of life. The world in which we live is a composite of two elements, physical and spiritual. These elements do not represent an irreconcilable duality. They are not opposing forces in constant strife with each other, rather, they complement each other. The physical serves the spiritual and the spiritual elevates the physical. The supreme challenge of Torah living is to combine the physical with the spiritual; to make holy that which is not yet holy.

CHAPTER 3: *Mishnah 5* 197

The Jewish concept of holiness separates Judaism from other religions and philosophies. Thinkers and theologians of all ages have dealt with the idea of the sacred and the profane. Most often, they saw the two as incompatible realms. The pagan world dealt with the problem by deifying nature. The sun, the moon, rivers, trees, mountains, birds, snakes, animals, etc., were worshipped as divine entities. The glorification of nature took on a special emphasis in ancient Greece. Greek art, which stressed the nude figure, was a paean to the gods. "No other religion — possibly excepting Catholicism — has so stimulated and influenced literature and art: almost every book or play, statue or building or vase, that has come down to us from ancient Greece touches upon religion in subject, purpose or inspiration" (*The Story of Civilization*, vol. II, Will Durant, Simon and Schuster Publ., 1966, p.217).

Christianity developed in reaction to the Greek and Roman emphasis upon the physical and the sensual. The body, once glorified, was viewed as the source of evil and sin. Denial of bodily pleasure became the highest virtue. "Holy" men and women were those who practiced celibacy and took vows of poverty. Spirituality can be achieved only by denial of the physical. The physical and the spiritual can never be harmonized or synthesized.

Judaism sees no duality in the physical and the spiritual, because all of existence derives from God's absolute unity. This idea is expounded in the Kabbalah, in Chasidic writings, and, in more recent times, in the writings of Rabbi Kook. Holiness resides in all of nature. There is no "holy and profane." Rather, there is the holy and the holy-in-potential. The Jew's task on earth is to elevate the physical world, to release the "sparks" of holiness that are concealed in nature. By living a life of mitzvot, the Jew sanctifies the world in which he lives. Eating is raised from the animal level with the sanctification of the hands and the recitation of a blessing. Sex is elevated from a biological need when it is viewed as the fusion of two souls within the context of marriage (*kiddushin*, i.e., sanctification). Nature, with its biological and physical aspects, provides man with a unique opportunity to spiritually elevate himself and the world in which he lives.

The path to holiness is paved with mitzvot. Every mitzvah that a Jew performs elevates him to a higher spiritual rung. Before performing a mitzvah, a Jew recites the blessing: "Blessed are You... who has sanctified us with His commandments...." Commandments have the power to sanctify because these are the deeds that link the Commander with the commanded. A Jew donning *tefillin*, for example, feels a personal connection with God. As he binds the leather straps around his arm and head, he feels bound up with the Divine Presence. When he envelops himself in a *tallit*, he feels enwrapped by God's love. When he sanctifies Shabbat, he enters a sacred dimension of time. Each mitzvah, in a similar fashion, raises the individual from the mundane to the holy. In the words of our Sages: "When the Almighty establishes a mitzvah for Israel he increases their holiness" (*Mechiltah*, Ex. 22).

Holiness is also acquired by refraining from that which is forbidden. *Kedushah*, "holiness," is defined as separation. "And the Lord spoke unto Moses saying: Speak to the entire congregation of the Children of Israel, and say to them, You shall be holy; for I, the Lord your God, am holy" (Lev. 19:1-2). Rashi interprets the verse to mean: "Separate yourselves from immorality and sin." Rashi views the commandment to be holy as a continuation of the previous chapter, which speaks of the laws of immorality.

Nachmanides gives a broader definition of "You shall be holy." He interprets this commandment to mean that a Jew must practice self-restraint even in matters which are permitted to him. Overindulgence and excessive pleasure-seeking prevent the attainment of holiness. He writes: "The Torah has admonished us against immorality and forbidden foods, but permitted sexual intercourse between man and his wife, and the eating of certain meat and wine. If so, a man of desire could consider this to be permission to be passionately addicted to sexual intercourse with his wife... and speak freely of all profanities, since this prohibition has not been expressly mentioned in the Torah, and thus he will become a sordid person within the permissible realm of the Torah!" (translation by Charles B. Chavel, Shilo, 1974). Nachmanides suggests that a person should strive for holiness by practicing moderation in matters which are permitted. He should not overly indulge in sexual intercourse (as the Sages advised: "So that Torah scholars should not be with their wives like roosters" [Berachot 22a]), he should drink wine in moderation, avoid impurity, guard his mouth and tongue from excessive eating and lewd talk, and practice personal cleanliness and hygiene.

CLEANLINESS AND GODLINESS
Cleanliness does lead to godliness. In the words of the Sages: "Purity leads to holiness, and holiness leads to humility" (Jerusalem Talmud, Sh'kalim 3:3). Hillel the Elder used to take leave of his students by telling them that he was going off to perform a mitzvah. "What mitzvah?" they would ask. "To take a bath," he would answer. Hillel explained the importance of bathing and personal hygiene in the following manner: "If the icons of kings which are erected in the theaters and circuses are scoured and washed by the person appointed to look after them, and, he, as a result, is paid, and even privileged to be in the company of the great men of the kingdom — how much more so I, who have been created in the image and likeness; as it is written, 'For in the image of God made He man' (Gen. 9:6)." (*Lev. Rabbah* 34:3). Rabbi Elazar states: "let a man always consider himself as though the Holy One dwells within him" (Ta'anit 11a-b). The human body is the sanctuary of the Divine Presence. Self-respect and self-dignity go hand in hand with respect for the Almighty, and more so during prayer and Torah study when we commune with the divine that dwells within. That is why the halachah rules that a person must wash his hands before praying and a *kohain* with soiled hands may not recite the priestly blessing, as it says: "Lift up your hands in holiness and bless the Lord" (Ps. 134:2).

The commandment "Be holy" is unique in that it pervades every aspect of life. It is a mitzvah that is not limited to a single ritual or deed. It governs our conduct in private and in public. It teaches self-restraint and moderation. It ensures good health and personal hygiene. It is a mitzvah that escorts the Jew in all walks of life. Even in a place that is most likely to be devoid of holiness, such as an army camp, where the pressures of war make men lose sight of civil behavior, the Torah insists: "Your camps shall be holy."

The Practical Law

1. If a person is bathing nude in clear water and wishes to drink, he must cover the lower part of his body with a garment before making a blessing (*Orach Chaim* 74:2). He may also fold his arms so that his "heart does not see his nakedness" (*ibid.*, 3).

2. He must also cover his head, but not with his hand (*Mishnah B'rurah, ibid.*, no. 8).

3. If the water is muddy, he need not cover himself to pray, provided there is no foul smell (*ibid.*).

4. It is forbidden to recite *Sh'mah* in the presence of urine unless he spills at least a *r'vee'it* of water on it (*ibid.*, 77:1).

5. It is forbidden to pray in view of human feces. If the feces is behind him, he may pray as long as he is at least four cubits out of range of the smell (*ibid.*, 79:1).

6. It is forbidden to pray where there is a foul odor caused by rancid or polluted water (*ibid.*, 86).

Mishnah 6

A *zav*[1] who had a seminal discharge, a menstruant who discharged semen,[2] and a woman who had sexual intercourse and then became menstruant, require ritual immersion.[3] R. Judah exempts them.[4]

זָב שֶׁרָאָה קֶרִי, וְנִדָּה שֶׁפָּלְטָה שִׁכְבַת זֶרַע, וְהַמְשַׁמֶּשֶׁת שֶׁרָאֲתָה נִדָּה — צְרִיכִין טְבִילָה. וְרַבִּי יְהוּדָה פּוֹטֵר:

1. ZAV — A man who had a seminal flux associated with illness. Nachmanides, in his Torah commentary, describes it as a serious contagious disease. Some translators associate it with gonorrhea.
2. WHO DISCHARGED SEMEN — Having had intercourse before the onset of her menstrual period. A discharge of semen within three days of intercourse causes impurity.
3. REQUIRE RITUAL IMMERSION — Before studying Torah and praying.
4. EXEMPTS THEM — From ritual immersion.

The Letter of the Law

The mishnah applies to the time when Ezra's enactment was observed.

The *zav* and the *niddah* (menstruant woman) are in a state of impurity (*tumah*). Both remain in a state of impurity for a period of seven days, after which they must ritually immerse in a *mikveh* to become pure (*tahor*). If a man has a seminal emission, or if a woman discharges semen after intercourse, their state of impurity lasts only until nightfall, after which they immerse and are pure. In short, the state of impurity caused by semen lasts for one day, while that of a flux or menstruation lasts for seven days.

It would seem logical, prima facie, that if one is rendered impure because of semen (a man who had an emission or a woman who discharged semen after intercourse) and has an additional impurity which lasts for seven days (*zav* or *niddah*), immersion for the semen would not permit Torah study and prayer because the other impurity still remains. Such is not the case. The mishnah establishes the principle that Ezra's enactment applies only to semen. Other impurities have no bearing whatsoever on the permissibility to pray and study Torah. Thus, a person should immerse to relieve the semen impurity even while remaining in a state of impurity due to other causes. The reason for this principle is because Ezra's enactment was not based on the laws of impurity. As explained earlier (mishnah 4), Torah cannot become impure. His enactment was rather intended to prevent overindulgence in sexual activity on the part of scholars. The state of impurity of the *zav* and the *niddah*, therefore, has no bearing on Ezra's enactment.

R. Judah disagrees. He contends that immersion for a lesser impurity makes no sense if the greater impurity still remains. Thus, no ritual immersion is required in all the cases listed in the mishnah. The Talmud takes R. Judah's opinion one step further. Even if a person had a seminal emission, at which time the obligation to immerse begins, and later contracted a greater impurity, he no longer is obligated to immerse for the seminal impurity (Berachot 26a).

It must be noted that R. Judah disagrees with the *Tannah Kamah* only insofar as Torah study is concerned. We learned previously, in mishnah 4, that, according to R. Judah, Ezra's enactment never applied to prayer. Only with regard to Torah study is immersion relevant.

The Spirit of the Law

TYPES OF PURITY AND IMPURITY
There are three main sources of impurity: dead bodies, *tzara'at* (usually defined as leprosy), and issues from the sexual organs.
Dead Bodies
The highest degree of impurity is that of a corpse. Carcasses of animals that have not been ritually slaughtered and eight kinds of dead reptiles are also impure. Contact with any of these renders a person, clothing,

vessels, and food impure. In the case of a corpse, even being in the same room causes impurity.

Tzara'at

A person with certain symptoms of leprosy is declared impure. *Tzara'at* is probably not identical with the disease of leprosy. *Tzara'at* may also appear on clothing and buildings and thereby render them impure.

Issues from the Sexual Organs

The *niddah* (a woman from the onset of her menstruation), the *zavah* (a woman who menstruates at a time other than her period), the *zav* (a man who had a seminal flux associated with illness), the *ba'al keri* (a man who had a seminal emission as a result of intercourse or any other reason), the woman who discharged semen after intercourse, and the woman after childbirth — all are impure to varying degrees.

ASSOCIATION WITH DEATH

All forms of impurity share a common theme; all are associated with death. The corpse and the carcasses of animals and dead reptiles clearly represent the grisly presence of death. *Tzara'at* shows symptoms of dying flesh on the body of the leper. The life-giving potential of millions of sperm cells is lost in a seminal discharge. Menstruation is a "whisper of death" caused by the unfertilized ovum leaving the body. Childbirth delivers life into the world. But from the perspective of the mother's body, a living fetus has departed. The life-force within her womb has been surrendered. The fact that the duration of impurity following the birth of a daughter is fourteen days, while that following of a son is seven days, is due to the fact that a daughter has more life potential within her body, for someday she too will bear children.

APPLICATIONS OF THE LAWS OF IMPURITY

The laws of purity and impurity were applicable only when the Temple stood. Maimonides explains: "All that is written in the Torah and in traditional writings of the laws of the impure and the pure is relevant only to the Temple, its sacred objects, heave-offerings and second tithes. Those who were impure were prohibited from entering into the Temple and from eating holy food, heave-offerings, and second tithes. Ordinary foods (which became impure), however, are not forbidden at all. It is permitted to eat ordinary food that is impure and to drink liquids that are impure.... Similarly, it is permitted to touch all impurities and to become impure because of them, because the Torah forbade only the descendants of Aaron and the Nazarite from becoming impure from a corpse, implying that for everybody else it is permissible and even *kohanim* and Nazarites may incur impurity from other impure things, with the exception of a corpse.... Even though it is permissible to eat impure foods and to drink impure drinks, the early pious ones would eat ordinary food in purity and guarded against all impurities all their lives. They are called 'The Separate Ones.' This is a special holiness.... Separation leads to purity of the body by avoiding evil deeds, and purity of the body leads to holiness of the soul by avoiding evil thoughts, and holiness of the soul leads to becoming like the Divine Presence, as it is written: 'And you shall sanctify yourselves and be holy... for I the Lord make you holy' (Lev. 20:7-8)" (*Mishneh Torah*, Laws of Impurity of Foods 16:8,9,12).

LAWS OF IMPURITY TODAY
The laws of impurity have little application at the present time. The absence of the Temple and sacred foods make the study of these laws theoretical. The ashes of the red heifer which were a necessary ingredient in the purification ritual of corpse impurity no longer exist. As a result, it is assumed that everyone has incurred corpse impurity. That is why it is forbidden to enter the Temple area on the Temple Mount today.

The *kohain* is forbidden to come in contact with a corpse even today. He may not enter a room in which a corpse is lying, nor may he walk near the graves in a cemetery. This prohibition, however, is unrelated to the laws of impurity. It is a unique prohibition for the *kohain*, irrespective of the laws of impurity. Similarly, the laws of *niddah* which require physical separation of husband and wife from the onset of menstruation until immersion in a *mikveh* are not due to impurity, but rather to a specific prohibition related to *niddah*.

LESSON OF THE LAWS OF IMPURITY
Unlike many religions whose focus is primarily on death, Judaism is a religion of life. Torah is called "a Tree of Life." Life is sacred; death is

unholy. Associations with death are grim reminders of man's mortality. Feelings of sadness and depression are evoked by a visit to a cemetery. All forms of impurity bear witness to the frustration of life. These are reminders of man's physical limitations and inevitable end. Such feelings can spill over into the spiritual realm. The presence of death can make a person feel morally and spiritually defeated. It can make him surrender his noble qualities and conclude: "That which befalls men befalls the beasts, one thing befalls them, as the one dies the other dies; there is but one spirit for all; so that a man has no pre-eminence over a beast: for all is vanity" (Eccl. 3:19). Such a conclusion is destructive. It prevents the human being from soaring to spiritual heights. It removes his dignity and leads him to a life of hedonism and pleasure seeking. "What purpose is there to life?" he asks himself. "My end is no better than the dead dog lying on the highway. Let me eat, drink, and be merry, for tomorrow I will die."

The Temple was a monument to life. It was an imposing symbol of sanctity and moral freedom. It bore witness to the spiritual heights which a human can attain. Being in the Temple elevated the human being to the proximity of God's presence. The *kohain*, as officiant and moral guide, was a living symbol of man's spiritual freedom. He taught, by personal example, that life is sacred, that even mundane foods can be made sacred, that even a lowly animal can be raised upon God's altar. *Tumah*, impurity, was antithetical to everything for which the Temple and the *kohain* stood. *Tumah* may not enter the sanctuary.

Rabbi Samson Raphael Hirsch expresses this idea as the Temple's message for every Jew: "Be not depressed, let not the fact of the death of physical life rob you of, or make you have doubts of, the consciousness of the freedom of your moral spiritual life, the freedom of your god-like spiritual self which does not come under the force and power of death. The Mikdosh which God has established for you, and its holy things which He gives you, guarantee in His name the truth of your moral spiritual consciousness which invites you — surrounded though you are with all the most compelling forces of your physical nature — to serve your God, with the complete freedom of will of your spiritual self. Both spheres, that of impurity, your physical lack of free-will, your having willy-nilly to submit to physical forces, and that of purity, your complete free will in moral and spiritual matters, both are truths, both come from God, the One Creator of physical Nature and spiritual life. They only become lies when you mix them. You belong to both realms, but beware of setting foot in the one with the breath of the other upon you. Physically you are unfree, but morally you are free, and while you are alive, God has wedded your unfree physical forces to the free mastery of your god-like free moral energy for the service of His Sanctuary of the Torah. Physical truths are only valid for physical existence. But your human existence reaches beyond, over the realm of purely physical being. It is ennobled by God, Who is free, with the breath of god-like freedom of will, and in that realm the true laws of physical matter and forces become untrue" (Commentary on Lev. 5:13).

The Practical Law

1. All who are impure are obligated to recite *Sh'mah* and its blessings even while in a state of impurity.... Ezra and his court enacted that one who had a seminal emission is an exception to the rule of the other forms of impurity, and he alone must immerse before reciting words of Torah. This enactment did not spread through all of Israel and most of the community was not able to observe it; therefore, it was nullified. All of Israel is now accustomed to recite Torah and *Sh'mah* after seminal emission, because words of Torah cannot become impure, but remain pure forever, as it is written: "Is not my word like fire, says the Lord" (Jeremiah 23:29). Just as fire cannot become impure, so too, words of Torah cannot become impure (*Mishneh Torah*, Laws of *Sh'mah*, 4:8).

2. One who had a seminal emission is permitted to study Torah, recite *Sh'mah*, and pray. Such is the widespread practice (*Orach Chaim* 88:1).

3. There are pious people who still observe Ezra's enactment and immerse in a *mikveh* after a seminal emission (*ibid., Mishnah B'rurah,* no. 4).

Chapter Four

Introduction

The first three chapters of Tractate Berachot deal mainly with the laws of *Sh'mah*. Chapter 4 addresses itself to some of the essential aspects of the *Amidah*. As is the case with *Sh'mah*, the first aspect of the *Amidah* discussed by the Mishnah is the appropriate times for prayer. When the Sages established fixed times and formulations for prayer, certain problems arose. Fixed prayer inhibits freedom of self-expression. It also tends to make prayer perfunctory, and sometimes even burdensome. Mishnah 2 provides an example of the individual's privilege to formulate his own personal prayer. Mishnah 4 warns against making prayer a "fixed routine." Two versions of the *Amidah* existed in Mishnaic times, a complete form which contained eighteen individual blessings, and an abridged form which condensed the twelve central blessings into a single blessing. In mishnah 3, the Tanna'im dispute which of the two versions must be recited on a daily basis. Prayer must be directed toward our Father in heaven. The Holy of Holies in the Temple was a symbolic reminder of the Divine Presence here on earth. In it was the Holy Ark, which contained the Stone Tablets which Moses brought down from Sinai, and upon it rested the Cherubim. Thus, the Holy of Holies became the focal point of prayer for Jews throughout the world. Even after its destruction, the site remains holy and continues to be the lodestone of Jewish prayer. This concept is discussed in the laws of mishnayot 5 and 6. The *Mussaf* service of Shabbat, festivals, and New Moons is directly related to the *Mussaf* offering in the Temple. As the *Mussaf* was a public offering, the question arose — does *Mussaf* require a *minyan*? This is a subject of debate in mishnah 7.

Mishnah 1 / משנה א

The morning prayer[1] may be said until midday.[2] R. Judah says: Until four hours.[3] The afternoon prayer[4] may be said until evening.[5] R. Judah says: Until half of the *Minchah* period.[6] The evening prayer[7]

תְּפִלַּת הַשַּׁחַר, עַד חֲצוֹת; רַבִּי יְהוּדָה אוֹמֵר: עַד אַרְבַּע שָׁעוֹת. תְּפִלַּת הַמִּנְחָה עַד הָעֶרֶב; רַבִּי יְהוּדָה אוֹמֵר, עַד פְּלַג הַמִּנְחָה. תְּפִלַּת

1. MORNING PRAYER — *Shacharit*. "Prayer" refers specifically to the *Amidah* prayer (the *Sh'monah Esray*).
2. UNTIL MIDDAY — Half the length of the day.
   There are two opinions as to the definition of the length of the day:
   1) from dawn until the stars appear (Magen Avraham).
   2) from sunrise to sunset (Vilna Gaon).
   The length of the day varies with the seasons and geographical location.
   The time period for the Morning Prayer begins at sunrise. If one must pray earlier, he may begin the *Amidah* after dawn.
3. FOUR HOURS — The day is divided into twelve units of one "hour" each. Four hours is a third of the length of the day.
4. AFTERNOON PRAYER — *Minchah*, from the Hebrew *Menuchah*, "rest," alluding to the sun coming to rest (Nachmanides).
5. UNTIL EVENING — Sunset. The time period for *Minchah* begins one half-hour after midday.
6. HALF OF THE *MINCHAH* PERIOD — There are two afternoon *Minchah* periods, *Minchah* Major and *Minchah* Minor. *Minchah* Major is from six and a half hours after the start of the day until evening. *Minchah* Minor is from nine and a half hours until evening. The origin of these two *Minchah* periods relates to the time in which the afternoon *Tamid* offering was brought in the Temple. Normally, the *Tamid* was brought from after nine and a half hours until evening. This is called the *Minchah* Minor. On the fourteenth of Nissan, however, when the Paschal lamb had to be sacrificed, the *Tamid* was sacrificed earlier, after six and a half hours. This time period from six and a half hours until evening is called *Minchah* Major.
   R. Judah says that *Minchah* may be said until half the *Minchah* Minor period, viz., an hour and a quarter before evening.
7. EVENING PRAYER — *Arvit* (or, *Ma'ariv*).

has no fixed time.[8] The *Mussaf* prayer[9] may be said all day. R. Judah says: Until seven hours.[10]

הָעֶרֶב אֵין לָהּ קֶבַע. וְשֶׁל מוּסָפִין כָּל הַיּוֹם. רַבִּי יְהוּדָה אוֹמֵר: עַד שֶׁבַע שָׁעוֹת:

8. NO FIXED TIME — I.e., all night long.
9. *MUSSAF* PRAYER — The *Mussaf* ("Additional") prayer is recited on Shabbat, festivals, and New Moons.
10. UNTIL SEVEN HOURS — I.e., one hour after midday. The time period for the *Mussaf* prayer begins at sunrise.

The Letter of the Law

PRAYER: A BIBLICAL OR A RABBINIC OBLIGATION?

According to Maimonides, prayer is a Biblical obligation. He writes in *Sefer Ha'mitzvot*: "The fifth mitzvah which we are commanded is to serve the One Above. This mitzvah is repeated several times, as it says, 'And you shall serve the Lord your God' (Ex. 23:25), and it says, 'And Him shall you serve' (Deut. 13:5), and it says, 'and Him shall you serve' (*ibid.*, 6:13), and it says, 'and to serve Him' (*ibid.*, 11:13). And even though this mitzvah is one of the general mitzvot, as we explained in our fourth principle, it has a specific meaning, i.e., prayer." Maimonides explains further in his *Mishneh Torah*: "It is a positive commandment to pray every day, as it is written, 'And you shall serve the Lord your God' (Ex. 23:25). From the oral tradition we have learned that 'service' means prayer, as it is written, 'And to serve Him with all your heart' (Deut. 11:13). Our Sages said: 'What kind of service is in the heart? It is prayer' (Ta'anit 2a)" (*Mishneh Torah*, Laws of Prayer, 1:1).

Nachmanides differs with Maimonides. He is of the opinion that prayer is not a Biblical commandment, but rather a privilege. God's attributes of mercy and kindness bestow upon us the right to pray, with the knowledge that the Creator hears and answers our prayers. The mitzvah "and to serve Him with all your heart" (Deut. 11:13) is unrelated to daily prayer. It means that we are to serve God with sincerity and devotion. To serve with the heart means to serve with no ulterior motive for personal gain. It is similar to the commandment "And you shall love the Lord your God with all your heart, with all your soul, and with all your might" (Deut. 6:5).

Though Nachmanides insists that prayer is rabbinically prescribed, he does concede that under circumstances of distress and danger, there is a Biblical injunction to pray. He bases his opinion upon the verse: "When you go into battle in your land against the invading enemy, you shall sound the trumpets and be remembered before the Lord your God, and you shall be saved from your enemies" (Num. 10:9) He concludes, "It is a mitzvah, in time of troubles, that we affirm that He, may He be blessed and elevated, hears prayer and will save us from trouble with prayer and cries" (*Sefer Ha'mitzvot, ad. loc.*).

THE TIMES OF PRAYER

A Jew prays three times daily: morning, afternoon, and evening. What is the source from which the Rabbis derived the requirement for prayer three times a day? The Talmud offers two opinions: "R. Yosi ben Chanina said: The prayers were established by the forefathers. R. Joshua ben Levi said: The prayers were established to correspond with the daily offerings. There is a *baraita* that supports R. Yosi ben Chanina and a *baraita* that supports R. Joshua ben Levi:

The *baraita* supporting R. Yosi ben Chanina —

"Abraham established the morning prayer, as it says: 'And Abraham arose early in the morning (and went) to the place where he had stood before the Lord' (Gen. 19:27). 'Standing' means prayer, as it says: 'And Phinehas stood and prayed' (Ps. 106:30). Isaac established the afternoon prayer, as it says: 'And Isaac went out to converse (*lasuach*) in the field before evening' (Gen. 24:62). 'Conversing' (*sicha*) means prayer, as its says: 'A prayer of the afflicted when he is faint and pours forth his prayer (*sicho*) before the Lord' (Ps. 102:1). Jacob established the evening prayer, as it says: 'And he came (*vah'yifgah*) to the place and lodged there' (Gen. 28:11). 'Coming' (*p'giah*) means prayer, as it says: 'As for you, do not pray for this people, nor raise crying or prayer for them, and do not come (*tifgah*) to me' (Jeremiah 7:16)."

CHAPTER 4: *Mishnah 1* 213

The *baraita* supporting R. Joshua ben Levi —

"Why did they say that the morning prayer may be said until midday? Because the Morning (*Shacharit*) offering was offered up until midday. R. Judah says: Until four hours, because the Morning offering was offered until four hours. Why did they say that the afternoon prayer may be said until evening? Because the Afternoon (*Minchah*) offering was offered until evening.... And why did they say that the evening prayer has no fixed time? Because the limbs and the fats that were not consumed (on the altar) at evening were burned all through the night. And why did they say that the Additional prayers may be said all day? Because the Additional (*Mussaf*) offering was offered at any time during the day. R. Judah says: Until seven hours, because the Additional offering was offered until seven hours" (Berachot 26b).

Maimonides codified the times of prayer in his *Mishneh Torah*: "...And so they (The Men of the Great Assembly) established that the number of prayers should be the same as the number of offerings. Two prayers every day to correspond with the two daily offerings and, on the days that there was a *Mussaf* offering, they established a third prayer to correspond with the *Mussaf* offering. The prayer that corresponds with the daily morning offering is called the morning prayer. And the prayer corresponding with the daily afternoon offering is called the afternoon prayer, and the prayer corresponding with the *Mussaf* offerings is called the *Mussaf* prayer. And so they established that a person should pray once at night because the limbs of the afternoon offering were consumed all through the night...." (*Mishneh Torah*, Laws of Prayer 1:5-6).

In his Laws of Prayer, Maimonides cites the opinion of R. Joshua ben Levi, who sees prayer as being rooted in the Temple sacrifices. This opinion does not, however, contradict that of R. Yosi ben Chanina. The two complement each other. That is why Maimonides writes elsewhere that prayer is derived from the Patriarchs: "... And he (Abraham) prayed *Shacharit*. Isaac... added another prayer before evening. Jacob... prayed *Arvit*" (*ibid.*, Laws of Kings, 9:1). Maimonides thus maintains that both the Patriarchs and the Temple sacrifices teach us the origins of prayer.

The Spirit of the Law

THE CONTROVERSY BETWEEN MAIMONIDES AND NACHMANIDES

Rabbi Joseph B. Soloveitchik explains the dispute between Maimonides and Nachmanides in the following manner: Both agree in concept that the obligation to pray is based upon the human need for divine intervention. Both opinions concur that we are enjoined to turn to God in times of distress. Nachmanides, however, defines "times of distress" as extreme situations, such as war, drought, famine or illness. Maimonides views "times of distress" as the perennial human condition. Every human being suffers daily from fears and anxieties. Mortal man, consciously and unconsciously, is forced to deal with insecurities and worries. Every day is a "time of distress." Thus, there is a Biblical injunction to pray daily.

Rabbi Abraham R. Besdin, in his reconstruction of Rabbi Soloveitchik's lectures in *Reflections of the Rav* writes as follows:

"The views of Maimonides and Nachmanides can be reconciled. Both regard prayer as meaningful only if it is derived from a sense of *tzarah*. They differ in their understanding of the word. Maimonides regarded daily life itself as being existentially in straits, including in the sensitive person feelings of despair, a brooding sense of life's meaninglessness, absurdity, lack of fulfillment. It is a persistent *tzarah*, which exists *behkol yom*, daily. The word *tzarah* connotes more than external trouble; it suggests an emotional and intellectual condition in which man sees himself as hopelessly trapped in a vast, impersonal universe, desolate without hope. Certainly, the Psalmist's cry, *min hametzar karati Yah*, 'Out of my straits, I have called upon the Lord' (118:5), refers to an inner, rather than an externally induced, state of constriction and oppression.

"Out of the sense of discomfiture prayer emerges. Offered in comfort and security, prayer is a paradox, modern methods of suburban worship and plush synagogues notwithstanding. The desire for proximity of wife and children at services comes from a need for security and comfort. Real prayer is derived from loneliness, and a sense of dependence. Thus, while Nachmanides dealt only with 'surface crisis,' public distress, *tzarot tzibbur*, Maimonides regarded all life as a 'depth crisis,' a *tzarat yahid*" (*Reflections of the Rav*, Abraham R. Besdin, Dept. of Torah Education and Culture in the Diaspora of the WZO, 1979, pp. 80-81).

TWO SOURCES OF PRAYER; THE PATRIARCHS AND TEMPLE SACRIFICE

The Patriarchs are exemplars of prayer. Not simply with the utterance of words, but with their daily devotion to God they lived prayerful lives. If prayer is viewed as a form of communication with the Divine, Abraham, Isaac, and Jacob were constantly praying. They prayed through acts of kindness, benevolence, and courage. They expressed faith in the One God and emulated His goodness at a time when mankind was submerged in a world of paganism, idolatry, and supersitition.

Abraham, Isaac, and Jacob were the fathers of prayer. Prayer for them was a spontaneous outpouring of the heart. It was the truest expression of their inner personalities and their life experiences. Abraham represents the dawn of Jewish history. His appearance on the world's stage ushered in an age of spiritual enlightenment. He was the trailblazer who ushered in a new day of unbounded faith and unsurpassed ethics. It is appropriate that the morning prayer be attributed to him. Isaac played a role that was different from that of his father. His unique strength lay in his ability to reinforce the revolutionary example of his father, Abraham. Unlike the sons of so many greats who flee from their father's shadow, Isaac chose to bask in his father's radiance. In the most agonizing event in the Bible, Isaac faithfully submitted to God's command and his father's knife. Later, he cheerfully accepted the wife chosen for him by his father's servant. And when the Philistines filled the wells of Abraham with earth, Isaac chose to re-dig them rather than dig new wells. His life was a continuation of his father's initiatives, as the afternoon is a continuation of morning's beginnings. Jacob's life was a long night of darkness and despair punctuated with brief gleams of joyful radiance. Pursued by a vengeful brother, swindled by an unscrupulous uncle, bereft of his beloved Rachel, grieved by the disappearance of his favorite son, and finally exiled in his last years to the gilded ghetto of

Goshen, Jacob endured in faith and prayer. To him belongs the evening prayer.

The words connoting prayer for each of the Patriarchs are illuminating. For Abraham, prayer was *amidah*, standing up, rising. For Isaac, prayer was *su'ach*, bending down, or *si'ach*, a bush or shrub. Both meanings imply humble submission. For Jacob, prayer was the result of *p'giah*, encountering obstacles.

The sacrificial offerings in the Temple provide a second source for prayer three times daily. Prayer is not a substitute for sacrifices. Daily prayer was well established during Temple days. The Sages, however, saw a close kinship between prayer and sacrifices. The Hebrew word for sacrifice is *korban*. The word is derived from the root *krv* which means "near." The *korban* in ancient times was a means by which a Jew drew near to God. His Peace offering was a token of love. Gratitude was expressed with a Thanksgiving offering. Repentance and the Sin offering bridged the gap between God and the sinner. Prayer is the modern day sacrifice that brings the Jew *karov*, ever near to the Lord.

When a person wishes to communicate with a distant loved one he may do so by writing a letter or making a phone call. These are verbal forms of communicating one's feelings of love and devotion. Sending a gift is another way of communicating feelings. A bouquet of flowers, a box of chocolate, or a meaningful present delivers a communication of love that is sometimes difficult to put into words. In ancient times, the sacrifice was a gift of love. Nowadays, without a Temple, prayer is a communication of love.

For the Patriarchs, prayer was a spontaneous outpouring of faith. It was a natural expression of their daily dialogue with the Almighty. Their special relationships with God resulted in inspirational prayer. But inspiration comes rarely to the average individual. That is why the Talmud chose a second source for the times of prayer. The sacrifices were Biblically ordained daily occurrences. They teach us the obligation and duty to pray daily, even when inspiration is lacking. The sacrifices place a responsibility of daily prayer upon the Jew, even when he feels incapable of spontaneous spiritual expression.

A THIRD SOURCE FOR DAILY PRAYER

There is yet a third source for prayer three times daily. The Jerusalem

Talmud (Berachot 4:1) states that a Jew prays morning, afternoon, and evening in correspondence with the three phases of the day: sunrise, sunset, and evening. Prayer, according to the Jerusalem Talmud, makes us mindful of the everchanging wonders of nature. The rising and setting of the sun, so often taken for granted, is a source of religious inspiration. The phases of the day evoke wonder and awe. They attest to the omnipotence of the Creator who "renews creation in His goodness, every day" (morning service). If we allow ourselves to feel awed by nature's beauties and wonders, we cannot help but feel inspired to pray.

THE TIMES OF PRAYER LINKED TO *SH'MAH*

The luminary Talmudist, philosopher, and mathematician of the sixteenth century, R. Judah Loew ben Bezalel, known as the Maharal of Prague, offers a marvelous conceptualization of daily prayer which, in effect, links the times of prayer with the *Sh'mah*. He writes as follows:

"One may ask, why are the three prayers specifically at these times? It can be explained in a simple manner. It is fitting that a person should submit himself to God in worship with his body, his soul, and his wealth, as it is written, 'And you shall love the Lord your God with all your heart, with all your soul, and with all your might.' The body is alluded to with the words 'all your heart,' as our Rabbis of blessed memory explained: 'With your two impulses, with the good impulse and the evil impulse.' It is understood that the evil impulse is in a person's body. And 'with all your soul,' even if He takes your soul, and 'with all your might,' even if He takes your wealth. Morning sleep is ever so sweet. When a person is sleeping in the morning and he longs to continue sleeping, he is in an utterly physical state. There is nothing more physical than one who is sleeping, because he has nothing left in his body, as his soul is not functioning at all. But a person must strengthen himself and arise from his sleep and pray. In so doing, he submits his body to the Lord, may He be blessed, by controlling his body.

"The afternoon prayer is in the midst of the day, when a person is occupied with his business which he loves so much. When he interrupts his business to pray, he submits his wealth to the Lord, may He be blessed. And when it is evening, when a person is already exhausted from his business activities and worries about that which he experienced until then, his soul seeks rest. This pertains to the soul, because the soul is the mistress of labor and movement, as I have explained many times before.... Despite this, he submits his soul to the Lord, may He be blessed, and prays. Thus, by means of these three prayers, a person submits all that he has — his body, his wealth, his soul — to the Lord, may He be blessed" (*Writings of the Maharal of Prague*, selected by A. Karib, published by Mosad Harav Kook, 1960, vol. 2, pp. 186-187).

Abudraham, in his *Siddur* commentary, links the *Sh'mah* with daily prayer by means of an interesting play on the word "*Sh'mah*," spelled *shin, mem, ayin*. *Shin* is the first letter of *Shacharit*, the morning prayer, *mem* is the first letter of *Minchah*, the afternoon prayer, and *ayin* is the first letter of *Arvit*, the evening prayer.

The Practical Law

1. The *Amidah* (*Sh'moneh Esray*) of *Shacharit* should not be recited before sunrise. If one mistakenly prayed earlier, or had to pray earlier due to circumstances — if "the face of the east is illuminated" he has fulfilled his obligation. Some authorities say that if he prayed after *alote ha'shachar*, the crack of dawn (approximately 72 minutes before sunrise) he has discharged his obligation (*Orach Chaim* 89:1).

2. The *Amidah* may be recited until four hours, i.e., one third the length of the day (measured from dawn until the stars appear [*Magen Avraham*], or from sunrise until sunset [*Vilna Gaon*] (*ibid.*).

3. If one prayed the *Amidah* after the fourth hour, even though he has forfeited praying at the proper time, he has fulfilled his obligation of prayer (*ibid.*). When one prays at this time he should mentally stipulate that his prayer is a "voluntary" prayer (*ibid., Mishnah B'rurah*, no. 6).

4. Under no circumstances should one pray after midday (*Orach Chaim, ibid.*). If one erred and prayed within one half hour after midday, he has discharged his obligation (*ibid., Mishnah B'rurah*, no. 7).

5. If a person, due to error or circumstances, did not pray the *Shacharit Amidah* he must recite a second *Amidah* after *Minchah* to make up for the *Shacharit* he missed (*ibid.*).

CHAPTER 4: *Mishnah 1*

6. The *Amidah* of *Minchah* should not be recited before one half-hour after midday (*Orach Chaim* 233:1). If one prayed during the half-hour period after midday, he need not repeat his prayer (*ibid., Mishnah B'rurah*, no. 2).

7. It is preferable to pray *Minchah* before *plag ha'minchah* (an hour and a quarter before sunset or before the stars appear). Every effort should be made to pray before sunset (*Orach Chaim, ibid., Mishnah B'rurah*, no. 14).

8. It is preferable to pray *Minchah* alone before sunset than to pray *Minchah* with a *Minyan* after sunset (*ibid.*).

9. The period from sunset until nightfall has a questionable status as to it being day or night. thus, if one prays after sunset he should mentally stipulate that if it is still day, his prayer should be counted as the *Minchah* prayer, and if it is already night, his prayer should be counted as the *Arvit* prayer, in which case, the *Amidah* after nightfall will be considered a "make up" for the *Minchah* that was missed (*Biur Halachah, ibid.*).

10. Under no circumstances may one pray *Minchah* after a quarter of an hour before nightfall (*Mishnah B'rurah, ibid.*).

11. If a person forgot to pray *Minchah*, he must recite a second *Amidah* after *Arvit* (*Orach Chaim*, 234:2).

12. One should pray *Arvit* after nightfall. If one prays *Arvit* after sunset he has fulfilled his obligation. If, due to circumstances, he must pray earlier than sunset, he may pray no earlier than an hour and a quarter before evening (sunset or nightfall) provided that he has prayed *Minchah* before this time (*ibid.*, 233:1).

13. When *Arvit* is prayed before nightfall, one must remember to recite *Sh'mah* again after nightfall (*ibid.*, 235:1).

14. *Arvit* may be prayed until dawn (*ibid.* 235:4, *Mishnah B'rurah*, no. 34).

15. If one neglected to pray *Arvit*, he must pray a second *Amidah* after the *Shacharit Amidah*. (*ibid.* 108:2).

16. The *Mussaf Amidah* should be recited after *Shacharit*. If one prayed *Mussaf* before *Shacharit*, he has discharged his obligation (*ibid.* 286:1).

17. *Mussaf* should not be delayed beyond the end of the seventh hour. If the seventh hour has elapsed, *Mussaf* may be recited until sundown (*ibid.*).

18. There is no "make up" for *Mussaf* (*ibid.*).

Mishnah 2 / מִשְׁנָה ב

R. Nechunyah ben Hakanah used to offer a brief prayer when he entered the *Beit Midrash*[1] and when he left. They[2] said to him: What is the nature of this prayer? He replied: When I enter I pray that no mishap occur because of me[3] and when I leave I give thanks for my portion in life.[4]

רַבִּי נְחוּנְיָא בֶּן הַקָּנָה הָיָה מִתְפַּלֵּל בִּכְנִיסָתוֹ לְבֵית הַמִּדְרָשׁ וּבִיצִיאָתוֹ תְּפִלָּה קְצָרָה. אָמְרוּ לוֹ: מַה מָּקוֹם לִתְפִלָּה זוֹ? אָמַר לָהֶם: בִּכְנִיסָתִי אֲנִי מִתְפַּלֵּל שֶׁלֹּא תֶאֱרַע תַּקָּלָה עַל יָדִי, וּבִיצִיאָתִי אֲנִי נוֹתֵן הוֹדָיָה עַל חֶלְקִי:

1. *BEIT MIDRASH* — Academy.
2. THEY — The students.
3. NO MISHAP OCCUR BECAUSE OF ME — That I not err in my teaching and thereby cause others to sin by rejoicing over my error.
4. MY PORTION IN LIFE — That I am privileged to devote my life to studying and teaching Torah.

The Letter of The Law

The *baraita* provides us with a more complete text of R. Nechunyah's prayers: "Upon entering what would he say? 'May it be Your will, Lord, my God, that I not err in my studies, that I not make a mistake in halachah, and that my colleagues rejoice with me. Let me not declare the impure pure, nor the pure impure. Let not my colleagues make a mistake in halachah and let me rejoice with them!' Upon leaving what would he say? 'I am thankful unto You, Lord, my God, that You have placed my portion in life amongst those who sit in the *beit midrash*, and

CHAPTER 4: *Mishnah 2*

not amongst the idlers. I arise early and they arise early. I arise early to words of Torah and they arise early to frivolous talk. I labor and they labor. I labor and receive reward. They labor and receive no reward. I run and they run. I run to life in the World to Come. They run to the pit of destruction' " (Berachot 28b).

The Jerusalem Talmud contains a variant text of R. Nechunyah's prayers: "Upon entering he would say: 'May it be Your will, Lord, my God and God of my fathers, that I not be impatient with my colleagues nor may they be impatient with me, that we not declare impure that which is pure nor declare pure that which is impure, that we not prohibit that which is permitted nor permit that which is prohibited— so that I not be embarrassed in this world and the next world.' Upon leaving he would say: 'I am thankful unto You, Lord, my God, and God of my fathers, that You have set my portion in life amongst those who dwell in the *beit midrash* and the synagogue, and, You did not set my portion in life in the theaters and the circuses. For I labor and they labor. I am diligent and they are diligent. I labor to inherit Paradise and they labor for the pit of destruction' " (Berachot 4:2).

The opening words, "*Mahu ohmer*," of the above *baraita* are somewhat ambiguous. "*Mahu ohmer*" may mean, "What would he (R. Nechunyah) say?", or, it may mean "What should one say?" Maimonides prefers the latter translation and deems it a requirement to utter R. Nechunyah's prayers upon entering and upon leaving the *beit midrash*.

The juxtaposition of mishnah 1 and mishnah 2 alludes to the idea that immediately after praying, a Jew should go to the *beit midrash* to study Torah. "R. Levi ben Chiya said: He who leaves the synagogue and enters the *beit midrash* to engage in Torah study will be privileged to greet the Divine Presence, as it says: 'Those who go from strength to strength will be seen unto God in Zion' (Ps. 84:8)" (Berachot 64a).

It is quite reasonable for the great R. Nechunyah to offer thanks for his portion that enables him to devote his life to Torah study. Why, however, did he find it necessary to deprecate others who engage in wordly activities and business endeavors? This seems out of character for the humble saint who told his students that he attributes his longevity to the fact that "I never allowed myself to be honored at the expense of another's degradation..." (Megillah 28a).

Rabbi Israel Lipschutz (1782-1860) raises this very question in his commentary on the Mishnah, *Tiferet Yisrael*, and offers the following psychological insight:

"When a person sits in solitude in a *beit midrash*, in the rear of a sacred house of study, when everyone is out in the streets and marketplaces running to and fro, when merchants and laborers hurry about in their business pursuits diligently pursuing money and material things, he, the Torah scholar, truly feels isolated. When he leaves the *beit midrash* to go outside he appears in his own eyes, and even more so in the eyes of his wife and family, as a lazy idler, a slacker in life's work. It is, therefore, important that the Torah scholar speak to himself with words that penetrate his innermost soul, that he should feel the greatness of his importance, that he is like an eagle who flies high above those who tread upon the earth in temporal vanities. It is for this reason that the holy, godly Tannah (R. Nechunyah) cast deprecating words upon those who spend their lives occupied with this-wordly matters and referred to them in his expression of gratitude to the Almighty for his portion in life."

The Spirit of the Law

THE IMPORTANCE OF TORAH STUDY
Three Crowns

R. Nechunyah's prayers dramatically express the supreme value Judaism places upon Torah study. Torah study is not merely an intellectual exercise or a pursuit of intellectual curiosity. It is a Jew's most noble endeavor, his most precious occupation. A Jew can wear no crown that is more beautiful or more ennobling then the crown of Torah. Maimonides writes: "Israel was crowned with three crowns: the crown of Torah, the crown of the high priesthood, and the crown of kingship. The crown of the high priesthood was granted to Aaron... the crown of kingship was granted to David... but the crown of Torah is reserved for and available to every Jew... the crown of Torah is greater than the other two" (*Mishneh Torah*, Laws of Torah Study, 3:1).

Every culture looks to an ideal type who is valued and envied above all others. Such an ideal person embodies the qualities and attributes most cherished in that culture. In some societies it is the brave warrior; in others, the nobility and aristocracy; and in others, the rich and famous. Judaism never paid the highest homage to any of the above. The Jewish "hero" is the sage, the Torah scholar, the *talmid chacham*. Neither birth, nor wealth, nor might, nor power can capture the esteem and reverence of the Jewish community. Rather, it is Torah wisdom that elevates the individual to high office. "Greater is the *talmid chacham* of illegitimate birth than the ignoramous High Priest" (*ibid.*, 3:2).

THE PRACTICAL ASPECT OF TORAH STUDY
It is obvious that one cannot be an observant Jew without having accumulated a wealth of Torah knowledge. Judaism is a very intricate, complex system that spans every aspect of life. It is a veritable way of life. One simply cannot perform his religious duties properly without extensive study and training. Every day's activities, from rising in the morning until retiring at night, are governed by halachah. Religious rituals, such as prayers and blessings, donning *tefillin*, etc., have myriads of laws, and the way one conducts himself in business, with neighbors, with family, etc., also falls into religious modes of behavior. Thus, for a Jew to conduct himself in a proper religious manner, he must invest himself in an extensive period of Torah study. The great sage Hillel put it succinctly: "An ignoramous cannot be pious" (*Ethics of the Fathers* 2:6). In light of the need of many years of intensive study before one can practice his religion properly, the built-in failure of afternoon Hebrew School and Sunday School education for children is apparent. Within those frameworks, the most an inspiring teacher can hope to accomplish is to whet the appetites of his students for future study.

Which is greater — study or deed? This question was discussed and debated by the great Sages: "R. Tarfon and the elders were gathered in the attic of Nitzah's house in Lydda when this question was raised before them: Which is greater — study or deed?" (Kiddushin 40b). The consensus was that study is a necessary prerequisite of deed. Without Torah knowledge, observance is impossible.

Our generation is witness to a phenomenon known as "the *Ba'al T'shuvah* movement." Thousands of young Jewish men and women who come from assimilated backgrounds are returning to their religious roots. A large network of yeshivot, both in Israel and in the Diaspora, has been established to meet the needs of these people. Not long ago, the Lubavitch headquarters at 770 Eastern Parkway, Brooklyn, and Chabad houses on college campuses were among the very few addresses to which *ba'alay t'shuvah* could turn. Today, thank God, scores of yeshivot, each with its own particular religious emphasis and flavor, are available for those returning to Judaism. What characterizes these institutions, above all else, is their strong emphasis upon study. Knowing the sources, exploring the texts, becoming familiar with the original Hebrew — these are the keys to understanding what Judaism is all about. The emphasis of study for religious tyros should be upon the practical aspects of Judaism. More time should be devoted to the "hows" than to the "whys." Studying the "hows" of the mitzvot should certainly precede their observance. "If a person has not yet studied and asks whether he should study first or practice, he should be told to study first because 'an ignoramous cannot be pious.' But, for a person who has already studied, deed is greater than study " (*Tosafot, ibid.*).

TORAH FOR TORAH'S SAKE

"Greater is study because study leads to deed." Greater, too, is study for study's sake. Not all study should relate to relevant topics. Torah is relevant because it is Torah. Most of the vast Talmudic literature has no practical application today. The Orders of *Kodashim* and *Taharot* apply only in Temple times. Most of *Nezikin* is not practiced today. Parts of *Nashim* are inoperative and, with the exception of Tractate *Berachot*, most of the Order of *Zeraim* relates to the agricultural laws of Eretz Yisrael. Yet, no part of Torah is less important than any other.

What makes all of Torah relevant? Torah is divine wisdom. Both the Written Law and Oral Law were given by God to Moses at Mt. Sinai. Torah study affords us the wonderful opportunity to glimpse into the divine Mind of the Almighty. Each word, each thought, each concept radiates with a spark of the divine. God no longer communicates to us through prophets. But He continues to communicate through His eternal Torah. This is what makes prayer and Torah study inextricably linked together. Both are forms of communication. In prayer, it is man who initiates communication. In Torah study, it is God who initiates.

Rabbi Shneur Zalman of Lyady in his *Sefer Tanya* describes Torah as a manifestation of God in the physical world. The human mind is incapable of grasping the essence of God. The closest the human being can come to comprehending God is through the study of Torah and the observance of mitzvot. He writes: "The Holy One, blessed be He, contracted His Wisdom and Will into the 613 mitzvot of the Torah, and in their laws and in the combination of letters of the Bible and in their interpretations in the *aggadot* and *midrashim* of the Sages, so that the soul in the body would be capable of comprehending them and observing them as much as is possible.... And even though the Torah is garbed in the physical world, it is as though one were embracing the King. It makes no difference in the degree of closeness and attachment to the King whether He is wearing one garment or several garments, so long as the 'body' of the King is in them, or if the King embraces him with His arm, even though it is covered with clothing...." (*Tanya*, chap. 84).

Studying Torah for Torah's sake is the ideal for which every student should strive. Not for honor and glory, not for the title "Rabbi," not for wealth and power should one study Torah. In the words of R. Tzadok: "Do not make Torah a crown for self-aggrandizement, nor a spade with which to dig." The mild Hillel warns: "He who makes unworthy use of the crown of Torah shall perish" (*Ethics of the Fathers* 4:5).

No greater tribute has been paid to the one who studies Torah for Torah's sake than that of R. Meir: "Whoever occupies himself with the study of Torah for its own sake merits many things; and not only that, but the entire world is worthwhile because of him. He is called friend, beloved, one who loves the Omnipresent God, one who loves mankind; he brings joy to the Omnipresent God and joy to mankind. It clothes him with humility and reverence, and prepares him to become righteous, pious, upright, and faithful; and it distances him from sin and brings him near to merit. People benefit from his advice, wisdom, understanding, and strength.... And it gives him sovereignty and dominion, and profound judgment. The secrets of Torah are revealed to him; and he becomes an ever-increasing spring and as a river that never runs dry. He becomes modest, patient, and forgiving of insult. It makes him great and exalted above all creations" (*Ethics of the Fathers* 6:1).

REWARDS FOR TORAH STUDY

The rewards for Torah study are immeasurable. Torah brings both physical and spiritual benefits. The rewards for Torah study are granted in this world and in the World to Come. These are but a small sample of the blessings derived from Torah study:

1. Reward in this world and the World to Come —

"These are the things for which a person eats of their fruits in this world and the principal remains in the World to Come: Honoring one's father and mother, kind deeds, bringing peace between man and neighbor — but the study of Torah equals them all" (Pe'ah 1:1).

2. The prevention of sin —

"Torah may be compared to medicine. As an illustration, a person hit his son, making a wound, and said: 'My son, as long as you keep the bandage on your wound, you may eat and drink and bathe as you wish and you have nothing to fear. But if you remove the bandage, the wound will become infected.' So did the Holy One, blessed be He, say to Israel: 'My children, I have created the Evil Inclination and I have created Torah as an antidote. If you engage in Torah you will not be delivered into its power. But if you do not engage in Torah, you will be delivered into its power. Its sole preoccupation is with you, but you have the power to rule over it' " (Kiddushin 30b).

3. Physical healing —

"R. Joshua ben Levi said: If a person is travelling alone without an escort, he should engage in Torah. If his head hurts, he should engage in Torah. If his throat hurts, he should engage in Torah. If his stomach aches, he should engage in Torah. If his bones hurt, he should engage in Torah. If his entire body hurts, he should engage in Torah" (Eruvin 54a).

4. Protection for one's home —

"Any house in which words of Torah may be heard at night will never be destroyed" (*ibid.*, 18b).

5. Guaranteed reward —

"R. Tarfon used to say: It is not your responsibility to finish the work, but neither are you free to neglect it. If you studied much Torah you will receive much reward. And the Master of your work can be trusted to compensate you for your work" (*Ethics of the Fathers* 2:16).

6. Freedom —

" 'And the Tablets were the work of God, and the writing was the writing of God, engraved (*charut*) upon the Tablets' (Ex. 32:16) — Do not read *charut*, engraved, but, *cherut*, freedom — for the only one who is free is the one who engages in the study of Torah" (*Ethics of the Fathers* 6:2).

7. Freedom from wordly cares —

"R. Nechunyah ben Hakanah (the Tannah of our mishnah) said: Whoever accepts upon himself the yoke of Torah will have the yoke of the government and the yoke of worldly cares removed from him; but whoever casts off the yoke of Torah will have the yoke of the government and the yoke of worldly cares placed upon him" (*Ethics of the Fathers* 3:5).

AN ADMONITION FROM THE THIRTEENTH CENTURY

The neglect of Torah study is probably one of the most serious afflictions of modern Jewry. Lack of education and widespread ignorance create the breeding ground for assimilation and intermarriage. But even in the circles of observant Jews who are committed to Torah, Torah study is often very low on the scale of priorities. All too many yeshiva graduates fail to devote a serious amount of time to Torah study. As a result, they forget much of what they have learned in their younger years. Even worse, their attitude towards mitzvah observance and the quality of their daily prayer slowly petrify over the years until these are reduced to cold stone. Would that as many Jews who seek to improve the health of their bodies through jogging and exercise would seek to improve the health of their spirits through Torah study.

The problem is not a new one. The problem of insufficient Torah study is perhaps more pronounced today, but the problem has existed for centuries. One of the great scholars and preachers of 13th century Spain was R. Bachya ben Asher, the author of *Kad Hakemach*. In this scholarly compendium of Torah topics, R. Bachya writes: "Man was created primarily to study Torah. Therefore, one should be disconcerted by the sinful neglect of the study of the Torah by the majority of people. Most people concentrate all their efforts upon vanity and totally forget their duty to set aside regular hours for study on the Sabbaths and festivals and to study occasionally on weekdays and even nights. One should consider that if he received a written communication from a mortal king and he was unsure of its meaning, he would certainly endeavor with all his might to understand it. If this is true with respect to the writing of a mortal king, who is alive today and dead tomorrow, it is so much more true of the Torah, the writing of the King of kings, for the Torah is man's life and deliverance, as it is written, 'For that is thy life and the length of thy days!' Our Sages commented: 'Every day, a Heavenly Voice bursts forth from Mount Horeb (Sinai) and proclaims: 'Woe to men for their contempt of the Torah.' Thus you learn that man was primarily created to engage in the study of Torah" (*Encyclopedia of Torah Thoughts*, C.B. Chavel, Shilo Publ., 1980, pp. 650-651).

"The law of the Eternal is perfect, restoring the soul; the testimony of the Eternal is faithful, teaching wisdom to the simple. The precepts of the Eternal are right, rejoicing the heart; the commandment of the Eternal is pure, enlightening the eyes. The fear of the Eternal is pure, enduring forever; the ordinances of the Eternal are true, they are righteous altogether" (Ps. 19:8-10).

R. Bachya, quoting a Midrashic source, interprets these verses as a beautiful tribute to the Oral Law as embodied in the Six Orders of the Mishnah. He writes: "David mentions here six expressions which describe the Torah as follows: law, testimony, precepts, commandment, fear and ordinance. These six key words correspond to the six Orders of the Mishnah, as the Sages have commented in Midrash Tehillim: *The law of the Eternal is perfect* corresponds to the Order of *Nashim* (Women). *The testimony of the Eternal is faithful* corresponds to the Order of *Zeraim* (Seeds), for the farmer who plants his seeds demonstrates his faith in the life of this world. *The precepts of the Eternal are right, rejoicing the heart* corresponds to the Order of *Mo'ed* (Festivals). This section is comprised of the laws of prayer, the Sukkah, the palm branch, and the festivals, concerning which it is written, *And thou shalt rejoice in thy feast. The commandment of the Eternal is pure, enlightening the eyes* corresponds to the Order of

Kodashim (Consecrated Things), which provides enlightenment in distinguishing between the non-sacred and the sacred. *The fear of the Eternal is pure* corresponds to the Order of *Taharoth* (Purities). *The ordinances of the Eternal are true* corresponds to the Order of *Nezikin* (Damages), which deals with all civil laws. These six Orders of the Mishnah correspond to the six periods in the order of the world: *cold and heat, summer and winter, and day and night.* The six Orders of the Mishnah embody the Oral Law, for on account of the magnitude of the Torah, the Oral Law is indispensible, since without it the Written Law could not be explained, as the Sages commented: God made a covenant with Israel only for the sake of the Oral Law, as it is said, *According to these words have I made a covenant with thee and with Israel"* (ibid., pp. 649-650).

LOVE FOR TORAH AND HUMANITY

Rashi interprets the words of R. Nechunyah as quoted in the *baraita* to read: "... that I not make a mistake in halachah that my colleagues will rejoice." In other words, R. Nechunyah was not only praying on his own behalf that he not make an error. He was also concerned lest his colleagues sin by rejoicing over his mistake. Such a prayer indicates the intense degree of caring for others in R. Nechunyah's soul. He did not wish to be the source of another's sin. He was not concerned about personal embarrassment, but he was deeply concerned with the possibility of his colleagues falling to the human weakness of laughing at the embarrassment of another. Even scholars are subject to this human frailty. It is forbidden to delight even when an enemy suffers shame — "Do not rejoice when your enemy falls" (Proverbs 24:17). To love one's neighbor is to empathize and feel the hurt of another.

R. Nechunyah lived to a ripe old age. His students asked him to what does he owe his longevity. His answer is quite telling of his character: "I never allowed myself to be honored at the expense of another's degradation. I never went to sleep without forgiving others, and I never placed too much importance on money" (Megillah 28a).

The Practical Law

1. He who enters a *beit midrash* prays: "May it be Your Will, Lord our God and God of our fathers, that I not make a mistake in halachah...."

Upon leaving he says: "I am thankful to you, Lord my God, that you have placed my portion in life amongst those who sit in the *beit midrash (Orach Chaim* 110:8).

2. A formula for entering a *beit midrash* is quoted by the *Mishnah B'rurah*:

"May it be Your Will, Lord our God and God of our fathers, that you enlighten our eyes with the light of your Torah and spare me from errors and mistakes, both in laws of forbidden-permitted and in monetary laws, both in teaching and in learning. Open my eyes that I may see the wonders of your Torah. As for mistakes which I have already made, bring me to truth. Do not hide the truth from my mouth in any way, for the Lord gives wisdom, from His mouth comes knowledge and understanding."

When learning with a group of people one should also request that he not rejoice at their mistakes, nor they rejoice at his mistakes (*Mishnah B'rurah, ibid.*, no. 35).

Mishnah 3

Rabban Gamliel says: A person is required to pray the Eighteen Benedictions[1] every day. R. Joshua says: The abbreviated version.[2] R. Akiva says: If he is fluent[3] he must pray the eighteen benedictions; if not, he may pray the abbreviated version.

משנה ג

רַבָּן גַּמְלִיאֵל אוֹמֵר: בְּכָל יוֹם מִתְפַּלֵּל אָדָם שְׁמוֹנֶה עֶשְׂרֵה. רַבִּי יְהוֹשֻׁעַ אוֹמֵר: מֵעֵין שְׁמוֹנֶה עֶשְׂרֵה. רַבִּי עֲקִיבָא אוֹמֵר: אִם שְׁגוּרָה תְפִלָּתוֹ בְּפִיו, יִתְפַּלֵּל שְׁמוֹנֶה עֶשְׂרֵה; וְאִם לָאו — מֵעֵין שְׁמוֹנֶה עֶשְׂרֵה:

---

1. EIGHTEEN BENEDICTIONS — The *Amidah*, or Standing Prayer.
2. ABBREVIATED VERSION — See the "Letter of the Law" for the text.
3. FLUENT — Familiar with the prayer and can recite it in a facile manner.

The Letter of the Law

In Mishnaic times, the prayers were recited by rote as there were no prayerbooks. Thus, it was an important issue as to whether an abridged version of the *Amidah* may be recited or whether the full text was required. R. Akiva takes a practical approach. It is preferable for one who is fluent in his prayers to recite the entire *Amidah*. For one who is not fluent, however, it is better that he recite the abridged version.

THE ORIGIN OF THE AMIDAH

Maimonides traces the historical development of the Eighteen Benedictions: "People used to pray according to their ability. Some would pray once a day. Others prayed often. Everyone prayed facing in the direction of the Temple, wherever he was. And so it was from the time of Moses until the time of Ezra.

"When the Jewish people was exiled in the days of the evil Nebuchadnezzar, they became assimilated in Persia and Greece and in other countries. They raised children in the lands of the non-Jewish nations. These children were confused in their language. Their speech was corrupted by a mixture of many languages. They lost their ability to speak properly in one language without mistakes.... Thus, if one would pray, he would not be able to request his needs or praise the Holy One, blessed be He, in Hebrew without mixing in other languages. When Ezra and his court saw this, they arose and established the Eighteen Blessings in a proper order. The first three praise God, the last three offer thanksgiving, and the middle ones request all the basic needs of the individual and the community. This was done, so that the prayers would be accessible to everyone and that others may learn them, and so that the prayers of the inarticulate ones may be complete like the prayers of those who are eloquent. It is for this reason, that all the blessings and prayers were arranged for all of Israel, so that every blessing will be prepared for those who are inarticulate" (*Mishneh Torah*, Laws of Prayer, 1:3-5).

WHY EIGHTEEN?
A variety of sources are given both in the Babylonian and Jerusalem Talmuds for the number eighteen. Each source relates to a specific aspect of prayer.

1. The Name of the Lord appears eighteen times in Psalm 29 (Berachot 28b).
2. The Name of the Lord appears eighteen times in the *Sh'mah (ibid.)*.
3. There are eighteen vertebrae in the spine (*ibid.*). The Jerusalem Talmud explains the connection with prayer: "When a person stands and prays, he must bow all his vertebrae. What is the reason? Because it says: 'All my bones will say, O Lord, who is like unto You?' " (Ps. 35:10) (Berachot 4:3).
4. The names "Abraham, Isaac, and Jacob" appear together eighteen times in the Torah (*ibid.*).
5. Eighteen commands were given in the construction of the Tabernacle (*ibid.*).

6. There are eighteen Psalms before the verse "The Lord will answer you on the day of trouble" (Ps. 20) (Psalms 1 and 2 are counted as a single Psalm) (*ibid.*).

THE NINETEENTH BENEDICTION

The name *Sh'moneh Esray*, or "Eighteen Benedictions," is in fact, a misnomer. There are *nineteen* blessings in the *Sh'moneh Esray*. The twelfth blessing, called *Birkat Haminim*, "the blessing concerning heretics," is a later addition. The Talmud relates: "Shimon Hapakuli arranged the Eighteen Blessings before Rabban Gamliel in Yavne. Rabban Gamliel said to the Sages: 'Is there anyone who knows how to formulate *Birkat Haminim*?' Samuel the Younger (*Hakatan*, "the Minor," called by that name either because of his extreme humility or because he was considered a minor version of the Prophet Samuel) arose and formulated it" (Berachot 28b).

Scholars differ widely as to the origin of this added blessing. It was clearly directed against the enemies of the Jewish people. To date, at least nine versions of the blessing are known. It seems likely that the text was changed to apply to current enemies. In some versions, divine judgment is invoked upon apostates; in others, upon slanderers. "Heretics," "enemies," "sinners," "arrogant ones" are, in one version or another, condemned. It is likely that Sadducees, Judeo-Christians, and Roman government informers were, in their times, the targets of the wrath of God and Israel.

Yet the name *Sh'moneh Esray* endures. Rabbi Tzvi Yehuda Kook explained the reason for this phenomenon. *Birkat Haminim* was never intended to become a permanent addition to the *Sh'moneh Esray*. It was composed with the hope that all evil would soon cease and the blessing be made obsolete. Once evil is eliminated, the *Birkat Haminim* will pass into oblivion. Thus the very name *Sh'moneh Esray* provides the Jew with the optimistic view that someday evil will, indeed, perish.

There is another, and probably more accurate, name given to the prayer, i.e., *Amidah*, or "Standing Prayer." This name is derived from a source in Tractate *Soferim* (16:12) and is currently used by Sephardim.

THE STRUCTURE OF THE AMIDAH

The nineteen blessings of the *Amidah* are divided into three sections: 1) Praise, 2) Petition, and 3) Thanksgiving.

I. **Praise**
 1. Protector and Redeemer
 2. Resurrects the dead
 3. Holy

II. **Petition**
 1. Knowledge
 2. Repentance
 3. Forgiveness
 4. Redemption
 5. Healing
 6. Prosperity
 7. Ingathering of the exiles
 8. Restoring justice
 9. Punishing the slanderers and enemies of Israel
 10. Rewarding the righteous
 11. Rebuilding of Jerusalem
 12. Coming of the Messiah
 13. Hearing prayers

III. **Thanksgiving**
 1. Return of the Divine Presence to Zion
 2. Thanksgiving
 3. Peace

The Petition section of the *Amidah* is subdivided into categories. The first six blessings relate to one's personal needs. The second six blessings relate to national needs. Of the six petitions for personal needs, the first three are of a spiritual nature, the second three are of a worldly nature. Of the six petitions for national needs, the first three deal with the physical well-being of Eretz Yisrael. The second three deal with the spiritual welfare of our national homeland. The thirteenth blessing is a summary request that God hear all our prayers. It also provides an opportunity for the individual to insert a personal prayer in his own words.

In terms of individual needs, spiritual welfare precedes worldly welfare. A person with a healthy soul is more likely to receive the blessing of a healthy body. Many people are concerned primarily with their physical and material needs and neglect their spiritual well-being. That is why emphasis is first placed upon petitions for spiritual welfare. On the national level, however, the Sages understood that the physical needs of Eretz Yisrael must be fulfilled before spiritual redemption will come. The process of redemption begins with the return of Jews in the Diaspora to their homeland. Israel must first be inhabited and developed by its people. This is the stage of redemption in which we find ourselves today. When Israel is strong and secure physically, there will be a spiritual renaissance that will culminate in the coming of the Messiah. Redemption is a slow, agonizing process that requires patience, endurance, and the concerted effort of the Jewish people.

PSALM 29

It is worth noting that the "Eighteen Benedictions" are recited on weekdays. On Shabbat and festivals, however, the *Amidah* contains seven blessings. The first three blessings of praise and the last three blessings of thanksgiving are constant. The thirteen central blessings of petition are substituted with a single blessing on the sanctification of Shabbat and festivals. Psalm 29, with its eighteen references to the name of the Lord, is also cited as a Biblical source for the seven benedictions. The Psalm refers to the "Voice of the Lord" seven times. Having the distinction of being the source for both the weekday *Amidah* and the Shabbat and festival *Amidah*, Psalm 29 is given a special place in the Friday evening *Kabbalat Shabbat* prayer. In this manner, Psalm 29 forms the link between the weekdays and the Shabbat. A special tribute is paid to this Psalm in the custom to stand during its recitation.

The Book of Chronicles records the song of thanksgiving that King David sang when the Holy Ark was transferred to its permanent home in Jerusalem. Contained in David's song are two verses which are almost identical to the first two verses of Psalm 29. "Ascribe to the Lord, you families of nations, ascribe to the Lord honor and strength. Ascribe to the Lord the honor of His Name; lift an offering and come before Him, bow down to the Lord in the beauty of holiness" (I Chron. 16:28-29). That momentous event which saw the Holy Ark brought to the holy city of Jerusalem is eternally recalled in Jewish prayer.

Not only the number eighteen, but also the themes of six of the blessings of the *Amidah* find their roots in Psalm 29: "Ascribe to the Lord you sons of the powerful" (v. 1) alludes to the first blessing, which speaks of the Patriarchs. "Ascribe to the Lord honor and strength" (v. 1) alludes to the second blessing which speaks of God's might. "Ascribe to the Lord the honor of his Name, bow to the Lord in the beauty of holiness" (v. 2) alludes to the third blessing, which speaks of God's holiness. "The voice of the Lord breaks the cedars" (v. 5) alludes to the ninth blessing, which speaks of abundance of food. The Jerusalem Talmud interprets this verse to mean that God will destroy the powerful manipulators of food prices, thereby making food inexpensive and plentiful (Berachot 2:4). The twelfth blessing, which speaks of the subduing of evildoers, is alluded to by "the God of honor thunders" (v. 3). Finally, the nineteenth blessing which speaks of peace, is alluded to by the words of the Psalm, "The Lord will bless His people with peace" (v. 11).

In addition to being recited on Friday evening in the *Kabbalat Shabbat*, Psalm 29 is recited, and often sung, prior to the return of the Torah scroll to the Holy Ark before the Shabbat morning *Mussaf* service. Because of its association with Shabbat through the seven "voices" (see above), its association with King David bringing the Holy Ark to Jerusalem, and its allusion to the giving of the Torah at Mt. Sinai in the words, "He causes them (the mountains) to dance" (v. 6), it is most befitting to recite Psalm 29 at that particular juncture in the Shabbat prayers, as well.

THE ABBREVIATED VERSION
The Talmud offers two opinions as to the meaning of "the abbreviated version." According to Rav, the three blessings of Praise and the three blessings of Thanksgiving are not abridged. Only the thirteen blessings of Petition are abbreviated, i.e., shortened. Sh'muel concurs that the first and third sections remain intact. The blessings of petition, however, are reduced to an abridged single blessing which contains all thirteen themes. The text of Sh'muel's version reads as follows: "Lord, our God, help us to understand Your ways, turn our hearts to fear You, forgive us that we may be redeemed, take away our pains, prosper us in the dwellings of Your land, gather in our fellow Jews from the

Diaspora, teach those who have gone astray, raise Your Hand against the evildoers, and let the righteous rejoice in the construction of Your city, and in the rebuilding of Your Sanctuary, and in the flourishing of the glory of Your servant David, and in the preparation of a lamp for the son of Jesse, Your annointed one; answer us even before we call. Blessed are You, O Lord, who hears prayer"(Berachot 29a).

The Spirit of the Law

PRAYER IN THE PLURAL
One of the striking features of the *Amidah*'s blessings is that they are all in the plural form. When a Jew prays, even in solitude and privacy, he prays with, and for, the entire Jewish people: "Forgive us," "Heal us," "Hear our voice," etc. Jewish prayer forms a relationship not only with God, but with *Am Yisrael*, the Jewish people, as well. As he addresses himself to God, the worshipper calls to mind every Jew living in the present, the ancestors of the past, and the community of the future. This is why praying with a *minyan* is so very important. Each *minyan*, each congregation, is a microcosm of the entire Jewish people. But even when a Jew prays in private, his soul is bound up with the fate of his people. Prayer, even in solitude, is a collective experience.

There is a fundamental principle quoted in the Talmud: "All Jews are responsible for one another" (Shevuot 39a). Jews should feel a natural kinship for one another, a kinship that is expressed in mutual concern for the physical and spiritual welfare of fellow Jews. To be a Jew is to be a member of a collective body. The pain and anguish of even a single Jew behind the Iron Curtain or any other land of oppression should be felt by Jews all over the world. It is not surprising that even when confronted with immediate danger and crisis, the Jew prays not only for himself but for every Jew who finds himself in distress. (See R. Joshua's prayer, *infra,* 4:4). In the Confessional Prayers of Yom Kippur, the plural form is employed, as well. Even when confessing one's personal sins, the individual expresses a vital concern for the sins and transgressions of his fellow. How true is the declaration in the Blessing of the New Month: *Chaverim Kol Yisrael*, "All Jews are friends." The word *chaver*, "friend," also means "connected." In a most literal sense, the Jewish people is spiritually connected by an indissoluble bond. No religious act more dramatically expresses the unity of the Jewish people than the act of prayer.

It was the practice of the great Kabbalist, the *Ari ha-kadosh*, R. Isaac Luria of 16th century Safed, to meditate on the mitzvah "Love thy neighbor as thyself" before beginning his prayers. By joining prayer with love for his fellow Jew, the *Ari ha-kadosh* felt confident that his prayer would be more meaningful and more effective.

R. Judah Halevi sees the Jewish people as a single organism. Every Jew is a part of that organism called *K'lal Yisrael*. When the nation as a whole is healthy, all its parts are healthy. When a single part is infected or diseased, all parts suffer. Thus, a Jew must pray not only for himself, but for his entire people (*Kuzari* 3:19).

Rabbi Joseph B. Soloveitchik underscores the essential aspect of praying for others in his famous essay *The Lonely Man of Faith*: "Man should avoid praying for himself alone. The plural of prayer is of central halachic significance. When disaster strikes, one must not be immersed completely in his own passional destiny, thinking exclusively of himself, being concerned only with himself, and petitioning God merely for himself. The formulation of efficacious and noble prayer is human solidarity and sympathy.... If God abandons his transcendental numinous solitude, He wills man to do likewise and to step out of his isolation and aloneness. Job did not understand this simple postulate. 'And it was so, when the days of their feasting were gone about, that Job sent and sanctified them, and rose up early in the morning, and, offered burnt offerings according to the number of them all.' He did pray, he did offer sacrifices, but only for his household. Job failed to understand the covenantal nature of the prayer community in which destinies are dovetailed, suffering or joy is shared and prayers merge into one petition on behalf of all. As we all know, Job's sacrifices were not accepted, Job's prayers remained unheard, and Job... met with catastrophe and the great whirlwind uprooted him and his household. Only then did he discover the great covenantal experience of being together, praying together and for one another. 'And the Lord turned the captivity of Job, when he prayed for his friends; also the Lord gave Job twice as much as he had before' " (*The Lonely Man of Faith*, Rabbi J.B. Soloveitchik, *Tradition*, vol. 7, no. 2, Summer, 1965).

CHAPTER 4: *Mishnah 3*

THE AMIDAH; PRAYER OF THE ANGELS

The book *Shibalay Haleket* records a Midrash that associates each of the blessings in the *Amidah* with events that occurred in the early history of the Jewish people. All the blessings are attributed to the angels who praised the Lord upon each occurrence.

"Blessed are You, O Lord —

1. Shield of Abraham — When Abraham was rescued from the fiery furnace.
2. Who brings the dead back to life — When Isaac was revived upon the altar.
3. The holy God — When Jacob dreamed of the ladder upon the holy site which he called "the Gate of Heaven."
4. Who grants knowledge — When Joseph miraculously learned seventy languages in Egypt.
5. Who desires repentance — When Reuven repented for sinning with his father's concubine.
6. Who is merciful and greatly forgives — When Judah acknowledged Tamar's innocence and his own guilt.
7. Redeemer of Israel — When the Almighty saw the suffering of the Israelites in Egypt and said: "I shall redeem you."
8. The Healer of the sick — When Abraham was healed after his circumcision.
9. Who blesses the years — When Isaac's produce multiplied a hundred-fold.
10. Who gathers the dispersed of His people Israel — When Jacob went to Egypt and his family was reunited.
11. Who loves righteousness and justice — When the laws of justice were given to the Jewish people at Mt. Sinai.
12. Who subdues the evildoers — When the Egyptians drowned in the Red Sea.
13. The support and trust of the righteous — When the Almighty promised Jacob that Joseph will be present at the time of his death and will place his hand over Jacob's eyes.
14. Builder of Jerusalem — When King Solomon built the Temple.
15. Who causes the strength of salvation to grow — When the Israelites were saved at the Red Sea.

16. **Who hears prayer** — When the Almighty heard the moaning of the Israelite slaves in Egypt.

17. **Who returns His Divine Presence to Zion** — When the Tabernacle was erected and the Divine Presence descended between the two Cherubs.

18. **Your Name is good and it is befitting to thank You** — When King Solomon installed the Holy Ark in the Holy of Holies and offered thanks to the Almighty.

19. **Who blesses His people Israel with peace** — When the Israelites entered the Promised Land and the blessing of peace was ultimately realized.

The Practical Law

1. If a person should be in difficult circumstances in which he is not able to pray the full *Amidah* properly, e.g., if he is travelling, or, if he is afraid of being interrupted, he should pray the abridged *Amidah*, i.e., the first three blessings, the shortened version of the thirteen blessings of petition (*havinaynu*, "Lord, our God, help us to understand, etc.") and the last three blessings (*Orach Chaim* 110:1).

2. *Havinaynu* may not be recited during the winter months when the prayer for rain is added, nor on the conclusion of Shabbat and festivals, when *atah chonantahnu* ("You have favored us...") is added (*ibid.*).

Mishnah 4

R. Eliezer says: He whose prayers are a fixed routine[1] offers no supplication.[2] R. Joshua says: If one is travelling in a perilous place[3] he should pray a short prayer. He should say: "Save, O Lord, your people, the remnant of Israel.[4] May their needs be before you at every dangerous crossroad. Blessed are You, O Lord, who hears prayer."

משנה ד

רַבִּי אֱלִיעֶזֶר אוֹמֵר: הָעוֹשֶׂה תְּפִלָּתוֹ קֶבַע, אֵין תְּפִלָּתוֹ תַּחֲנוּנִים. רַבִּי יְהוֹשֻׁעַ אוֹמֵר: הַמְהַלֵּךְ בִּמְקוֹם סַכָּנָה, מִתְפַּלֵּל תְּפִלָּה קְצָרָה. אוֹמֵר "הוֹשַׁע הַשֵּׁם אֶת עַמְּךָ אֶת שְׁאֵרִית יִשְׂרָאֵל; בְּכָל פָּרָשַׁת הָעִבּוּר יִהְיוּ צָרְכֵיהֶם לְפָנֶיךָ. בָּרוּךְ אַתָּה ה' שׁוֹמֵעַ תְּפִלָּה":

1. A FIXED ROUTINE — A burden. He prays merely to fulfill his obligation.
2. NO SUPPLICATION — He fails to capture the essence of prayer which is a sincere entreaty of divine mercy.
3. PERILOUS PLACE — Where there is danger of being robbed or physically harmed.
4. SAVE, O LORD . . . ISRAEL — A quote from Jeremiah 31:6.

The Letter of the Law

"A FIXED ROUTINE"

The Talmud (Berachot 29b) offers several interpretations of the expression *kevah*, "a fixed routine." One interpretation views a "fixed routine" as a "burden." In other words, when a Jew prays merely to fulfill an obligation, hurrying to finish in order to go about his business, his prayer is empty and hollow. Such prayer is merely a burden that is waiting to be cast off as quickly as possible. A second explanation defines "a fixed routine" as perfunctory prayer, void of feeling and supplication. It refers to people who recite their daily prayers by rote and give little thought to their essence, which is heartfelt supplication before the King of kings. A third interpretation sees "a fixed routine" as prayer without nuance. One should not recite the *Amidah* without adding a personal plea in the blessing "Hear our voice." Prayer should contain a personal element and should not be limited to a standard text. A final view of "a fixed routine" is prayer that does not coincide with the rising and setting of the sun. It is at the transitional points of the day that prayer is most favored. The glory of nature, the Creator's handiwork, is most apparent as every new day is born at dawn and as the curtain of darkness descends at day's end. These are the times when prayer is enhanced by the awesome spectacle of creation.

R. Eliezer's dictum is paralleled by R. Shimon in Ethics of the Fathers (2:13), "Be scrupulous when reciting *Sh'mah* and *Tefillah (Amidah)*. When you pray, do not make your prayer a fixed routine, but, entreat God's mercy and offer supplication before the Almighty, as it is written, 'For He is gracious and compassionate, patient, abundant in kindness and repenting of evil' (Joel 2:13)."

R. Eliezer's statement is interpreted by R. Joseph Ashkenazi (Safed, 1525-1577; quoted in *Melechet Shlomo*) in a totally different light. He sees our mishnah as a continuation of the previous mishnah. Whereas Rabban Gamliel, R. Joshua, and R. Akiva debate whether it is required to pray the full text of the *Amidah* or the abridged version, R. Eliezer maintains that the worshipper should not restrict himself to one form or the other, as this would make his prayer a "fixed routine."

R. Joseph Heineman, in a contemporary study on prayer, wrote that the *Amidah* had not yet been formulated into a specific text at the time in which the *Tannaim* lived, i.e., at the end of the first century of the Common Era. The number of blessings was established, but the text was fluid. The worshipper "authored" his own prayers. R. Eliezer discourages a person from making his prayer routine by repeating the same formula every time he prays. Better that he be creative in his worship and develop new expressions of communication with God (J. Heineman, *Iyunay Tefillah*, Magnus Press, Hebrew University, 1983, pp. 77-79).

"AT EVERY DANGEROUS CROSSROAD"

The Talmud interprets the text *parashat ha'ibur*, to mean, "at every turn they make to sin, may their needs still be before You and may You fulfill their requests." Inherent in R. Joshua's prayer is the concept that God is merciful and compassionate, that He hears the prayers even of those who sin against Him. This is reminiscent of the verse cited earlier, "For He is gracious and compassionate, patient, abundant in kindness and repenting of evil" (Joel 2:13). A Jew prays in the *Selichot* prayers before Rosh Hashanah: "We knock on Your door, poor and destitute." Though we are poor in merit and destitute of mitzvot, the Almighty opens the door to our prayers and graciously accepts them.

R. JOSHUA'S PRAYER

As a point of interest, there are eighteen words in R. Joshua's prayer which is said in time of emergency.

The Spirit of the Law

SINCERE AND SPONTANEOUS PRAYER

Prayer is a special gift that is granted to the human being by the Almighty. Prayer is a privilege that permits the mortal creature to confront the Eternal Creator in dialogue. It is a privilege that grants the human being the right to establish an I — Thou relationship with the Master of the Universe. Prayer spans the chasm between the finite and the infinite, between the mortal and the Eternal. It is a magic carpet that lifts man from his mundane world and carries him to celestial heights.

This is true only if prayer is sincere and heartfelt. The power of prayer is effective only when it is truly a "service of the heart." In prayer, the medium is the message. When prayer is spontaneous, emotional, meditative, contemplative, devout — it is a veritable communication beam between man and God. But, if prayer is a "fixed routine," if it is mere lip service bereft of feeling and thought, it is then an empty shell, a body without a soul. So writes Rabbeinu Bachya in his *Duties of the Heart*: "When the worshipper prays with his tongue, and his heart is occupied with matters other than prayer, his prayer is like a body without a spirit, like a shell without a heart" (*Sha'ar Cheshbon Hanefesh*, chap. 3, *Cheshbon* 9).

The problem of prayer without devotion is not new. The Prophet Isaiah decries, "the nation that draws near, with its mouth and lips it honors Me, but its heart is distant from Me" (Isaiah 29:13). The Talmud was keenly aware of how difficult it is to pray with devotion. When prayer was established with a specific text and a three times daily schedule, it became an even greater challenge to achieve the spontaneity and sincerity that prayer requires (See *infra*, 5:1).

GOD, THE MERCIFUL PARENT

The Almighty is a merciful Father who hears the prayers of His children. But He is also a stern Father who rebukes, admonishes, and punishes His children who go astray. Love and discipline are gracefully interwoven in the fabric of God's rule over the world. "As a father has mercy upon his children, so may you have mercy upon us." This *Selichot* prayer appeals to the Almighty as a loving parent who forgives the erring child. It is interesting to note that the appeal is to the mercy of a father, and not that of a mother. The Hebrew word *rachamim*, mercy, is derived from *rechem*, womb. Would not the prayer have greater impact if it appealed to the mercy of a mother, rather than that of a father? Paternal love is different, however, from maternal love. A mother expresses her love in warmth and affection. She is forgiving and understanding. No sin can quench the fire of love for her child. Even the mother of Sisera, the ruthless Canaanite general, sits anxiously by her window, peering into the distance, awaiting the return of her son from battle. "Why is his chariot so long in coming, why are the sounds of his wheels so late?" (Judges 5:28) she wails. Sisera's mother is so vivid a portrayal of maternal love, that the Sages enacted that the *shofar* be sounded one hundred times on Rosh Hashanah to correspond with the one hundred times Sisera's mother wailed for her lost son.

A father loves differently. The mother's attribute of mercy is mitigated by the father's attribute of justice. "I was a son to my father, a delicate darling to my mother" (Proverbs 4:3). A father is usually not all-forgiving. His affection is often expressed in discipline and admonition. A healthy balance between maternal affection and paternal discipline is viewed by King Solomon as the key to wisdom. "Hear my son the discipline of your father, and do not abandon the teachings of your mother" (Proverbs 1:8).

The Talmud deals with a seeming contradiction between the order in which father and mother are mentioned in the Torah. In the Ten Commandments, father is mentioned first: "Honor your father and your mother" (Exodus 20:12). But, in the Torah portion of *K'doshim*, mother is mentioned first: "A man shall revere his mother and father" (Leviticus 19:3). The Talmud explains that there is no contradiction here, but rather a matter of emphasis. It is human nature to honor a mother more than a father because she speaks kindly to her child. Thus, as far as honor is concerned, the father is mentioned first for added emphasis. At the same time, it is human nature to revere the father more than the mother because he instructs in the lessons of Torah. Thus, as far as reverence is concerned, mother is mentioned first for added emphasis. It should be added that "honor" is defined as deeds of affection, such as feeding, clothing and escorting. "Reverence" is defined as refraining from being disrespectful or discourteous (Kiddushin 30b, 31a).

Solomon's wisdom is elaborated upon by our Sages in the Midrash. "He who spares the rod hates his son; he who loves his son disciplines him early" (Proverbs 13:24). Three fathers are cited for not having disciplined their sons; all three witnessed the bitter fruits of their misplaced kindness. Abraham refrained from chastising Ishmael. As a result, Ishmael behaved so corruptly that in the end Abraham had to expel him from his home with merely a loaf of bread and a flask of water. Isaac withheld discipline from Esau. As a result, Esau despised his birthright, rejected the basic tenets of his father's beliefs, and came near to killing his brother. King David did not rebuke Absalom. As a result, Absalom sought to kill his father, slept with David's concubines, and was directly responsible for the deaths of tens of thousands of Jews in a tragic revolt. Also, King David's failure to hurt the feelings of his son Adonijah ultimately cost Adonijah his life.

The Midrash adds that the latter part of the verse, "He who loves his son disciplines him early," refers to the Almighty. God's love for Israel is expressed in the suffering that Israel must endure. Suffering removes the dross of arrogance and evil. Suffering humbles and inspires repentance. The Hebrew slave in Egypt was not able to see the good in his suffering. But when he experienced the Exodus, he was able to see the "Hand of God" like no other Jew before his time or after (*Ex. Rabbah*, 1:1).

The Merciful Father hears the cries of His children even when misdeeds have distanced them from Him. R. Meir disputes R. Judah's contention that we are called God's children only when we conduct ourselves as loving children. R. Meir contends that a child who misbehaves is still a child. "Children are you unto the Lord your God" (Deut. 14:1), whether obedient or rebellious (Kiddushin 36a). Furthermore, says R. Meir, we see from another verse that the Father-child relationship between God and Israel is not lost when Israel sins. "Their punishment is not His doing, it is His children's blemish" (Deut. 32:5). Even though they are blemished with sin, they are still called "His children" (*Sifre*). R. Abba states that a Jew who has sinned has not lost his identity as a Jew. "Even if he sins, he is a Jew... as the saying goes, 'A myrtle amongst the thorns is still called a myrtle' " (Sanhedrin 44a).

The Practical Law

1. One should pray in a calm, supplicating manner, as a poor person standing at the door. His prayer should not seem as a burden which he is eager to be done with (*Orach Chaim*, 98:3).
2. If one is travelling in a place where there is danger of attack by wild animals or robbers, he should pray: "The needs of Your people Israel are many and they do not know how to express their prayers properly. May it be Your will, O Lord our God, that You provide each and every one with his livelihood and to each and everybody according to its needs. Blessed are you, O Lord, who hears prayer" (*ibid.*, 110:3).
3. This prayer may be said while walking; if, however, it is possible to stop, he should stop (*ibid.*).
4. When he has reached his destination and has settled down he must recite the *Amidah* (*ibid.*) provided that the time for the *Amidah* has not elapsed (*Mishnah B'rurah, ibid.* no. 14).

Mishnah 5

If one is riding on a donkey[1] he must dismount. If he is unable to dismount[2] he must turn his face;[3] and if he is unable to turn his face[4] he must focus his thoughts towards the Holy of Holies.[5]

משנה ה

הָיָה רוֹכֵב עַל הַחֲמוֹר, יֵרֵד; וְאִם אֵינוֹ יָכוֹל לֵירֵד, יַחֲזִיר אֶת פָּנָיו; וְאִם אֵינוֹ יָכוֹל לְהַחֲזִיר אֶת פָּנָיו, יְכַוֵּן אֶת לִבּוֹ כְּנֶגֶד בֵּית קֹדֶשׁ הַקֳּדָשִׁים:

1. RIDING ON A DONKEY — And it is time to pray.
2. UNABLE TO DISMOUNT — E.g., there is no one to hold the donkey while he prays.
3. TURN HIS FACE — Towards Jerusalem and the site of the Temple.
4. UNABLE TO TURN HIS FACE — E.g., he must pay attention to the path on which he is riding.
5. TOWARDS THE HOLY OF HOLIES — The inner sanctum of the Temple.

The Letter of the Law

The Talmud quotes a *baraita* that details the law of the mishnah and bases the details on King Solomon's prayer on the occasion of his completing the construction of the Temple: "A blind person or one who does not know the direction should direct his heart towards his Father in heaven, as it says, 'and they shall pray to the Lord' (I Kings 8:44). He who is standing outside Eretz Yisrael should direct his heart towards Eretz Yisrael, as it says, 'and they shall pray to You towards their land' (*ibid.* v. 48). He who is standing in Eretz Yisrael should direct his heart towards Jerusalem, as it says, 'and they shall pray to the Lord towards the city which You have chosen' (*ibid.*, v. 44). He who is standing in Jerusalem should direct his heart towards the Temple, as it says, 'and they shall pray towards this House' (II Chron. 6:32). He who is standing in the Temple should direct his heart towards the Holy of Holies, as it says, 'and they shall pray toward this place' (I Kings 8:35). He who is standing in the Holy of Holies should direct his heart towards the place of the Ark Cover. He who is standing behind the House of the Ark Cover should imagine himself to be in front of the Ark Cover. Thus, if he is standing in the east, he should turn to the west; if in the west, he should turn his face to the east; if in the south, he should turn his face to the north; if in the north, he should turn his face to the south. In this way, all of Israel will be turning their hearts towards one place" (Berachot 30a).

Maimonides succinctly states: "He who is in the Diaspora, should face Eretz Yisrael; he who is in Eretz Yisrael, should face Jerusalem; he who is in Jerusalem, should face the Temple; and he who is in the Temple, should face the Holy of Holies. A blind person, or one who does not know the direction, or one who is travelling on a ship, should direct his thoughts towards the Divine Presence and pray" (*Mishneh Torah*, Laws of Prayer 5:3).

The Spirit of the Law

THE CENTRALITY OF ERETZ YISRAEL IN PRAYER

This mishnah is a glorious testimony to the centrality of Eretz Yisrael, Jerusalem, and the Temple in prayer. The law that requires the Jew of the Diaspora to face Eretz Yisrael when praying is one of the many factors that kept the dream of a return to Zion burning in the hearts of our people for nearly two thousand years of exile. Three times a day, the Jew is reminded of the centrality of Eretz Yisrael and his own peripheral religious existence outside of Eretz Yisrael. The Diaspora Jew builds his synagogue facing Zion. And no matter where he lives, in whichever continent and country he resides, when he utters the words, "May our eyes see Your return to Zion in mercy," his face and heart are directed towards Zion. The *Siddur* and prayer have been wellsprings of Zionism for more than two millenia. Daily prayer is a constant reminder to the Diaspora Jew of his obligation to fulfill the mitzvah of settling in Eretz Yisrael. R. Yaakov Emden (1697-1776) is quite emphatic on this point in his *Siddur* commentary. He writes: "It is known that there is an obligation upon the worshipper to direct his body towards Jerusalem.... Thus, every Jew must absolutely resolve in his heart to go up and settle in Eretz Yisrael... and to yearn to be privileged to pray there before the sanctuary of the King. For though it is destroyed, the Divine Presence has not departed from there" (*Siddur Beit El*, Altuna, 1745).

In addition to the powerful Zionist message contained in this law, there is another essential and meaningful lesson, as well. All prayers lead to Jerusalem when all Jews face Jerusalem. And when all Jews face Jerusalem, all Jews face each other. And when Jews face each other, they are reminiscent of the Cherubim that rested on top of the Holy Ark: "and their faces shall look at one another" (Ex. 25:20). There, in the inner sanctum of the Holy of Holies, the dwelling place of the Divine Presence, stood the only graven images permitted in all of Judaism. The Cherubim do not symbolize God, for God may never be reduced to a physical representation. They symbolize the Jewish people with their innocent childlike faces looking at one another in love and affection. Here resides the focal point of Jewish prayer, for prayer forges the unity of the Jewish people. Jews throughout the world share a common language and a common direction for prayer. In the *Siddur*, language and homeland merge into a harmonious synthesis.

Early Reform Judaism failed to appreciate the significance of language and homeland. The Frankfurt Conference of 1845 rejected Hebrew as the language for prayer. Forty years later, the Pittsburg Platform officially rejected the return to Eretz Yisrael. It wasn't until the Columbus Platform of 1937 that the Reform movement recognized the vital importance of language and homeland. Hebrew was to be retained in prayer (not exclusively, but rather nominally) and it recognized "the obligation of all Jewry to aid in (Palestine's) upbuilding as a Jewish homeland..." Would that all Jews today joined in a bond of unity, in a sacred triad of language, homeland and prayer.

LOFTY FOCAL POINTS
Jews throughout the world pray in the direction of a single focal point which is the symbol of supreme sanctity — the site upon which the

Holy of Holies once stood. A two-dimensional diagram would picture four concentric circles representing Diaspora, Eretz Yisrael, Jerusalem, and the Temple, respectively. A fixed point in the center would be the Holy of Holies. A more accurate representation could be demonstrated with a three-dimensional model; four rings, one smaller than the other, resting on each other, with a peaked summit on top representing the Holy of Holies. The model would look like a four-tiered mountain with its peak pointed towards heaven. Perhaps this was the imagery in the mind of the Psalmist who rhetorically asked, "Who shall ascend the mountain of the Lord, who shall stand in His holy place?" (Ps. 24:3). The elevation of "the mountain of the Lord" is not meant in a literal sense. It is a symbol of the spiritual ascent that man must make in his lifelong climb towards God. In prayer and in daily life, the Jew should focus his mind and attention upon Eretz Yisrael, Jerusalem, the Holy Temple, and the Holy of Holies, and upon the sanctity which they represent.

The Rabbis viewed Eretz Yisrael as being the "navel of the world." They said: "Just as the navel is located at the center of the human body, so is Eretz Yisrael located in the center of the world, as it says, 'Those who dwell upon the navel of the earth' (Ezekiel 38:12). The creation of the world emanated from there, as it says, 'A Psalm of Asaf. The Mighty One, God, the Lord, spoke and He called the earth from the rising sun unto its setting. From Zion, the perfect beauty, God appeared' (Ps. 50:1-2). Eretz Yisrael is located in the center of the world; Jerusalem at the center of Eretz Yisrael; the Temple at the center of Jerusalem; the Sanctuary at the center of the Temple; and the Foundation Stone from which the world was created is located in front of the Ark" (*Midrash Tanchumah, K'doshim* 10). In typical Midrashic style, the Rabbis did not view Eretz Yisrael as the literal "center of the earth," but rather the center of holiness and the Divine Presence. The prophetic allusion to the "navel of the world" intimates that just as the navel is that part of the anatomy from which the fetus draws sustenance from the mother, so too, Eretz Yisrael is the place from which the world derives its spiritual sustenance from the Creator.

The imaginary three-dimensional model referred to earlier suggests elevations. Indeed, the Rabbis viewed Eretz Yisrael as being higher than all other lands. The Midrash states: "Because the Temple is higher than every place, it is the best place" (*Sifre*, Deut. 7:12). The Talmud, too, ascribes loftiness to Eretz Yisrael: "Eretz Yisrael is higher than all lands, as it is written, 'Therefore, days are coming, speaks the Lord, and they will no longer say, 'As the Lord lives, who has brought the children of Israel up from the land of Egypt,' but instead, 'As the Lord lives, who has brought and has led the seed of the House of Israel up from the land of the north and from all the lands to which I dispersed them' (Jeremiah 23:7-8)." Here, too, the words are not meant in a literal sense. Eretz Yisrael is not geographically and topographically higher than all other lands. What the rabbis are teaching is that Eretz Yisrael stands on a spiritual level that is loftier and more sublime than any other land. And even within Eretz Yisrael there exist spiritual planes, each higher than the next.

The Practical Law

1. When a person arises to pray, if he is outside of Eretz Yisrael he should face Eretz Yisrael and direct his thoughts also towards Jerusalem, the Temple, and the Holy of Holies; if he is in Eretz Yisrael he should face Jerusalem and direct his thoughts also towards the Temple and the Holy of Holies; if he is in Jerusalem he should face the Temple and direct his thoughts also towards the Holy of Holies; if he is standing behind the Ark Cover he should face the Ark Cover (*Orach Chaim* 94:1).

2. One who does not know the direction should direct his thoughts to his Father in heaven (*ibid.*, 3).

3. One who is riding on a donkey need not dismount in order to pray, even if he has someone to hold his donkey. It is better that he pray while riding. If he is sitting on a boat or on a wagon — if he can stand, he should stand. If not, he should sit where he is and pray. If he is walking on foot, he should pray while walking, even if he is not facing Jerusalem and even if he is not in danger, because a delay in his journey may upset him and he will not be able to concentrate on his prayers. Everything is relative to the situation and his state of mind. Some are stringent about stopping for *Avot* (the first blessing of the *Amidah*). It is proper to follow their practice if there is no physical danger (*ibid.*, 4).

Mishnah 6

משנה ו

If one is sitting in a boat, or in a wagon, or on a raft,[1] he should direct his thoughts[2] towards the Holy of Holies.

הָיָה יוֹשֵׁב בִּסְפִינָה אוֹ בְקָרוֹן אוֹ בְאַסְדָּה — יְכַוֵּן אֶת לִבּוֹ כְּנֶגֶד בֵּית קֹדֶשׁ הַקֳּדָשִׁים:

1. IN A BOAT... WAGON... RAFT — Where conditions do not allow for standing for fear of falling.
2. HIS THOUGHTS — While sitting.

The Letter of the Law

This mishnah is a continuation of mishnah 5.

The halachah recognizes that it is not always possible to perform a mitzvah in a proper manner. Mitigating circumstances sometimes prevent the performance of a mitzvah in the optimum way. In matters pertaining to prayer, concentration and devotion are most essential. The form and manner are secondary. *Rachmanah libah ba'ee*, "the Merciful One wants the heart." The quality of prayer does not depend upon style, posture, swaying movements, or dress. These are only outward manifestations. The soul of prayer is a spiritual connection with the Almighty. The outer form should be a reflection of, and not a substitute for *avodah sheh'b'lev*, "service of the heart." *Kavanah* must not be sacrificed for the sake of standing in the proper manner.

The Practical Law

1. See above, 4:5, "The Practical Law," no. 3.

Mishnah 7 / משנה ז

R. Elazar ben Azariah says: The *Mussaf* prayer may be said only in the presence of a congregation.[1] The Sages say: In the presence of a congregation or not in the presence of a congregation.[2] R. Judah says in his name:[3] wherever there is a congregation, the individual is exempt from the *Mussaf* prayer.

רַבִּי אֶלְעָזָר בֶּן עֲזַרְיָה אוֹמֵר, אֵין תְּפִלַּת הַמּוּסָפִין אֶלָּא בְּחֶבֶר עִיר. וַחֲכָמִים אוֹמְרִים: בְּחֶבֶר עִיר וְשֶׁלֹּא בְחֶבֶר עִיר. רַבִּי יְהוּדָה אוֹמֵר מִשְּׁמוֹ: כָּל מָקוֹם שֶׁיֵּשׁ חֶבֶר עִיר, הַיָּחִיד פָּטוּר מִתְּפִלַּת הַמּוּסָפִין:

1. CONGREGATION — Hebrew: *chaver eer,* i.e., a *minyan,* a quorum of ten men.
2. ... OR NOT IN THE PRESENCE OF A CONGREGATION — The *Mussaf* prayer may be said privately, as well.
3. IN HIS NAME — In the name of R. Elazar ben Azariah.

The Letter of the Law

Three opinions are formulated in the Mishnah with regard to an individual's obligation to pray *Mussaf*. According to the first interpretation of R. Elazar ben Azariah's opinion, the individual is precluded from *Mussaf*. *Mussaf* is an exclusively congregational prayer. R. Judah's interpretation of R. Elazar ben Azariah is that the individual is exempt from *Mussaf* only where there is a congregation that is praying *Mussaf*. In such a case, the congregational Reader fulfills the obligation of the individual. In a place, however, where there is no congregation, the individual is obligated to pray *Mussaf*.

The Sages differ with both interpretations of R. Elazar ben Azariah. In their view, the individual is obligated to pray *Mussaf*, whether or not there is a congregation that is praying *Mussaf*.

No distinction is made with regard to *Shacharit, Mincha,* and *Arvit* as far as the obligation of the congregation and the individual is concerned. It is only with regard to *Mussaf* that we find R. Elazar ben Azariah making such a distinction. In his view, *Mussaf* is intrinsically different from other prayers. The essence of the morning, afternoon, and evening prayers is the supplication which they contain. As far as supplication is concerned, the individual is obligated to express his needs as is the congregation. And even on Shabbat and festivals, when there is no supplication in the *Amidah*, these prayers correspond with the weekday prayers that do contain supplication. *Mussaf*, however, is *sui generis*. The *Mussaf* is a commemoration of the Additional offering that was brought in the Temple. The *Mussaf* was a communal offering. Thus, the *Mussaf* prayer must be a communal prayer. The individual may not pray *Mussaf*. This is the opinion of the first interpretation of R. Elazar ben Azariah.

According to R. Judah, the individual is not precluded from *Mussaf*. When there is no congregation he, indeed, must pray. When, however, there is a congregation praying *Mussaf*, the congregation's Reader fulfills the obligation of the individual who is not present. The communal proxy is preferred over the individual's prayer. The Sages, on the other hand, reject the notion that a distinction should be made between the individual and the congregation insofar as *Mussaf* is concerned. *Mussaf* is essentially no different from other prayers. Just as the individual must pray *Shacharit, Minchah,* and *Arvit* when not praying with a *minyan*, so must he pray *Mussaf*. The absence of supplication is irrelevant as far as the obligation to pray is concerned.

The Spirit of the Law

There is a fundamental dispute between R. Elazar ben Azariah and the Sages as to the question: What gives man the right to pray? Prayer is a privilege. Not every subject may have an audience with the king and not every citizen is privileged to address the president. Why then

CHAPTER 4: *Mishnah 7*

should we presume that everyone has a right to address the King of kings whenever he so chooses? Is it not presumptuous to assume that we have the freedom to approach the Almighty at whim? A Chasidic tale speaks of the Apter *Rebbe* who came late to morning prayers. The Chasidim asked him why he arrived so late. He answered: "When I awoke in the morning I began to utter the prayer 'I give thanks before You.' I then stopped and began to ponder, 'Who am I that I should have the right to express my gratitude toward the Almighty?' I pondered this question for a long time and when I could find no answer, I got up and came to the synagogue to pray."

Prayer is, indeed, a privilege. This privilege is granted by the Almighty when the individual approaches with humility and pours forth his needs and wants. The broken heart is the key that opens the heavenly gates: "On the day the Temple was destroyed, the gates of prayer were closed. And even though the gates of prayer were closed, the gates of tears were not closed" (Bava Metziah 59a). Our heavenly Father hears the cries of all His children. "And the Children of Israel sighed from the work and they cried; and their cry rose up to God" (Ex. 2:23). And just as the Almighty hears the cries of the nation, so too does He hear the cries of the individual: "The Lord is near to all who call to Him" (Ps. 145:18). When King Hezekiah was informed by Isaiah that he will die of his illness, "he turned his face to the wall and prayed to the Lord" (II Kings 20:2). God heard his prayers and he was healed: "I have heard your prayer, I have seen your tears, behold, I will heal you" (*ibid.*, v. 5). Both R. Elazar ben Azariah and the Sages concur that prayers of supplication may be said by the individual, as well as by the community. Though the *Shacharit, Minchah*, and *Arvit* prayers of Shabbat do not contain supplication, they, in fact, correspond to the weekday prayers that do. *Mussaf*, however, is a prayer that is devoted entirely to praise and thanksgiving and is unrelated to supplication. Herein lies the dispute between R. Elazar ben Azariah and the Sages. R. Elazar maintains that the privilege of praise is granted only to the community, as the Psalmist says: "Bless God in the congregations, the Lord from the fountain of Israel" (Ps. 68:27). The individual is not granted the right to praise God unless his praise is accompanied by supplication. The Sages, on the other hand, see each individual Jew as a representative of the Community of Israel because he is "from the fountain of Israel." As a member of *Am Yisrael*, he is privileged with a unique son-Father relationship with God and his praise is as welcome as his supplication. Thus, *Mussaf*, a prayer of praise, may be said by the individual, as well as, by the community.

The Practical Law

1. Every individual is obligated to pray *Mussaf*, whether or not there is a congregation in the city (*Orach Chaim* 286:2).